THE
COMET'S
TALE

A Novel About Sojourner Truth

BY
Jacqueline Sheehan

Greenforge Books

ISBN-13: 978-0984716531
ISBN-10: 098471653X
LCCN: 2012932187

For information, address Jaqueline Sheehan c/o The Bent Agency 204 Park Place, Number Two, Brooklyn, New York 11238.

CHAPTER ONE

HURLEY, NEW YORK

I rode to earth on the backside of a comet. Mau Mau Bett saw me blaze across the sky and disappear into the moon, where I reined in the comet with my strong arms, tightened my thighs to make the comet turn and then scorched back again across the sky. With the last light of the comet, for I had nearly burned it up dashing around the moon, I rode until I saw a man as tall as a tree holding a burning pine knot in a smooth stone mortar. Next to him was a woman holding out her apron. I landed headfirst into her outstretched cloth, turning her apron black with my heat.

Mau Mau said every child is born a different way. Some are born by water, some by lightning, some by blizzards, and some squeeze in through the cracks in the wall. You never know until the baby arrives.

"How did Peter get here?" I asked.

"On a strong wind."

Strong wind was right enough. The first thing every morning, Peter woke me with his farting. He started before he woke up and because we slept together, I was the one most affected. Peter was also as warm as burning wood. It was a challenge to stay warm in our cellar home and Peter's farting or drooling on my neck was small inconvenience for his comfort.

The wet from the ground often seeped up between the boards that Bomefree and Mau Mau set on the dirt floor. It rained so hard in the land of Charles Hardenbergh that our cellar home was more often a pond than a refuge for people.

The boards were hewn by Bomefree and each one was earned by his extra work on top of his expected work for Master Charles. Every plank of wood was time spent when Bomefree squeezed out his own labors, often in the middle of the night. Peter and I slept on a sack filled with hay as did Bomefree and Mau Mau. Living in a cellar is easiest for frogs and lizards (of which we had a continual parade) who thrive in the mud and mold. At times we could have housed fish as well. If it was raining when we went to sleep, Peter and I could be sure that the water would seep through to us before morning. Peter was such a sound sleeper that often he did not notice the wet until after he woke. He was prone to say, "Isabella wet the bed again." He knew I had not wet the bed. He also knew I could not answer him back in a loud voice. Our voices were never to carry beyond our cellar. Mau Mau had beat that knowledge into us early on.

Mau Mau said that when Peter slept, his spirit traveled far. It was my job to hold onto his warm body until his spirit returned. She said people who can sleep so deeply in this hard life are blessed.

Our mother fretted about the water in our home, but what I remember most is the smell of her skin not the unrelenting dampness. Later in my life, I would smell perfume, some of which came from France, and none of it compared to the skin and hair of my mother. She was named Mau Mau Bett by Colonel Hardenbergh. Her mother named her Elizabeth although none but my father ever called her by her given name.

Mr. Charles came by us when I was a baby and Peter was not yet born. We were owned first by Colonel Hardenburgh and when he died, his son Mr. Charles gained us. I do not remember our first home with the Colonel, which was a

4

cottage with a small plot of garden space allotted to us for growing the extra that we needed. My ten older brothers and sisters were born in the cottage; all sold off or given as gifts to other Dutch folks before I was born. The Colonel named me Isabella after a queen he was partial to talking about. Mau Mau said that the few other slaves already called us the white people's niggers because of the favored status of Bomefree and her. The old man naming me after a long dead queen from a place I later learned was called Spain only served to create a distance between us and the other colored people in Hurley. It was not easy for anyone to stay long away from Mau Mau, even if they felt that she was favored. To the disenchanted, she told them that that the Colonel was an old man and his thinking was starting to wander with his age so why else would he name a colored child after a queen? To me she whispered, "He finally got one right."

Mr. Charles was better than most and if we did not steal, lie, or act disrespectfully, our chances of not being unfairly beaten were good. A fair beating was one you deserved and the strokes were given in accordance with the behavior. A fair beating came as no surprise to anyone. An unfair beating was given out for something we did not do, or was one delivered with no relationship to the wrongful behavior.

My father was called Bomefree, which is Dutch for tree. He was said to be named for his tall height and his powerful strength. I once asked him what kind of tree he was, because Mau Mau told me of many different kinds of trees. He said he was just a plain tree.

Trees had sweet bark, or smooth skin, or leaves that danced and rattled in the breeze, or bubbles of pine that could burn bright if you were lucky enough to find one on a dark walk through the woods. My mother was very fond of the white birch. We were likely to find them crashed to the ground after a fierce wind storm, so it was not for their physical strength that my mother rubbed her cheek against the moon white bark. It was for their defiance and unlikeliness in the midst of the more brutish trees that could

5

survive lightning bolts, thick wet snow, or the porcupine ravaging teeth on the protective bark. The white birch chose to grow despite nature handing the worst conditions.

If my father was a tree, Bomefree was the kind of tree who grows on the edge of cliff and is turned different directions from the wind and it makes him hold on all the tighter as he digs his roots in harder and the trunk, roots and branches are grown gnarled and tough.

My first language was Dutch. In our part of New York, all the people, colored and white alike, spoke Dutch. It is a round language, smooth as river rocks, and there are still moments when I tumble back into Dutch when I talk to God. The first time I heard English, I was walking with my mother and Peter, carrying spun wool on instructions of Master Charles. We were all three bundled like oxen with the precious cargo of hard worked wool. A man on horseback pounded up to us on the road taking us out of Hurley. He pulled cruel on the reins, his horse striking a look that I had seen before, meaning that the horse was torn between wanting to throw off the man and fearful of the payment if he did. He spoke to us in slapping sounds as if he had no soft spot in his mouth or throat. He cracked away with his voice, getting agitated by degree as we stood waiting for sensible words to come out of him. He brought his horse closer to us, and I could smell the sweat on the animal's tired body. The man snapped his arm at Mau Mau and made more sounds, this time with a snarl to his lips. Finally she spoke to him, saying that we were taking spun wool to a farm a day's walk from where we stood. He arched an eyebrow at her, spoke again, she repeated her message more slowly, and he turned one ear toward her. I could see him thinking over the situation. He finally dismissed us with the flap of his hand and rode off. Mau Mau told us that people who lived farther away spoke in different words than we did but that there was no reason for us to have to learn it.

It was from Bomefree that I learned that trees do not live forever; they are born, live their life, then die. Bomefree was already in decline, his knuckles bulging and twisting by the time I grew to his waist.

I looked at my father's knuckles and then held out my arm to look at mine. My hands were smooth and the color of fire dried acorns, of which we had many. I squeezed my hand into a fist and my knuckles poked closer to the skin making the pointy places a lighter and lighter shade of acorn. Mau Mau's knuckles were smaller than my father's, but larger than those of most men including Master Charles. Her fingers were long and they went in the right direction, which Bomefree's no longer did. Mau Mau rubbed lard mixed with the bark of the quaking leaf tree into his aching joints and told him stories of summer heat and dry breezes in the land of my mother's people. The ashy color from his knees darkened and glowed with the warmth from Mau Mau's hands.

"Oh Elizabeth, tell us a story of the children. Tell us story that will make my bones young again."

Mau Mau held in her the lives of all her children, and all those who went before her who had time to leave her a story, a touch, or enough of a spark to be remembered. Mau Mau and Bomefree had ten children before Peter and me, most of whom were sold by the old Colonel while some were offered as gifts to the other Hardenberghs of Ulster County. The taking of each one of the children was chiseled in a story of pain and Mau Mau did not spare us such stories. But we never heard a story of a child's terrified screams without hearing a story of who this child was or how she was tied forever to Mau Mau and Bomefree and all of us.

Margaret was a first sister and we loved to hear of her in particular. To hear Mau Mau tell this story, or most of the story, warmed the bones of my old father. We sat close to my mother, in our cellar home, me with my head leaning up against her knee. Margaret was born on spring rain and flooded streams. All the snow was gone from around the cottage and all over the Colonel's large farm. No ice firmed the river to the east and all the animals and birds were furious to birth their babies. When Mau Mau walked to the big barn to collect eggs, she saw a Robins egg, pecked in half, free of its charge. When she picked up the blue shell, she knew her child would soon be on her way. It was a spring filled with birth after a cold, white winter where many animals had starved. The snow had been too deep for the deer to forage, making them easy targets for the farmers. So many of the weakened deer were shot that even the Colonel, who was a terrible marksman, had a surplus of venison and gave a withered hindquarter to Bomefree.

Margaret gushed into this world with the snowmelt from the west mountains. Mau Mau called her tadpole for she never stopped loving the water. If Mau Mau was set to spinning wool for weeks on end, Margaret (as the Colonel named her) could be kept quiet for hours if left with a small bucket of water. To this, Margaret would add twigs, grass, feathers, and these things she would chase about in the watery sea. Like all of us, Margaret was sturdy in bones and size. When she had gone through but a few springs, she could tote her wooden bucket herself, filling it with fresh water from the well. When she was a taller child, and before the Colonel could set her to work, she spent the warm months by the stream near the cottage until the pink soles of her feet were wrinkled into a terrible mess. She had such a way with the water creatures that she took to catching the trout in the stream. Nobody ever saw her catch fish but she said she held her hands in the water until they came to her. In the last summer before she was taken away, Margaret filled her old wooden bucket with trout and did so with great frequency. It was at this time that the Colonel began to note her strength and endurance and told Mau Mau that the time would soon come to sell Margaret.

It was at this point in the story that I began to tighten up in my stomach and my blood beat faster, always hoping that the story would have a different ending. I thought that if Mau Mau would tell the ending different, then Margaret would still be catching trout and I would run up to her and say

"Tadpole, Tadpole" even though I had never in my life seen her.

The Colonel said that he sure hoped that Mau Mau would produce more children like Margaret because she looked unusually strong and good tempered which is the best one can hope for with slaves. She was taken away by the Colonel's brother in law who saw fit to put a bag over Margaret when he drove off with her, but he didn't need to do that. She never made a sound, didn't speak again until the following summer, Bomefree heard, as he had ways of finding out about all his children. When he was told she wasn't talking, and was being beat for being feeble minded, he got permission from the Colonel to walk to where she was, which took him the full part of a day and a night. He brought her the wooden bucket and put it where her master couldn't see it. She spoke then and was no more trouble to them.

I missed Margaret terribly when I heard this story and the sadness that it brought up in me seemed to taste like fish and smell like tadpoles. But at least I knew her from Mau Mau's stories, and I knew her from the sadness and from the picture of pink soled feet in the stream outside a cottage when times were not so hard in some ways.

CHAPTER TWO

Master Charles never spoke a word to Mau Mau about
me and Peter, about us being sold off. If we did not
draw attention to ourselves, the thought of selling us might
not settle occur to Master Charles.

In our cellar home, we had both an entrance to the
outdoors and an entrance to the upstairs kitchen by way of a
stone stairway that made several turns. The stones were most
often glistening with water except for the hottest and driest
seasons when the cool stones became a comfort unknown to
the Hardenberghs upstairs. Mau Mau was the first to rise and
she did so long before sunrise. She was mostly an indoor
slave. Her day started with adding wood to the fire in the
kitchen and then preparing the cooked grain for breakfast.
When Peter was a baby, a time filled only with sketchy
memories for me, she had to nurse the Hardenbergh's baby
Karl first thing and make sure that Peter did not suckle at all
during the night. If her breasts were not full to bursting in the
morning, Mrs. Hardenbergh could have her beaten with the
whip or could have Mau Mau sleep outside their door to keep
her from baby Peter. The trouble was, Peter howled like a
wolf when he was hungry and could wake people from all
over the house if Mau Mau slipped out of his sight, or more
to the exact point, if her milk filled breasts moved out of his

10

hungry sight.

Most slave mothers who are nursing white babies will teach their babies not to cry, either by whipping them, or by making a sucking cloth mixed with goat's milk and watery mush. While most slave owners will no sooner kill a healthy slave baby than they would a healthy calf, we had heard stories of babies who were whipped if their mothers could not keep them quiet. The problem here was that the slave had to keep her baby healthy and valuable and yet not give her baby the nursing that the babe needed to stay healthy. No creature was in more danger of being killed off than an unhealthy colored baby.

Mau Mau taught me to give Peter the sucking cloth and to muffle any of his cries with a blanket. After she nursed Karl, emptied the chamber pots from each sleeping room, started the midday meal, and began the washing if it was the day for it, her breasts would fill up enough again to nurse Peter. His nose would be covered by snot and he'd be exhausted by crying and his probable lack of breathing air as I tried to cover his cries with a blanket. By then, I was about ready to throw him in the river myself.

I watched as Mau Mau cooed to him, letting him gulp away at her. She had found us in the barn, or maybe she had told me to take him to the barn and hide in the hay with him, I don't remember. But I do remember the three of us easing into the hay as Peter finally stopped his struggling. His baby hands clutched open, close, open, close as he sucked and his eyes with his thick, black eyelashes beat time to his hands. His belly heaved, making room for as much milk as possible. He then fell asleep every time, exhausted from crying, waiting and fighting me off with the moldy blanket.

"I don't know how this body makes enough milk for both these babies. Karl is a weak sucker and wastes half the milk down my dress. It's Peter who keeps my milk coming in so strong. He has a need to suck me dry," said my mother.

It was understood that Mau Mau could nurse Peter as long as Karl came first. She also knew never to nurse Peter so that Mrs. Hardenbergh could see. She said if she did, there would be extra work and extra trouble.

Slave babies are blessed when there is no white baby in the neighborhood who needs nursing. Mau Mau said I was able to have my fill until I took my first steps, crashing my head and bottom as a regular course. By then, another white baby was born to a daughter of the Colonel's (as we were still with him then) and she needed a wet nurse for the winter visit. Mau Mau said she beat me off the breast. "How?" I asked her as Peter's soft lips pulled on her breast, liking to drag her stretched teat straight from her body.

"Don't ask me now. You'll learn soon enough when your babies want your breast and the white babies have to have it." When Peter was older and both of us would take to wrestling with each other on the far side of the sheep herd if we were sent to watch the animals, he had a weak spot that would allow me to win. When he had me pinned down and it looked like all hope was off and he could be declared the winner, all I had to do was cover up his nose or his whole face if I was able. This flew him into a rage and would sometimes make him cry. I knew why he hated it so.

CHAPTER THREE

Keeping track of the sheep was a job where Peter and I found the most pleasure. We were out of sight of the farmhouse, not so much by distance but because the meadows were separated by a hill and a thick stand of trees. Our job was, among other things, to see that the arrival of new babies was reported to Mr. Daniel, the hired man. Mr. Daniel was a brown haired, white skinned man who managed the animals of the farm. If the lambs came out as they were supposed to, all wobbly legged at first then knocking their heads at their mother's teats, we could wait until we drove the sheep back to the barn late in the day to tell him of the event. During lambing season, when lambs were popping out every which way, the sheep were brought into a fenced area near the farmhouse. This was to protect the lambs from being eaten by wild cats who found them an easy meal.

Daniel rarely spoke to us. He might say, "sheep" or "fences". He spoke fewer words to us than he did to his dog, who drove the sheep hard by nipping near their heels. The dog was long-haired, and her soft dark fur hung off her sides, bobbing as she ran. She ran low to the ground, nipping if she needed to make them change direction, then lay in the grass watching, waiting for one of them to get out of order. Then she leapt into action and started all over again. She did not stay all day with the sheep as we did in the spring, only when it was time to drive them from one pasture to another.

The dog's name was Mutton. She had cream colored paws and snout. When Mutton was not working with the sheep, she was with Daniel. He had hand signals for Mutton that we learned one spring. Across the field, Daniel would raise his right arm, pointing it across his chest and we and Mutton knew to go right with the sheep. If he did the same thing with his left arm, we went off the other way. Our lessons were held in the outer field with Daniel booming out solitary commands.

It was toward the end of spring when Peter and I came to tell Daniel that two lambs arrived in the field. We raced across the meadow, through the opening in the trees and up the grassy lane to the barnyard. We started to tell him how exciting, how red was the blood and how the mother had eaten the sac around the lamb and other raw parts that looked like liver. He gave us the sign for "quiet and sit". We had been with Mutton for so long that both Peter and I sat in the dirt stopped talking. Mutton was given a fresh bone from the stew for her hard work. Peter and I were dismissed with the release sign from Daniel. We raced across the yard to the cellar door to find Mau Mau to tell her about the big liver thing that comes out of the sheep after the baby comes. We saw her standing in the window of the kitchen looking out at us. We knew not to go inside the house unless we were told, so we went in search of Bomefree. We found him stacking wood and we helped him as we told our birthing news.

That night, Mau Mau took to one of her crying spells from which she could not be consoled. When this happened, Bomefree was no help in relieving her. Her crying spell made my father crash about, slamming the iron pot to the floor when he burned his fingers on the handle. It was as if Mau Mau's spells hurt Bomefree's skin, scraping him deep, slicing open the shiny scars on his back that ran diagonally from shoulder to waist. He would do anything to make her stop, to stop the way her cries pierced his skin.

Mau Mau could work up a wail and if she was going to

wail, she would leave the cellar to get all the noise out of her, past the ear shot of Hardenbergh's house. In this case, she wrapped her shawl around her shoulders and head. She was moaning deep and rocking her upper body.

"They are not dogs. My children are not dogs," she said.

I didn't know what struck this sorrow in her because I knew we weren't dogs. Peter and I looked at each other sideways and wondered where our mother got the idea that we were dogs. Mostly we wondered if we were in trouble and would have to answer for it in the strap or the stick.

Peter said, "Mutton is a dog."

Peter liked to clear up muddy waters. I could see he offered this bit of news as a way to save the situation.

This made our mother moan again and Bomefree hissed, "It's not my fault Betsy. What can I do, what do you expect me to do?"

She was in the doorway, bending her head, ready to shrink down her tall form to make her way out our door. The whites of her eyes were shot through with red till I feared blood would run out the corners and down her face.

"I will not have them trained like dogs. They were not born into this world to be trained as dogs."

Bomefree stood still, the cold night air pouring over him. He was halted by the words of our mother.

"I will do it, I will speak to Mr. Hardenbergh."

Mau Mau left the cellar door and ran into the cold spring night, leaving us to ponder what had gone wrong and what was the price we would pay. The rules of existence had been made clear to us by our parents; if we were not working, then stay clear of the Hardenberghs or any of the white people. If the white people told us to do something, we were not to question them. It was Mau Mau's hope that if everything went without trouble, we might all be able to stay together at the Hardenbergh's farm. Mau Mau would not be having more children arriving by water, wind, or from comets. I didn't understand how she knew this but I didn't question her wisdom. Because we were to be her last children, Mr.

Hardenbergh might be reluctant to sell us.

There was also talk of a new law that might let slave families stay together. Mau Mau told us about this law (which she explained was a rule that white people decide on) because she had heard about it from Mr. and Mrs.Hardenburgh's arguments. They had considerable arguments, followed by further loud noises from their bedroom.

Mr. Hardenbergh traveled to Albany to help with the making of laws, particularly about the unfairness he saw happening to the Dutch.

"We are being squeezed out of our right to farm. We are slowly giving every damn thing away. We were the first ones here. We brought the slaves here. We shall do as we damn well please," said Master Charles.

I had this part memorized. He said this all the time. It came up with every visit from his brother Emory, with the men after church every Sunday, every time he prepared for a trip up river to Albany, and as a way to start an argument with Mrs.Hardenbergh.

She was a yellow haired woman one head shorter than Mau Mau. What with her yellow hair, light skin and blue eyes, she had a ghost-like appearance. As I understood ghosts from Peggy the hired girl, they were light and almost see through. That's just what Mrs. Hardenburgh seemed like to me. From across the yard, I couldn't see her eyebrows, lips, or eyes.

I also memorized what Mrs. Hardenburgh answered back to her husband during their evening arguments.

"The Negroes will be the death of us. We have some good ones here, but I've seen others in New York City, in Albany, who have murder in their eyes. It's too much work taking care of them, feeding them, selling off the little ones. We have the hired help. If you weren't so tight with the money, we'd only have the hired help."

Their arguments about slaves were never any different. They might interrupt each other, repeat what they just said, accuse each other of being crazy, lazy, too lenient with slaves, ruining the blacks for sale, and worse.

The day after Mau Mau's crying spell, Bomefree was awake before any of us, drinking a root tea that Mau Mau hoped would relieve the stiffening and twisting of his fingers and joints. He sat on the chair he had made from alder wood. In his younger days, Bomefree was known for the furniture that he made of willow, alder, and pine. He bartered chairs and tables among the hired help and the few traveling tinkers who appeared in our part of the valley for which he got cloth, dried meat, sewing needles, and other comforts of life. The chair in which he now sat was tall backed and high seated for his long legs.

My father smoked a clay pipe. Not often and never before noon. His soft, full lips tugged at the stem of the pipe, drawing in the tobacco that he was allowed to grow for his own use. To see Bomefree smoking so early in the day meant something was off. I went outside in the dim light.

I pumped a bucket of water from the well and drank a ladle full of it to wash away the thick taste of sleep. I carried the bucket down to the cellar, emptied it into the jug by the door, and poured the rest into the kettle hung over the fire. I kept Bomefree in my sight the whole time. He had not moved except to gaze into the small fire and tap his pipe from time to time. I looked over at Mau Mau's sleeping mat. She lay facing the wall, her knees pulled close to her body, making her look folded up. From the quietness that came from her, I knew she was awake.

I went back to the well to pump another bucket of water for the Hardenbergh's kitchen. This was Mau Mau's job but she had recently turned it over to me. She said it was important to have the jugs filled with fresh water in the kitchen, to have the water going hot over the fire for tea and porridge, and it was especially important not to spill any water, which Mrs. Hardenburgh regarded as a sign of slovenliness.

My mother was a confusion to me. She picked jobs for

me based on her idea of what would please the Hardenburgh's. But she said she walked a narrow bridge because she didn't want them to sell me off. So I needed to be valuable just to them and to no one else. Mau Mau's consuming passion was to keep us all together. I did not spill a drop of water from the bucket, not even when I lifted the latch on the kitchen door, or poured the water into the kettle.

Bomefree was gone when I returned and Mau Mau was shaking out her cotton dress with sharp snaps. "Wake your brother, Isabella. How can he sleep through my noise?"

Peter and I took flatbread in our pockets and headed out to the sheep corral where Mr.Daniel was opening the gate to drive the animals to pasture. The lambs were trotting close to their mothers. We spent a good part of the day watching how the lambs pull hard on the sheep's teats, yanking milk. I tried to get Peter to pretend to be a lamb and to tug hard at the teats with his mouth but the sheep wouldn't let him get that close. He came close to getting his head kicked by hard hooves.

When Peter and I drove the sheep and the lambs back across the two meadows and through the opening in the stone wall leading back to the farm, we could see Daniel and Mr. Hardenbergh standing together. Bomefree was stiff and off to one side. Mutton was with us of course, nipping at the heels of the sheep, keeping them from running off in the wrong direction. One more lamb had been born. We delivered the news to Daniel as we had been instructed to do.

"One more lamb, Mr. Daniel. She stood as soon as she hit the ground."

Mr. Hardenbergh and Mr. Daniel paid no attention to my news of good fortune for the farm.

"Show me what these children have learned Daniel. I don't quite understand what you've been teaching them."

Mr. Daniel said, "Get" and Mutton ran to the center of the farm yard and lay down, keeping her eyes dead center on Mr. Daniel. Peter and I scrambled after her and squatted on either side of her. We kept our eyes on Daniel too.

Mau Mau had given us no warning of this. Was this one of the things that would make Mr. Charles sell us off or was this one of the skills that he would particularly need, letting us stay together? Should we show him how we know every command of Daniel's? What if we do and the next day a wagon pulls up for me or for Peter of for both of us? A wagon had come for each one of my sisters and brothers. Should we feign ignorance?

Peter and I stole a look at each other over Mutton's head. "Do it," I hissed at him.

Daniel raised his right arm and the three of us ran off in that direction, following the point of his hand.

"Show me what they do with sheep. Bring out the sheep," said our master.

I looked at Mr. Daniel. He nodded. I lifted the latch on the rail fence and let out a handful of sheep, hoping that it was the right amount.

"No lambs you idiot," said Daniel.

This was the longest string of words he had ever spoken to me. I wanted to tell him that I knew not to run the lambs needlessly but that it was impossible to get the mothers out without the new babies. Daniel did not take being spoken to and certainly not in front of Mr. Charles Hardenbergh. I picked up the two lambs that bleated to their mamas and put them back into the fenced area.

With most of the sheep now in the yard, Mr. Daniel demonstrated what we could do. At his hand signs, we drove the sheep to the left and to the right. We split the herd in half, Mutton taking one half of the sheep to the barn side of the yard, Peter and me taking the others to the orchard side of the yard. Each action was followed by our rapt attention on Daniel as we squatted and waited for the next command.

Mutton had a distinct advantage over Peter and me; the sheep knew about her sharp teeth and her warning bark. We had no such tools available to us. The result was that the sheep minded Mutton better than they did us. Daniel had recently tried giving us two willow sticks to snap at the sheeps' legs. The sticks proved useless. The dog and the sheep spoke a true and clear language that Peter and I could only pretend to know.

I dreaded the thought of Mau Mau watching our pitiful display but I dared not take my eyes off Daniel for fear of making our showing worse than it was. Mutton's sheep were cowering obediently in a far corner while our bunch had shaken two sheep loose and Peter ran ragged to get them back in the group.

To make oneself useless as a slave had dire consequences that we had heard about for as long as I could remember. If we proved useless to Mr. Hardenburgh, we would be sold off, despite the protests of our parents. The worst to happen was that we could be sold south. Every slave we knew feared this more than the lash, more than separation from family. Being sold to places with names like Georgia, Alabama, or Maryland meant disappearing into a bottomless well called plantation. And whatever was on plantations was so bad that slaves from the south were risking life and limb to run away and they were running north.

Two things happened at once; Daniel gave a new hand signal that Peter and I had not seen before and I caught sight of Mau Mau coming out of the kitchen with the fire poker in her hand. She was coming up behind Mr. Daniel. I saw Mutton advance to Mr. Daniel then stop short and crouch down. "Go!" I said to Peter without moving my lips. I said it in my new deep voice. We advanced even with Mutton then squatted down low on all fours as much like Mutton as we could. I looked up to see a stone eyed Mau Mau closing in behind Mr. Daniel and Mr. Hardenbergh. She wasn't watching us at all which suited me fine for I was so ashamed of being bested by Mutton.

Then Bomefree was at her side, fast for my father given that his walk was troubled with stiffness. One of his long arms grabbed the iron poker, the other settled on her shoulder and pulled her in close.

"Mr. Hardenbergh, sir. My children are making a

sorrowful display of their herding abilities. Mr. Daniel has a fine dog who could herd the animals all by herself with a slight bit of help knowing when to bring them in to the farm."

The two white men turned to face Mau Mau and Bomefree. Peter and I stay put. We had not been given the release sign.

"You know we breed strong, tall children. Why, Isabella could start learning both the laundry with Mau Mau and the wheat scything with me. She is taller all ready than all her sisters and brothers at this age."

Bomefree paused to give time for this suggestion to filter in.

"And Peter here could tend the eel pots in the river. Not too young at all, no sir. And a boy is never too young to work with me stripping the bark off the cut wood."

Mau Mau peeled his hand off her shoulder and walked past the group of men straight toward us. I thought we were done for, I saw so much anger in her face.

"Get up children, get up my children," she said.

She held out a hand to each of us. I, of course, got the one with the soot from the poker. We looked past her skirts to see if Daniel gave the release sign. His back was to us and I could see he was holding his arms across his front.

"I said get up!"

Mau Mau never had to tell us twice to do anything and I wanted to tell her that we were doing what Mr. Daniel told us to do which is what she always told us to do. Peter moved first. Being younger, being closer to the insides of our mother, he moved without thinking it out like I had to do, being the older one. When I saw Peter's hand get swallowed up in the great hand of my mother, I found my hand flying to her like a bird.

We adjusted ourselves to walk with Mau Mau as she led up back to our cellar door. I felt Mr. Daniel's eyes burning into my back. We passed Mutton. I stuck my tongue out at her and crossed my eyes, daring her to move.

CHAPTER FOUR

Mr. Daniel made life particularly hard for us after we stopped herding with Mutton. And Mau Mau was most often the target of his intentions. We no longer had access to the extra eggs from the hen house as we had before. The eggs were broken before Mau Mau could get to them. She became quieter after our sheep herding performance. I didn't know if Peter and I had shamed her into silence, or if Mr. Daniel's tricks wore her down. I took pains to avoid Mr. Daniel after I saw his eyes piercing evil into my mother and me. Bomefree said he was vengeful. That meant mean tricks were to be expected forever from Mr. Daniel.

Peter and I took to our new work with a mix of feelings. Peter, although three years younger than me, seemed to get the better work. He now hauled in the eel pots. The pots were attached to a long line that could be hauled in either from the shore of the Rondout Creek where the eels came to spawn or from the boats when Mr. Hardenburgh wanted the pots set further out in the Rondout or in the Hudson River itself. He brought the thick meated catch to the table of Mrs. Hardenbergh, who told Bomefree that if Peter was old enough to haul in the eel pots, he was old enough to learn how to gut and prepare them. Peter did a lot of watching and Mau Mau did a lot of slicing and gutting.

In his other work, Peter spent time with Bomefree when

22

he was stripping bark from the logs to be hewn for lumber and then dried. I'd say Peter escaped from sheep herding and went to a loftier place.

My advancement from working with the sheep meant hauling a lot of water and learning the exacting art of laundry and cleaning from Mau Mau. We had more laundry than most households because the Hardenberghs ran a small hotel that served travelers. Two bedrooms were for guests of the hotel. When we did not have travelers, we often had family visitors, like the Hardenbergh's married daughter and grandchild. When we had travelers staying with us, Mau Mau's work took on a hectic pace and my job was to learn everything that she did. As my mother was getting a bit older, she hoped that I could take over in her place someday as well as take care of her and Bomefree in their old age. Old age for slaves frequently meant freedom. It was the only sort of freedom I had seen for colored people up to that time. Freedom meant being very old with gnarled up bones, being turned out by your owner, and told to make your own way. Bomefree said it was a sure path to death in the winter for old Negroes.

It was at about this time that waking every morning felt more important. The ability for us to stay together, for mother and father not to freeze out in a lean-to in the forest all hinged on me and Peter learning our jobs and becoming good slaves like our parents.

My biggest problem, according to Mau Mau, was learning to be silent. When serving food, walking through a room with visitors, or bringing hot water for the naked backside of Mrs. Hardenbergh, I was to be silent unless spoken to. This went not only for slaves, but for white servants and children as well. Silence did not come naturally to me and my new voice was growing deeper and louder by the day.

My mother looked like she was born and grew in silence. She floated through a room leaving her true self outside to watch clouds and talk to the trees, humming her soft old songs. She wore her hair pulled back from her face with a

23

long braid wrapped round the crown of her head. A sprinkling of searingly white hairs ran along her hairline on either side of her face. When she worked in the main house, she wore a white cloth bonnet, of the style that draped long flaps on either side of her face. When the wind roared down the Catskill Mountains or off the Hudson River, the flaps of her hat stood out like wings. Standing in the farmyard, with her white flaps sticking straight out and her white apron fluttering, she became a black faced bird, ready to leave us and fly north with the geese.

I dreamt once that a flock of geese came and asked my mother if she could fly. She said no, because she had no voice, which had somehow affected her wings. The geese said it was no matter and they lifted her up and flew her low over the house and the meadows. Her neck grew long like theirs but she made no sound when she opened her mouth.

I asked Mau Mau what such a dream meant. She said it meant that I best hurry and learn to be the best slave around.

I was the kind of child who was partial to being outside, as I think all but the most sickly of children are. I missed working with the sheep but I learned from the back hand of Mau Mau not to even mention my time with the sheep lest she go into a fit. Even Mr. Hardenbergh said that there would be no more talk of training children to be dogs.

What kept me outside were the times that Bomefree needed me to scythe the wheat, the hay, and the flax. Of course, I already could swing the short handled sickle and make the grasses whistle as I sliced them from the stem. The long handled scythe was the tool I was after and my father knew it.

"You need to grow this much more," he said, holding up the first knuckle of his thumb, "or you will be no use to me with the long handle."

This made me stand taller and straighter. Mau Mau said not to worry. Children grow most in the summer and more specifically, during the night when the spirit is away and not troubling the body.

"See if you aren't taller tomorrow morning," she said each day.

I marked a place with charcoal on the wall of the summer kitchen. The floor of our cellar home was too wobbly to be counted on for me to stand and then mark my growth on the wall. The summer kitchen was a sturdy floored shed in back of the main house. Our summers got steamy enough without Mau Mau heating a fire all day long in the main house for cooking.

The summer kitchen was as open as it could be and still keep out the rain. On the south side of the summer kitchen, facing the creek, big shutters were fastened after the leaves turned colors and fell; for the summer, they were flung wide open and covered only with canvas if it rained. I made my charcoal mark on the inner door frame each day as the summer progressed.

As I waited to grow taller, I continued under Mau Mau's tutelage. I delivered the bowls of cooked foods from the summer kitchen to the main house. I brought in the split wood from the woodpile. I stoked the open fire for roasting meats and boiling water. The two bread ovens on either side of the fireplace baked not only our breads but the finest pies as well.

We had travelers staying with us at the hotel part of the main house. The Pinkster holiday had just passed. Pinkster falls when summer was still out of reach and only the hardiest of flowers had popped their heads out of the cold, wet ground. It was our most joyous holiday, as well as our only holiday, where the slaves had several days off in a row, and wore bright clothes begged and borrowed from who knows where. Mau Mau told us of street fairs in some towns where a Negro king and queen were selected and given crowns of flowers. She also said some colored fools took to drinking rum and that if she ever caught wind of any of her children doing such wickedness she would turn them inside out, no matter how old they were.

Mau Mau had fresh laundry, sheets and all the white

25

clothes, washed and spread out over the bushes and low trees to bleach in the sun. It was just hot enough to open up the summer kitchen so we were busy setting it up for the season. Mrs. Hardenbergh said the guests were very important, from Albany. Mau Mau must make peach pies and one of the geese had to be killed, plucked, and roasted. We had our hands full.

Mau Mau sent me running this way and that, carrying bowls of flat breads to the main house with cold cooked beef.

"Eggs," she said, "Isabella, we've got to have more eggs today."

I forgot, and I suppose Mau Mau forgot too, that Mr. Daniel was feeling bested by us in front of Mr. Hardenbergh. He was particularly hateful to my mother, standing in her way when she was loaded with wet laundry or a pail of water, making her work twice as hard when it came time to render the lard from the butchered hogs, dropping the fat into the dirt. He made sure that none of his meanness was in evidence when the Hardenbergh's were about. But in the rush of the moment we both forgot about his mean and small ways.

Mau Mau saw my arms were filled with food for the main house. On top of that, Mrs. Hardenbergh yelled out for me to see if the sheets were dried yet and if they were, to carry them right up stairs. My mother wiped small bubbles of sweat off her forehead with her apron. "You go on in, I'll run and get the eggs," she said.

I got caught up in the flurry of guests arriving; four old men, friends of Mr. Hardenbergh's father, friends from the big war when we said good bye to the English, which to hear the Hardenbergh's tell it, was the best thing to happen since God. These old soldiers were coming straight from Albany and everyone was in a riot about them staying with us.

I helped set up the two rooms, brought water for the wash basins, double checked the night jars to make sure they were empty, and wiped down all the good plates with the tiny flowers on the rim. It was a long time before I got back out to the summer kitchen. I did everything right with Mrs.

Hardenbergh, no loud talking, and no spilling water.

Mau Mau was gone and the fire was nearly died out. The bowl of flour was just as she left it when she went to get the eggs. My stomach grew quick knots. My bare feet dug into the grass and dirt as I ran to the far side of the barn where the hen house sat.

Mr. Daniel emerged from the door and quickly closed it behind him as I nearly collided with him. I was glad for not bumping into him, as I could not imagine anyone touching Mr. Daniel except for Mutton.

"Looks like you're training to be the next house nigger," he said. "You make sure she teaches you everything."

Mr. Daniel gave me the cold stare and then he let his eyes settle not on my face but on my chest and even lower. The sound of a wagon pulling into the yard snapped his face up again and he was off.

I pushed open the rough wood door. The stink from the hen house always shocked my eyes and nose in the first moments. On the side farthest from the door was a heap of body and cloth on top of the chicken manure that was piled knee high until someone got ready to heave it out the door. A ray of sunlight flecked with straw dust hit a brown arm.

"Mau Mau?"

The crumpled body lifted her head and straw and clumps of manure were stuck to her hair. My mother had been face down. She turned her face away from me and vomited into the mess around her.

"Get me water. And my other dress. Check the fire on the way."

I did as she told me. I didn't know what Mr. Daniel had done but I knew it was very bad. When I brought fresh water and the clean dress, she was standing, leaning her back end against the first row of raised nesting for the chickens. She held her hands to her ribs on her right side. I helped her slide the torn and badly soiled dress off over her head. I yelped when I saw the bite marks on her shoulder and the bruises rising to the surface of her ribs.

27

"What happened? What did Mr. Daniels do to you?"

Even as I spoke, my eyes fastened on the blood streaks on the inside of her thighs and the thick wetness that turned chalky on the dry edges. I didn't want to know. I fought to keep the image out of my mind as I crooned over Mau Mau. I started at her head and washed her with cool water. I picked the chicken droppings and straw from her hair and hummed a cricket song. Mau Mau rocked back and forth, letting my cricket song chase away Mr. Daniels. Despite my crooning song, I knew what had happened and I hated Mr. Daniels. I grew old on that day, washing the damage from my mother.

Every farm child grows up seeing animals mate, seeing the large cock of a horse hanging down. Peter and I watched the pigs, the sheep, the horses, and the cows, plus some cats and dogs hump away on each other. Colored children on farms were not spared the coarsest words and they come back easily to me. The animals never looked like they enjoyed doing it what with one looking it was killing the other. Bomefree said that wasn't so. He said they do it to have babies. I suspected that people did such things because my parents sometimes hung a blanket between them and us at night and I heard strange and fretful sounds. But Mau Mau told me that babies came on spring winds and comets and such.

As I washed my mother's body, letting my cloth slip water over her breasts, her belly, and sopping up the blood and other wetness from her legs, I knew that Mr. Daniels had both beat my mother and humped away at her with his cock.

"Get the eggs," she said when she was cleaned and dressed again. I didn't know how my mother could keep such thoughts in her mind. She was already thinking about baking the cakes and making the necessary excuses to Mrs. Hardenbergh for the tardiness of the evening meal. She left behind her body's memory of her face in the dried clumps of chicken manure, and Mr. Daniel's teeth in the flesh of her shoulder.

"We will have to work extra hard today. You will have to

run, you hear me, run all day."

She didn't have to tell me. I would do anything for my mother. If she had told

me to kill Mr. Daniels, I would have done so. I would have chopped his neck with the ax as we later did to the goose. If she had said to bind his hands and feet with rope, fill his pockets with stones and throw him into the Swartekill Creek, I would have done so. But what she told me to do was to clean, cook, carry, serve and I did so.

For the evening supper, Mau Mau and I served in silence. I was ever watchful to help carry the heaviest platters. My mother moved like the mute swan of my dream, voiceless and full of grace. The guests talked about what they called the old days, about the great war for freedom from the English, the sheer terror of Kingston, our port town on the Hudson, being burned by the English and the smoke that could be seen from the yard of the Hardenbergh's farm. One old man, dressed in fine breeches, tall boots, and a fine vest over his shirt, said, "I would do it again, I would fight to the death for our freedom. If you don't have freedom in this life, then you are not truly a man."

I wanted to ask him if the same applied to a woman and a girl. If he had come a day earlier, it is likely that such a question might have spilled out of me. But today I was much older and the question stayed in my throat.

29

CHAPTER FIVE

I grew more than Bomefree said I needed to that summer.
He said a knuckle's length and I grew more. I was at the
age where girls grow so fast that you can hear both the corn
growing and their bones crackling on a summer night. I grew
tall enough to use the scythe right along with my father. In
late summer we sheared down the flax, the wheat, the hay.
He taught me the steady rhythm needed for all day working. I
naturally wanted to go fast and I wore myself out long before
noontime on the first day. Bomefree was still swinging his
scythe easy, low and letting his body go with it. His arthritis
even seemed to loosen up as his long self weaved slowly
back and forth. At first I thought he was just going slow
because he was old. There was a lot of talk about Bomefree
being old those days.

My father let me wear myself out on the first day, let me
get blistered up on my hands from holding the scythe too
tight. At night, as he rubbed herbed lard into my hands, he
said, "Are you ready to learn how to go slow and steady or
do you need to burn up more of your skin on fast? Step small
and let the scythe swing from one side to the other. Keep
your knees bent. Let the rhythm carry the scythe like the
clock in the house, back and forth."

I'm a fast learner on most things, painful slow on others.
Scything was one that I caught on to quickly. Mr.

Hardenbergh took to bragging about me, saying that it was good to have a nigger girl who could do field work and house work.

I took comfort in working hard even then. When I worked hard, I showed Mr. Hardenbergh that I was worth keeping. I also relieved some of my father's labor. Working til I was spent meant we could all live together forever.

My exact age at this point is unclear. No one wrote my birth in a book to catch it in time, or so Bomefree told me. He had been around a long time and this was something he was sure of; the birth of slaves did not get recorded in the black scratches of the owners.

Mr. Hardenbergh had a way of saying exactly how old a thing was or when a white person was born. It had to do with writing. Mrs. Hardenbergh did not have the skill of writing and was upset by the lack of it. She made sure her daughter had the schooling to write and read. I didn't pay much mind to either reading or writing as neither Mau Mau nor Bomefree were skilled in those areas so I saw no need to do so myself nor was it offered to me.

Writing was reserved for important things on the farm; the number of sheep born in the spring, the birth of a white granddaughter, the sale of land to one of the nephews. Was it possible that I might be written down in one of the special books as important? A flicker of me who could now cut down hay with the scythe felt important. I had never doubted my father before but the thought occurred to me that he might have missed the occasion of my birth being written down as he had been too busy working.

"Am I written in the book?" I asked Mrs. Hardenbergh as she sat working on her needle work, dipping in and out of the linen with bright indigo thread. I scraped corn kernels from the cobs with a knife. The two of us were on the back porch.

"What a strange thing to ask. Next time my daughter comes to visit, we'll have her take a look. Mr. Hardenbergh chides me and takes an upper hand about reading and writing. No point in fueling his fire."

Mrs. Anna came to visit on a Sunday and the three of us pored through Mr. Hardenbergh's book while he was gone to the river town of Kingston. Mrs. Hardenburgh and I squeezed our eyebrows in concentration as if we could decipher the writing.

"Let's see if we can find you in here Isabella. You'd be under property. Farm property...eel pots, two wagons.... now, property acquired from the estate of Johannes Hardenbergh, Negro girl child, weaned and walking. Why Isabella, father did write something down about you. You are in the book after all."

I was pleased to be in the book. The lack of exactness had no meaning for me. Mrs. Anna figured on her fingers, "Grandfather died in 1799, you might have been around two years old. That makes you almost ten years old. What do you think of that?'

"Will I always be a ten?" I was both pleased to be near ten and nervous that I didn't know what to make of being a ten.

Anna and Mrs. Hardenbergh laughed when I asked my question. Anna spoke slowly and more loudly to me as if I had suddenly gone hard of hearing.

"Ten is the number of years you have been alive. Next year you will be eleven years old, or there abouts. Do you understand Isabella?"

I nodded yes although I was afraid to let them know that I had not heard all this before and I needed time to let it simmer in me before I could make sense of it. Mrs. Hardenbergh told me to run along and help Mau Mau in the summer kitchen. As I stepped outside the kitchen, I heard the two women talking through the open window.

"Don't try and teach her things she can't learn. The colored minds stay like children forever. That's the way it is with all the coloreds."

I was going to stay just as I was forever. I wondered why my parents had not told me this. Mau Mau told me I was going to wear myself out thinking. Bomefree said he felt heat

32

coming off my head from all my tangled up thoughts. Now Mrs. Hardenbergh said my mind, as well as my mother's and my father's, was stuck forever as a child.

Bomefree and Mau Mau had much more in their minds than I did and I had more in my mind than Peter. Indeed, Peter seemed to be emptying his mind since tending the eel pots. But I could not imagine a mind more full than my mother's. She held the story of her travels from Africa, when she was a tiny girl and fed extra biscuits by the slave ship's crew, the stories of all my sisters and brothers from birth to the day each one was sold off, and the stories of Bomefree's people that even he had forgotten by now.

A revelation occurred to me. Mau Mau kept a good part of herself secret from the Hardenbergh's, so they did not know her great, filled mind. They did not know that Mau Mau could name a thing and bring it to life. And she could unname as well, which I only saw her do one time.

When I found my mother in the hen house and after I had cleaned her up and as we were walking out, she pinched my arm hard, her soiled clothes in my hands, me holding her up on her still unsteady legs.

"You cannot, hear me, cannot tell your father or anyone about this. When we cross the doorway, we will never speak of this again. Nothing happened here. That man does not exist. Do not call him by name."

I thought she would pull the skin right off my bony arm. The man who no longer existed, who I used to call Mr. Daniels, still lived and worked at the farm. And he didn't know what we had done to him by unnaming him but he knew something was wrong. I got so I could look clear through him so only a shadow of an outline was left to him.

What the no name man didn't know was that Mau Mau was a namer and so was I. My mother told me often enough that I was like her, able to name the sound that snow makes falling off the roof, or name the first feeling of autumn.

To name a thing is to give it meaning and life. To take away a name from a person is the same as slicing them open and letting their blood drain out. Pretty soon that person has no life left.

The no name man tried his evil stares on Mau Mau and me back when we could still see him, but after a time, there was no blood left in his eyes to make the stare solid. Mau Mau was far better at naming and unnaming than I was. It seemed that in her world, the no name man was gone, had turned into mist, like the billowing white blankets that hung along the rivers in the morning and were gone by noon time. As hard as I practiced the powers of Mau Mau, I still caught sight of him at times, the twitching muscles of his jaw, the way he would slam down a tool, making it jump, or the way he would squat in the shade of the barn door with one knee on the ground, one out like a table for whittling.

* * *

We harvested peaches that summer. I suppose peaches were grown every summer but the summer I was tall enough to use the scythe, the summer Mr. Daniels became unnamed, was the first summer I remember peaches.

Bomefree rigged up a peach picking basket that hung on a pole. At the end of the pole was a sharp blade with a rope and pulley and if you were careful, had good aim and good luck, the peach landed in the basket and not on the ground where it would be bruised before it softened. Because I was neither careful nor had good aim or luck, I was not allowed to use my father's great peach picker.

Mau Mau was famous for her peach pies, so famous that Mr. Hardenbergh read a letter to her from one of our guests at the Inn, who commented at great length about the sheer wonder of her peach pie. Mau Mau gave us one of the first smiles since the beginning of the summer.

We picked and dried everything there was to pick. We picked berries and made jam or preserves, we picked apples and dried them in the sun or set them aside for the cider press. The gristmill, powered by the new waterwheel on the

Swartekill, was now grinding daily. Most of the flour was sold, then enough was kept to last the farm till spring.

Early autumn on the Hardenberg farm was a busy time, filled with crisp apple smells as they were crushed in the cider press, sides of pork being smoked, and the beauty of gold, yellow, and red leaves making a miracle of color on our hills. I heard more laughter from the Hardenbergs this time of year as their bounty of crops was harvested and stockpiled or sold in Kingston on the dock. If I wasn't bundling wheat that my father and I scythed, I was helping to load apples through the cider press, or sacking grain to take to the grist mill on the Swartekill creek.

Peter was pulled off his eel pot duties for which he sulked terribly the first day. I think he forgot about work and was wishing to forget it forever. In our bed, after our parents were matching snores with each other, I told Peter that he was old enough to work as hard as me, and that if he didn't that he'd be sold south the very next day.

"Oh yes." I said. "I heard Mr. Hardenbergh say so just today. That he wouldn't have a useless nigger child here. He said if you didn't load sacks of wheat, haul wood, and water, and do everything your sister said, you'd be sold south by the time the first orange leaves fell."

Peter cried all night. I didn't regret telling this lie at the time. Peter ran from grain to wood to water all the next day and the days after. When I was convinced that Peter would keep working, I told him that Mr. Hardenberg was willing to keep him on if Peter would keep working this hard and especially if he listened to me. Peter didn't entirely believe that he was safe until long into the winter.

To get ready for winter after the flurry of activity in the fall, we had to chink the cracks in our walls with hay, mud, or slivers of wood. We also had to get warm clothes. Mrs. Hardenbergh asked Mau Mau to check all of us for shoes. For most of the summer, none of my family wore shoes. The soles of my feet grew happy and tough, my toes spread wide. Now Mau Mau tried to force last year's shoes on me. My feet had grown to match my height and despite serious efforts on her part and tears on my part, the shoes could not be made to cover my feet. Peter tried on my old boots and they fit with room to spare.

Mau Mau drew an outline of my feet on a board that was taken to the shoemaker in Hurley and the result was a sturdy pair of boots so big that I had to stuff the ends with wool. Mrs. Hardenbergh wanted these boots to last me more than one winter, maybe as many as three or four.

Next, Mau Mau readied us with clothes for the long winter. We used slave cloth mostly. Slave cloth was a rough hewn cloth with a wide weave, whether it be flax or cotton or wool. Mr. Hardenberg said the world had gone wild for cotton. Mrs. Hardenbergh bought two bolts of cotton and the weave was so tight that you couldn't tell that it was made from thread. She made her own dresses from a number of fine fabrics.

Mau Mau dyed my cloth yellow from onion skins so it wouldn't be so plain. I liked the gold color against my skin. With the sun turning late afternoon to long slanted rays, my skin and my gold cloth looked to be as fine a pair as ever I'd seen.

Mau Mau knew how to knit almost anything. She said a lot of colored people didn't know how. Starting in late summer, she spun the wool sheared from the sheep after it was carded. Winters around Kingston made wool as precious as gold. I would say that animal skins and wool were more valuable than anything except food. She spun, which I had not yet learned to do, then she got to keep some of the wool for us. She knitted the wool into boot liners, hand mitts, sweaters, shawls, and scarves.

She got us ready for winter, when we would wake to snow filtering through the openings in the wood slats. The snow would soon sit in coned piles near the walls, and the water would need to be brought inside at night to stay near thawing. My mother and I wore quilted britches beneath our wool skirts.

Winter came early, right on the tail of the last falling leaves and the last honking geese following the Hudson south. In truth, the winter, miserable though it may be, was a quieter time of year without as much work to do. Several times, Peter and I were called upstairs into the main house to hear stories told by visitors and to warm ourselves by the fire.

CHAPTER SIX

The howl that went up from the main house made me drop my early morning load of wood and run to the house. The wail sounded like an animal caught in a trap about to chew off its leg. Bomefree hit the front step at the same time as me. He pushed me back to the stone slab steps. I feared for him going in alone and so I waited a short time and then followed him.

The howling came from Mrs. Hardenberg who had awakened to find a cold and dead husband beside her in bed. I peeked in the bedroom and there was the dead man, open eyed and slack jawed. He was a blue gray color. The thought of our master falling to something as plain as death had not occurred to me as a possibility.

Spring was in the air and it seemed wrong to have so big a death when this season wanted to get a fresh start on life. Early signs of buds were everywhere and we were awash in mud from the melted snow.

Bomefree hitched up the wagon, slogging ankle deep in mud around the barn. He set out to Mrs. Anna's house, which would take him till mid day given the slowness of the roads. From there he went straight to the homes of the Hardenberg brothers. They were a quarrelsome pair of men, more stern than our master.

Mau Mau tended to the widow who wailed long into the

morning, crying on my mother's breast, soaking her dress front. I was set to making tea and a thin soup from the meat and vegetables of the night before that Mau Mau eventually spooned to Mrs. Hardenbergh.

Peter grabbed at my elbow. "What should I do?" he asked me.

"Stay in the kitchen with me, haul the kettle over the fire, keep the wood stocked, and be ready to run errands for Mau Mau."

The death of a master was something I knew nothing of and I relied on Mau Mau to tell us what to do. For the most of the morning, Peter and I sat by the fire in the kitchen, perched on the stone hearth, saying nothing, waiting with my eyes turned often to the hallway leading to the bedroom with the blue-gray dead man.

The missus slowed her crying and sat stunned in a wicker seated chair in the far side of the bedroom. I brought her a basin of water to wash herself.

"Your daughter will be here soon. And then after her, Mr. Hardenbergh's brothers will be here," said Mau Mau.

"Yes, I need to get ready, don't I?"

"Do you want to prepare the body with me?" asked Mau Mau. I didn't know how she prepared a body but it sounded serious.

"No. I've seen enough of his body in my lifetime," said the Missus.

She heaved her body out of the chair and over to the wash basin as if she were the weight of the mountains. My mother pulled her night dress over her head and started to wash her. I don't think my mother usually washed the missus. But she did then, in the way she would if a baby had vomited or when Peter had the terrible diarrhea. I watched from my place near the door and I think both of them forgot about me.

Mau Mau waited with the mistress until afternoon when Bomefree returned with Mrs. Anna. The daughter fell into her mother's arms and then the Missus seemed to be more herself and comforted her daughter.

39

Mau Mau set me to boiling water and bringing wet rags and a bucket into the bedroom.

"Close the door Isabella. Now come here and do as I say. First, say the Lord's Prayer with me."

My mother taught me to say the Lord's Prayer back before I can even remember. We said it every night and any other time the moment seemed right for Mau Mau, no matter where she was. I often saw her mouthing it, mutely, as she did the laundry, and more often, as she took to sitting outside under God's sky at night.

We said the prayer together, right next to the stiff, dead master who was then giving off a shocking odor. She took off the large sack of night dress that he wore to bed, back when he was among the living. I saw the certain evidence that he had messed himself. Mau Mau said that people do that when they die. The body lets go of everything it was holding in. She said when the spirit left the body, the body then became useless and could no longer hear, see, taste, remember, forget, or keep from messing the pants.

Having cleaned him, she and I dressed him in some of his fancier clothes, not the muddy work clothes of everyday. It was hardest to get him into his stockings and his pants.

The Hardenbergh family was well known in the area and the following day, a steady stream of people came to tell Mrs. Hardenbergh about their sadness for her and to say fine things about her husband. His body was laid out on a table in the main room, as far from the fireplace as we could put him. Bomefree said dead bodies do poorly in a warm room. As a final precaution, the fire was not lit in the main room and the door to the kitchen was closed up. It was here where I spent most of my time during those sad days. For once we were the warm ones in the steamy kitchen, and the white people wore their coats in the cold main room, sitting on their hands to keep them from turning as blue as Mr. Hardenbergh.

Peter had been absent too long from the kitchen and I needed him to bring in fresh cream and milk. I went to look for him when I overheard two visitors talking in low tones.

"It's a shame there is no son in this family," said one man. I had seen him before at the gristmill.

"There will be a fight over this, I know his brothers. Won't go easy on the widow," said a man who stepped gingerly down the stone steps into the muddy yard. They were both old men, with white hair, and thick white eyebrows that stuck straight out from their foreheads.

After the burial, the farm continued without the usual spring plans for planting. I asked Bomefree why no one was planting the early wheat.

"They'll be changes now. I've seen it before. Seen it enough times to wish I hadn't."

"Seen what?" I asked him. He fed tobacco into his clay pipe.

"When the master dies and there is no son to claim the land along with the widow, there's trouble to be had. Mr. Hardenbergh's brothers are getting ready to jump on this farm like black flies."

"What will happen to us?"

"Depends on more things than I know about." Bomefree smoked his pipe more often these days.

While Mau Mau no longer had to see the no-name man, I occasionally caught sight of the wisp of him left from being unnamed. I saw the thin outline of him talking more and more with the missus, something he had not done while the master was alive. His scent, a gamey cat smell, surprised me as it lingered on one of the kitchen chairs. I sniffed the seat of the chair and I knew he had been invited to sit, not just stand in the doorway.

Mrs. Hardenberg took to talking more and more with the no-name man, particularly in the evenings when she was apt to get sad and talk about her husband. At first, she relied almost entirely on Mau Mau in the quiet moments of the evening; crying and needing Mau Mau to hold her hand, to tell her that everything would be all right, that with enough help the farm could continue as it was, maybe sell off a piece or two. At any time, I might hear her tell Mau Mau the same thing, again and again.

"You are my saving grace. If it weren't for you and my daughter, I don't know how I would have gotten through these dark days. You are so like family Mau Mau," she said.

I knew that our fate was in the good hands of Mrs. Hardenberg, that Bomefree was mistaken about any misfortune coming our way. She could not get on without the warm comfort and wisdom of Mau Mau.

The news of the auction was delivered to Bomefree. I was not present when Mrs. Hardenberg told him, but I have imagined it many times. Did she look him in the eye, did she stand rigid, did she tell him in an off-hand sort of way, such as news of an early frost or a dry summer? Did he stand pegged to the ground, unable to move after she turned and left the rustling sound of her black widow's skirts dancing in the warm June air? Did he go first to Mau Mau or did he walk to the shelter of the woods and rage? I did not see him tell my mother that the property of the farm was to be auctioned to settle an inheritance dispute between Mrs. Hardenberg and the brothers of her late husband. I was not there when Mau Mau lost the strength of her unnaming skills due to her grief and terror and had to see Mr. Daniels all over again. It took full strength to unsee and Mau Mau's strength leaked out with the news of the auction.

All the farm animals and tools were to be auctioned. At first, all of us were to be auctioned as well. My Father was to be set free. There was not enough left of him to sell. Mau Mau being so much younger than Bomefree, could still be sold as a house slave. Her loyalty and good nature were known widely and she would fetch a good price. I didn't know why, but it was finally decided that Mau Mau could stay with Bomefree and care for him into his old age and that they could continue to live in the cellar home with the new owners of Hardenberg Inn. It was a great relief for me that my parents could stay together and that Bomefree would never die alone without his beloved Mau Mau. Even so, I took to vomiting most of the food I ate.

In all of my ten years, I had never seen an auction and so, could not picture what an auction would look like. I pressed my parents to tell me what to expect. My mother, who could speak of many things, who could keep stories in her head from the beginning of time, could not tell me what an auction looked like because she fell to crying when I mentioned it. It was left to Bomefree to tell me about them.

"People will come and look at all the things being sold, to see if they want to bid on any particular thing. Not everyone needs another herd of sheep. They might only need a work wagon or a wagon for special outings. Then the bidding will start when the auctioneer says to begin. Then they will haul something up to the center like the cider press and those who want it will bid what they can pay with the hope of paying the least."

"How will Peter and I be sold?" I asked my father.

"Just like I said, the same way. Them that wants a nigger girl will look at you good and hard then decide if they can bid on you. There's not many who can afford a slave so the bidding will be thin," said Bomefree.

"What if someone needs two nigger children? Then Peter and I will be sold together."

"Around here slaves are sold one by one, mother by mother, father by father and child by child. The selling part is something I have seen since I was much younger than you, younger than Peter. You will not be sold with Peter," he said. His clay pipe snapped in his hand as he finished talking. A new vein on his neck thumped madly, the skin around his eyes hunched up, and the furrows on his forehead were deep and dark like freshly tilled fields.

"Isabella, you need to get ready for being with new folks and new ways. Between now and the auction you listen to everything that we tell you and remember as much of it as you can. That is the best that can be done."

"How can I learn everything that you and Mau Mau know? I only started to learn the scythe. I don't know how to spin the wool. I don't know when to still my voice, when to be silent, when to say the rights words."

"Takes time daughter, takes time. Your new owner will let you know when you've done wrong. Then you learn, and correct yourself."

At night, Peter and I hung on to each other and stopped sleeping. We whispered all night long.

"We'll be sold together won't we sister? Anyone can see that together we will work a farm better than anyone. I'll listen to everything you tell me. You'll see," said my little brother.

We lay nose to nose. His brown eyes grew large and I swam in them searching for God to hear us both.

As the time grew closer to the auction, Mau Mau took us more often outdoors to her church, as she called it. She took us to a clearing past the house, off the path to the grist mill. She told us that God was in everything and everyplace. Peter and I sat huddled to her side under the stars, as she told us that God is in the leaf, the fish, the rock, and the wind.

"If you call to him, he can hear you. In this life, you must ask Him for help. Keep talking to God."

"Is God in the eels I bring to you?" asked Peter.

"Yes."

"Is God listening to us right now?"

"Yes."

"Can you get God to sell Isabella and me together on a farm close to you and Bomefree?" asked Peter.

"There is suffering in this life and I pray every day that our suffering will end. You might get sold to different places. But God promises to end our suffering when we die, when we go to heaven. You have to speak to God to tell Him you understand, that you understand how this life is," said Mau Mau.

Her instructions grew more feverish in the day before the auction.

"If you think that you will be lashed, tell God, and ask God to be with you. Tell him to heal your wounds quickly so that you can get back to work again and be ready for the day when suffering ends. If the cold is too harsh, talk to God and ask him to warm you."

She moaned and rocked till it was Peter and me comforting her, patting her with our four hands, rocking with her.

The day of the auction was quiet in our house. Peter and I had tried not to sleep the night before. We told ourselves to stay awake all night. I don't know why. Sometimes it is hard to go back to a child's way of thinking, how staying awake will keep evil away, how looking deep into Peter's eyes, sucking in his breath, would keep us together. In the end, it was Mau Mau and Bomefree who stayed awake all night and Peter and me who slept. I awoke to the silence of my mother's rigid form standing next to our kitchen table, her arms folded over her breasts. She stared straight into the wet wall. The June rains sent rivulets of water glistening down the wall, soaking the earth floor beneath us.

"Give them what food we have woman. Fill their pockets," said Bomefree. He left to lay down planks of wood to keep the people out of the mud in the barnyard when they arrived for the auction.

"What stories will you tell of Peter and me," I asked Mau Mau as she packed dried meat and flatbread in our pockets. The thought had just come to me that she would have to keep us in her head with stories and I wanted to know which ones she would tell.

She fell into Bomefree's chair with a sob, and hung her head, and called to God. Peter grabbed my hand as we stood in front of her.

Then she said, "Isabella, I will tell how you rode here on a fast comet and how your voice filled the barn and the house and how you are a namer. Peter, I will tell how you are a joyful soul and how you made the eels laugh."

As the day heated up and the people for the auction arrived in their wagons and on horseback, my family stood near the pile of tools, barrels and such. We did not speak. I was taken to the front and center after the sale of the cider press. I faced a sea of white people, mostly men with boots up to their knees. The auctioneer talked about someone who would last a long time, someone who came from a family of fine breeders, how fine an investment was to be made, how young and strong this person was, and I came to understand he meant me. I was all these things, some of which had no meaning for me.

My dress was pulled over my head and with a swift jerk. I was naked underneath. I heard Mau Mau gasp. I stood with the bothersome bugs trying to get in my eyes, trying to remember if my mother had told me about having to show myself naked to all the people and if so, what should I do.

"She doesn't have a mark on her," said a graveled voice from the crowd.

"Hardenbergh didn't know how to manage his colored ones, that's for sure," said another one.

I was asked to turn around. I was asked to open my mouth for the auctioneer to look at my teeth. My age was reported to the crowd. No bids were made. My sack dress was returned to me and I slid it back over my body.

"Who will start the bidding? Do I have $100?"

Silence. I wondered for the first time what would happen if no one wanted me. Could it be possible that I could simply go back with my family? As I pondered this I heard a familiar voice.

"Sell the nigger girl with the sheep," shouted Mr. Daniels from the back of the crowd. "She's got a way with the sheep."

I saw him as clearly as I ever had before he became unnamed. Mutton was by his side. His arms were folded over his chest and he was smiling and looking straight at Mau Mau as if there was no one else except the two of them. With the nod of approval from the Hardenbergh brothers, the sheep were included in my sale.

For the sum of one hundred dollars, the sheep and I were sold to John Neely, a man who spoke a brittle form of Dutch and mostly the foreign language of English. When the bidding for me and the sheep was over, I didn't know what to do. I started to walk back to my family.

"Get over here!" barked John Neely.

He was mounted on his horse and ready to leave. He rode his horse between me and Mau Mau, who was fast approaching.

"Get," he said again.

He herded me over to the sheep with his horse.

"We go," he said.

My knees grew weak and I was overcome with fear. I was leaving. Peter was not coming with me and he looked suddenly smaller next to Bomefree who had an iron grip on him. Who would look after him, keep an eye on him, sleep with him, wake him up? I would be lost without Mau Mau and Bomefree. I let loose with my large voice and I cried out for my mother. I could not see her for the bulk of John Neeley's copper horse but I heard her, I heard the scream tear out of her and into me.

The crack of his whip caught me by surprise. The whip did its job to drive me with the sheep. Everytime I turned to look back, he snapped the whip and spoke an English word that I did not understand. As we passed the last gate from the Hardenbergh's farm, we passed Mr. Daniels, who leaned against the stone wall. He must have cut across the field to get there so quick. He looked hard at me the whole time we passed. It was the last time I ever saw him. My war with John Neely had begun.

JACQUELINE SHEEHAN

CHAPTER SEVEN

John Neely spoke a young child's form of Dutch, enough to
tell me, "go, come here, sheep, eat, water, speak English."
We walked till the cool of the evening descended on us. I
knew to keep the sheep from wandering to one side while he
covered the other side. It was a saving grace that I was kept
busy on the journey to his home. Dusty work forced out the
sound of Mau Mau and the picture I had made up in my mind
of Peter being sold as I had been. When I had a moment to
think, I hoped that Peter would not be frightened to death by
his new owner.

John Neely's house was made of stone. I could see right
off that it was not so large a house as the Hardenbergh's. And
this was not so large a farm either. When we put the sheep
into the fence, I didn't know what to do next. I had eaten
most of the bread cakes in my pockets. I stayed in the front
yard of the house and watched his back as he scraped the
soles of his high boots on the sides of the gray stone steps.
He was most particular about his boots. He gave me a stern
look and went inside, leaving the door open. Keeping his
hand on the door frame, and poking his head out the door to
keep looking at me, he hollered into the house to someone. A
woman holding an infant came out the door. She had two
little children, both girls, hanging onto her skirts.

The missus took one look at me and scowled and let
loose with an army of angry words, none of which I

48

understood. I could only guess at their meaning. I wondered if the missus didn't like the looks of me, wondered if she had asked for a different kind of slave, a boy slave, or a grown up slave. I hung my head and tried to adjust my dress by running my hand down the front of it.

All the words spoken by John Neely from that moment on would be in English. I would on occasion meet with someone who spoke my warm, Dutch tongue, and when that would happen, my soul poured out to them. My world was about to become tight and small, a world where my thoughts and feelings stayed in my throat. I floated in a land of people who spoke incomprehensible words to me and could not bear a moment of patience or compassion when I did not understand.

I entered into a world of strange, chattering silence. I understood the sound of the crow better than the words of my new owners. The crow called to her mate and announced that a dry time was coming, that there would be no rain to drive the fat worms from the ground, or that a wild flock of insects were spotted along the edges of the Rondout Creek dancing along the boats that brought John Neely goods to sell in his store. The crows made more sense than the tight-lipped English speakers. The truth was, he spoke enough words of Dutch to do business with the members of the old Dutch families, but he let me know that in his house, only English was spoken.

There was one exception. I slept in a shed that looked hastily built on the kitchen side of the house. At night, the master opened the door to my little shed. He shoved me against the wall of the house. He stood close, facing me and said Dutch words that had to do with my most private parts. He said names for my chest and my arse that were Dutch but still new to me. I stood as still as I could. It was often dark when he came to say these words to me and I dared not move as he looked agitated and I did not want to cause further problems. He worked up a sweat and the moisture carried his scent to my nose. His smell was not so gamey as Mr. Daniels nor as pleasant as my father's. I prayed that the missus would call to him or that a tree would fall or lightning strike his barn and catch it on fire so that he would leave me in my silence. When he was sweated up and his jaw muscles looked like they would pop, he grabbed his manhood, moaned like he was in pain and then wet himself a little, all the while looking straight in my eyes.

I dared not move nor speak while he carried on. So to occupy my mind, I pictured myself washing laundry with Mau Mau or scything with Bomefree. I stared straight back at him with my eyes but my spirit was busy doing the good work with my family. After John Neely finished up, he went back to his English speaking. He was like two men; the one who sold his goods from the storefront on one side of the house and the one who came into my sleeping shed to stare in my face and point to my body.

In the first few days with him, I tried to appeal to him in Dutch, to ask him, "what is this called, how do you say broom, barrel, trivet, vinegar," but he cuffed me on my face with the side of his hand with a chopping motion. The first time he did this, I was stung both by the pain, and by the insult my body felt. I had been hit before, by my mother and my father to get my attention loud and clear, and by the swat of a frustrated Mrs. Hardenbergh who wanted me out of her way, but never with such deliberate motion as came from John Neely. His strike let me know that he looked for opportunities to hurt.

All of my words stayed inside me and echoed against my ribs and spine. I did what I imagined they wanted. I pointed to the hearth. I looked with one eyebrow raised at the woodpile, at the cold ham to be sliced and served, at the broom in the corner. My voice that had grown so large in my ten years backed up like a log jammed river. I was silent.

The Neely house was filled with talk and with a mistrust of me. Something had gone wrong between husband and wife. They fired words at each other and pointed at me nearly every day. I took this to mean that they disagreed, either at my purchase entirely, or at my price. In the rush of sounds, I waited for a repetition to emerge that I could connect with a person or a thing.

Then finally I thought I was saved by the baby daughter. "Mama," said the baby girl who walked on unsteady legs and smelled of sour britches. "Mama." I was so relieved to hear this word. Of course I knew it and it warmed my heart.

"Mama," I said to the baby, pointing to the mistress. The baby girl smiled an open mouthed smile. I crouched next to her and held out my hand. The crash of the broom on my shoulders caught me off balance and both the baby and I tipped over on the floor.

I sealed my lips and braced for the broom that crashed down on me again and again. To say Mama was wrong as well. I could not even say this familiar word.

CHAPTER EIGHT

Summer trailed off to autumn and I began to dream of Mau Mau and Bomefree and Peter. The dreams were so terrible that it was a relief to fully wake up to the day and to shake the terror of the dream from every part of me. I dreamt that Mau Mau, Bomefree and Peter lived in a new town where all the colored people had their own houses. My sisters and brothers were all living in the house. Mau Mau had her full voice and she was naming and unnaming people left and right. When I ran to her, she unnamed me so they couldn't see me. I was stunned to be the target of her unnaming. I smelled the pies that she made: peach, apple, blueberry. I tried to scream to them, but in the unnaming, my voice was lost as well and none of them could hear me. The sorrow I felt when waking from this dream was as deep as it was on the auction day, but worse because it seemed like it came from my own family not wanting me. I must have had this dream a dozen times during my life with John Neely.

It was only after these dreams that I welcomed my cold, wordless isolation with my owners, the daily cuffs from John Neely's fist, senseless English words that had no meaning for me and that now seemed too dangerous to learn. This was better than the terror of the blank stares of my family in my dreams. When awake, I pictured Mau Mau as she was, sending her love by way of the wind, trees, and stars. I pictured old Bomefree sucking on his clay pipe, but I could not picture Peter. I only prayed that his life was better than mine was with John Neely.

I held tight to the notion that God could hear me. Mau Mau told me, time after time, to talk to God, let God hear my voice. And if I could get God to hear me quick enough, I could survive anything. So I talked to God and asked to learn a word of English, and if I practiced the word, I learned it. I whispered the English words when I was alone, not daring to have another encounter with the missus and the broom. I learned the words for water, wood, fire, get out of here, and boat.

God also helped me prepare for particular things. It was early on that I learned that talking to God is the key but that you must additionally do something about the situation yourself. So I talked to God about John Neely's dirty talk and I learned to send my spirit back to my mother and father during those times. Between God and me, we fixed many situations in this way. I asked God to tell my mother that I was alive and that I thought of her and Bomefree from the moment I opened my eyes to the time I closed them at night.

I was the first slave that the Neelys ever had. I gleaned much of this from the tinker who drove by one day with his wares for sale: tin cans, glass bottles, wire, brooms, bottles of whiskey. He was an old Dutchman. He told me that John Neely was a man with finally enough wealth to buy a slave and that slaves cost plenty. The tinker already knew that I was bought for $100 along with the sheep.

The tinker told me that there were freed negroes south in New York City who were paid money for their work and who were never bought nor sold. Out of politeness, I listened, but did not believe a word of it. Surely Bomefree would have told me if such a thing could be true. Bomefree had only said that by the time freedom came to New York, he'd be long dead. The old Dutchman said that across the river and north into Massachusetts, all the slaves were free.

"Are they all starving and frozen solid in the winter?" I asked him.

"No. There are some who have their own places, some that live on with others as housekeepers and servants, some that do just as I do."

I did not want to appear rude to him so I listened to him without questioning his senses. I liked the old man, and it loosened up some of the logjam inside me to speak words at all or to hear any that I could understand without making my head hurt. He traveled to all the farms and houses and he agreed to let my parents know that I was working hard, listening and learning but that my learning of English was going slower than I had imagined. And I asked him to please bring back word of my family.

The seasons were turning again, summer into fall, when I saw that John Neely was making his business bigger. He bought goods from the ships that came into port and in turn, sold them to the local people. He bought cloth, dishes, sugar, furs from up north, paper, a few books, buttons, and such fine things as clocks. While he previously sold goods from his barn, he now moved his family to the back part of the house and made a nicer sort of store right in the front of the house that faced the street.

It was about this time when he made a trip of several days away from home. He often came home from one or two day trips with goods on his wagon. I was left alone with the missus for a long stretch of time. She had two girls who were younger than Peter and the baby, who was learning to walk.

I was relieved that John Neely was gone for more and more days because he was one less person I had to look out for. But as the days stretched on, the missus grew wary of me. She would not turn her back to me in the kitchen nor anywhere. Whichever way I faced, she would face me. We moved in an unfriendly dance, for I began to feel that I also needed to keep my face to her as well. We kept our backs to the wall, revolving around each other. I have seen dogs do this, with their hair raised up straight, putting forth a killing

54

menace, each dog terrified of the other, till one senses retreat, then the lunge, teeth sinking into neck or snout in a fury. With the missus, I knew it would be my neck and not hers that would feel the fangs.

I carried the water from the big bucket by the door to the kettle over the fire. I poured the water but I kept her in my sideways vision. She was holding the youngest, the baby girl called Hannah who drooled a steady stream of spit. I moved slowly, pacing myself, fearing the moment that she would try to tell me what to do next in the shattering English that I did not understand. I had already learned the outcome of speaking Dutch to her in my first few days.

Mrs. Neely had one piece of jewelry that she wore. It was a cameo, as I later learned, but never having seen one before, I had no Dutch word for it. It later became one of the English words that sank deep into my mind and had no Dutch twin. When I pointed to it one day, with a moment of forgetfulness of my situation, hoping that she would tell me the word for it, she sucked in air and grasped it.

The cameo hung by a ribbon around her neck. It was a black profile of a woman with her hair piled in curls on her head against a white background. I have learned since that cameos can go either way, black on white or white on black, but this one was black on white and it was the black face that made me point. The sudden warmth of seeing a black face, even though I could tell it was a just a white woman in deep shadow, played a trick on me and made me forget myself.

She stared at me with that terrible dog-about-to-be-attacked look, then jabbed a finger at me and spoke rapidly in the hard spitting sounds of English. She backed out of the room, rushed to her bedroom and slammed the door. The two little girls stared wide eyed at me from their places at the table. Both held spoons midway to their mouths, frightened by the angry words of their mother. The girls looked at each other and slid from their chairs, giving a wide berth to their mother's bedroom door and to me as they made their way out of the house. I wanted to tell them that their mama would calm down. When the missus came out later, the cameo was no longer around her neck.

The next day, the last before the return of John Neely, she flew into a fit first thing in the morning. Her long hair was unbraided and uncombed. She pointed to her throat. I understood her quickly. I shook my head to let her know I had not seen it. I didn't know how she lost her cameo, but she was wild when she couldn't find it. I made a show of looking in the kitchen shelf where she kept her plates and bowls, lifting each one, shrugging my shoulders in disappointment when I couldn't find the cameo. Mau Mau always said something could be sitting right in front of me and I wouldn't see it so I wanted to make a special effort in this case, to let her know that I would search for her missing cameo. We did not find it. I looked under each plate twice.

John Neely returned loaded down with goods in the back of his wagon the next day. He was in a rare mood where the girls knew they could come near him without suffering a cuff to the head. He was drunk on his possessions and acted like the lord of the land. He held out fancy clocks for his wife to see. He did not notice her stern mood.

I don't know what the whipping was for, but it was for one or both of two things. I had understood by then that the mistress felt I was the thief of her cameo. Even if English had purred off my tongue as well as could be, I stood no chance of her believing me. Because I could not tell her in words, I kept shaking my head side to side every time I thought the subject was coming up. After supper I cleaned the bowls and plates. John Neely asked for what I thought was the water dipper. I brought the water dipper to him and he slammed his fist against the table and threw the filled water dipper to the floor, spraying an arc of water across the room. He wanted something else but I didn't know what it was. The fury and the shouting froze me up against the wall.

John Neely grabbed my arm and shoved me out the door. I was afraid that we were going to my little shed and he would talk his talk to me again. But we went toward the barn in back of the house, him squeezing my arm and marching with his well oiled boots, yanking my arm this way and that. He lit the lantern in the barn, even though the days were still long and the light outside was strong. His barn had few windows to let in the light.

The center poles were thick and well hewn, much like the work of Bomefree. John Neely forced me to face one of the poles and hold out my hands. From his back pocket he pulled a leather strip and he tied my hand fast. I turned to look at him. I had never been tied before. His forehead was beaded with sweat and he was rolling up his sleeves.

"I did not take the cameo," I said in Dutch except for the word cameo, which came out in English. I knew he could understand what I said.

"No Dutch!" he shouted, and the first lash hit my back with what felt like many whips.

I turned and looked again. He held the worst whip I had ever seen. Green saplings had been stripped and hardened with fire, then bound together at the top with strips of rush and leather to form a handle. On the ends of some of the saplings were metal tips. I don't know how long it took him to make the whip, but I knew then that it had been a long time in the making and that John Neely had waited for the chance to use it, needing no reason really, but knowing that I would soon enough present him with a reason to make the whipping right enough in his mind.

He ripped down my dress and laid bare my back. The whip flew and tore at my skin. I heard the metal tips clank on my shoulder blade.

"No Dutch!" he shouted as he hauled back his arm and let the whip snap on my back again and again.

I tried to talk to God, as Mau Mau had said, but speaking out loud to God only infuriated him more. I wished I knew how to talk to God in English.

"No Dutch!" he roared when he heard me whispering to God.

I heard a high pitched sound after the crack of the lash.

The sound came from somewhere in the barn and I felt so sorry when I heard this poor animal's sound. The sound took me out of myself, and I could no longer talk to God. I worried that if he kept whipping me, I would have no skin on my back and that I would die without skin. I had never seen a creature alive without skin before.

The sound came again, high pitched screaming, yelping and my knees buckled and my head grew too heavy for my neck. The sound continued, the whining dog sound now, certainly it was a dog. I heard the whip drop to the ground and the animal sound continued. Finally I realized that the sound came out of my own lips but I don't know how. My lips and tongue spoke a language that was neither Dutch nor English.

He untied my hands. I was left in the barn for the night. I could not have moved if I wanted to. I must have slumped over to lie on my stomach for that is how I awoke the next day.

But I had a dream that night and to this day I remember it. A black bear came to me as I was floating face down in a big river. I floated with my head hung far into the water, breathing in the wet like it was air. My arms were dead weights and I could not move them. Birds tore at my back, ripping the skin and muscle from me until I was sure that only bone was left. The bear grabbed me with one great paw and tucked me under her arm, carrying me hanging like a rag. She smelled like rich earth and leaves and wild onions. She set me up on soft grass. She leaned over my shoulder and looked at my back. Then she licked me with her rough tongue and said to me, "This will keep you clean." She handed me a long strip of birch bark and I drank sweet sap from it, in the way that can be done only in dreams.

CHAPTER NINE

I don't know what let me sleep that night, if it was sleep, to let me dream of the black bear licking clean the gouges on my back. It could have been the shock that numbs the body. At the Hardenburghs' farm, I had seen one of their people, a boy who was visiting from Albany, run all the way across the field with an axe blade in his head. It had flown off a loose handle and lodged itself right over his ear. He said it didn't hurt him. He didn't live but the shock of it kept him from the pain. Mau Mau said the numbing comes from God.

The missus came the next day and the day after and put grease on my back. She found an old piece of muslin to lay over my back and wrap around my front. I could not look at her, thinking she believed I was the thief of her cameo. I was not and if I had known the English words for it I would have dared another whipping to tell her.

She brought me water and held me under the armpits when my legs kept buckling under me. Her way of touching was different than the way Mau Mau touched me. For the missus, the situation demanded that she touch me. I would be a wasted purchase if she let the open slashes on my back fester, or if I fell in the dirt landing on my back, adding further injury. This was touch without knowing me.

I stayed in the barn enough days for the thick scabs to cover nearly all of my back. In part, I welcomed the scabs, for worse than anything I feared my flesh being open to the world, and maggots in particular. But the scabs had their own price; they became hard as dry leather and they bit into the new raw flesh at every turn. The hardest thing was to raise my arms, which pulled at the core of each scab. I could again wear my dress, after some mending, and if I moved smooth, the dress did not catch on the scabs and tear the edges.

Autumn was making its arrival known. I felt it first in my shed at night, not so much a change in temperature, but a change in smell and sound. The peepers started all at once to say fall was coming. Mau Mau said the day the peepers stop is when the first frost comes at night.

The missus, her name was Agnes. So I called her Miss Agnes. Her black eye was what let me know her name. That's when I figured we had something in common.

She nursed me through the worst days of my back being raw and kept infections from setting in and most importantly, she kept me a distance from John Neely. When I was up and walking, she helped me with some English words. Her manner never softened, her spine remained rigid around me, and she only touched me when she had to for healing purposes, but she would not kill me and I knew that John Neeley would.

I had never seen a white woman struck in the face before. I heard the commotion coming from the house when I was outside returning from an errand. A bushel of apples had been traded for eggs. The Neelys' chickens had gotten loose and their eggs were laid all over creation, probably eaten by crows and fox and any sort of creature lucky enough to find the eggs. This left us shy of eggs for a time. We were rich in apples so I hauled apples to neighbors down the end of the street who had better luck keeping their chickens in the coop.

My basket was loaded with eggs as I pushed open the gate to the Neely place. I understood none of the angry words I heard but my stomach clenched up tight at the tone. John Neely had gone wild again.

I slipped back out the gate and walked fast to a thick trunked tree to hide behind. If I went into the house with the egg basket he would beat me for sure.

I heard the baby scream and the girls wail as they ran out of the house. The baby was left somewhere inside to fend for itself. The missus was putting up a fight, that much I could tell. She did not go quietly to a beating. I heard the smacks, crashing dishes, and furniture upended. If John Neely killed his wife, who would take care of his children? If he killed her, there would be no relief from my beatings, nor grease on my wounds, no milk for the baby. I wondered if the missus had a mother and a father somewhere who could help her or if everyone feared John Neely too much to speak against him.

I heard the stomp of his boots on the floor, and the earth pound as he leaped from the front steps. I stood as flat as I could against the far side of the tree away from his sight. I heard him hitch up his horse and heard him riding my way. I held my breath then started fast talking to God.

"God, pour me right into this tree. Make me into rumpled bark so John Neely won't see me. Make me not a girl, Lord, make me a tree!"

I closed my eyes tight and my skin melted into the bark. John Neeley rode like the devil past me. He rode the horse with no mercy for the cobblestones. I waited with my eyes closed.

"Thank you God. You and this tree saved my life."

I opened my eyes and the tree released me from her folded flesh. My heart pounded a steady thumping into my head, a song that I was truly alive, one more time, one more time saved.

Inside the house, the baby wailed a pitiful dirge. There was no sound of the missus. The girls hid behind bushes. I took the basket of eggs and walked on shaking legs to the house. I noticed that I had wet myself and that clear streaks ran down the insides of my legs, washing off a line of dust.

I stepped carefully into the kitchen and surveyed the wreckage of an upturned table and chairs and shards of the thick pottery on the fireplace hearth. The missus lay on her side with one leg pulled up tight, protecting her stomach. One hand lay across her breasts, another cupped her cheek. She stared in a puzzled way at an upturned chair that had suffered a crack.

I did not know that white men beat white woman. Mr. Hardenburgh had not beat Mrs. Hardenburgh and he was the only white man who I had known day in and day out for my whole life.

I took a wet cloth and hesitated. I didn't know if I should go to her or not. I went to find the baby, who had recently learned to walk but was unable to now from her fright. The thick scab was still on my back so I bent at my knees and held out my arms to the baby. She came to me and I scooped her onto one hip, hoping she wouldn't touch my back with her small round hands.

I carried her to the missus and slid myself to the floor next to her with the child. I took the wet cloth and held it to her face. She broke up crying and kept at it for a long time.

Late that afternoon, when we had cleaned up the kitchen and the children were as cared for as they could be, the missus sat in one of the uncracked chairs with her face as swollen as her skin could stretch. One eye was hard shut with no hope of opening for days. John Neely had knocked out a tooth and she held a cloth in her mouth to slow the bleeding.

I learned my first complete sentence in English.

She said, "I am Agnes." She pointed at her chest and looked directly at me for the first time with her one good eye. Her lips were swollen but I heard her just the same.

"I am Isabella," I said to her.

* * *

As the leaves turned and fell, I received no more beatings as grave as the whipping given to me in the barn. John Neely took on a boyish air around Agnes after he had beaten her with his fists. He stayed away one whole day and night and then brought back a silk purse and a great length of sky blue satin ribbon. At night, I heard him weeping. He was attentive to his wife, touching her arm as he walked by her. She stayed in the house completely until her blackened eye went from bloody red to dark browns, shades of blue and then an ailing shade of green. She taught me a sentence to say to visitors. "Mrs. Neely is resting." I said this again and again to the ladies with worried faces who called on her.

I tried to help her now without being asked. She was the one person who understood what it was like to be beat by John Neely. I could now pick up the baby without causing Miss Agnes a fright..

One day she said, "Isabella, the soup..." and she pointed at the cauldron over the fire which had started to boil and stick to the bottom of the pot. I tended the soup as soon as she asked me. John Neely looked at me strange, as if it never occured to him that I had a name. He had never bothered to learn my name from the auctioneer, no more than he would have inquired about the names for the sheep.

"Isabella?" he asked in a whining, mocking voice as if I shouldn't have a name.

"Isabella," said Miss Agnes with a tone of finality to her husband. I saw that she had her times with John when she could push a little more and he would give in without such a fuss as he often made about things. I was grateful that she took one of those moments on my behalf. Now he knew I had a name.

As the leaves fell and the winds coming off the Catskill Mountains turned sharp, I found it harder to stay warm in my shed at night. The family dog, a plain creature with round buggy eyes, stayed in the shed with me and we naturally slept closer as winter approached.

* * *

The first frost came early. Perhaps if I had had shoes, lived indoors with a thick quilt wrapped tight around me, I would not have noticed the first frost. As it was, the first frost cut into me with a shock. On the first frosted morning, I ran from my shed to the kitchen door with a load of kindling to start the fire. The Neelys expected to wake to a warm kitchen and I was more than glad to oblige them. Last winter had been the winter of my new boots. When I was sold in the summer, no one gave a thought to my boots. Now, I could think of little else.

My feet suffered the most. I wrapped a coarsely woven cloth around my feet as many times as the length allowed. If I slid and shuffled my feet, I could walk with the cloth. If I stayed indoors, sweeping, chopping food, cooking, scrubbing laundry, changing the baby, emptying ashes from the fireplace, then my feet were eased. The trips to the outdoors bore heavy on me and took a toll that let me think of little else.

As the ground froze solid, I felt every stone, stick, and frozen lump of earth. The worst thing was to get the rags wet, for then my feet had no hope of warmth.

Full winter was not yet on us. I appealed to Miss Agnes. I did not know the English word for shoes but pointed instead to hers. I knew that if she was in the right sort of mood, she would tell me the English word.

"Shoes," she said. She crossed her arms over her chest.

I liked the sound of this word, soft and ending with round lips. What I couldn't tell her was that I had a pair of shoes back at the Hardenberghs', if they had not been auctioned, or taken away from Mau Mau by Mrs. Hardenbergh when she left to live with her daughter. I hoped that my shoes were safe with Mau Mau. I wanted to make Miss Agnes understand that I didn't expect them to get me shoes, I just wanted my own. I showed her the bottom of the wet rags wrapped around my feet.

"No good," I said shaking my head from side to side for emphasis.

She turned on the heel of her warm shoes and left me in the kitchen, still shaking my head from side to side.

The clang of metal cups and buckets announced the

tinker, Mr. Clauson. I made sure I was the first one at the gate by the time he drove up. It saved Miss Agnes having to wade through Mr. Clauson's version of English. I prayed that he had word of my parents.

"Mr. Clauson!" I said, waving my arm.

"Isabella, if only everyone was as glad to see me as you are," he said reining in his horses. He set the brake and slid his legs around on the bench. His yellow hair was laced with white and it hung down on the collar of his wool coat, falling in waves, like the hay fields do when wind rolls over them.

My own hair was so unlike white folks'. Now that I had been without the attentions of my mother since early summer, I developed matted knots that were a trial to me. After the main beating by John Neely, my attentions went to how I moved, figuring out where the master was, when he would return, how much time I had before he would return, whether or not a dark cloud was in his mind or was it one of the rare times that he wanted his little girls to stand in front of him and recite their daily events. Would this be the night that he would come to my shed and point to my body parts and hold his face close to mine? I knew if I worked hard at figuring John Neely's ways, that I could improve my condition there. It was some time before I took notice of my poor matted hair because I had been so caught up in watching his every move.

Mr. Clauson told me news of my parents.

"Bomefree is a lucky man to have a good woman like Mau Mau Bett. He must be as old as the mountains. Mau Mau, she keeps him moving, she does."

"What of my brother Peter, do you have news of him?"

"Yah. He was sold to a fellow in Kingston, known for his fishing. But no one has seen Peter for an age now. I think he was sold up to Albany. Maybe Canada."

Albany! Canada! To think of Peter so far away, in a place I had never seen, tore at my heart. Mr. Clauson saw my tear filled eyes and distracted me with more of his talk and stories. To hear his sweet Dutch voice warmed my spirits. I

65

inquired about Mrs. Hardenburgh. I did not ask about Mr. Daniels out of respect for Mau Mau, but even without my asking, I learned that he had moved west. I sighed with relief to hear this, knowing that Mau Mau was safe.

Mr. Clauson got down off his wagon and checked the metal funnels that hung from the back side of the wagon.

"Isabella, we are heading straight into winter. You are dressed for apple picking season.Get more clothes on or the ill winds will find you."

I had a wool scrap that I fashioned into a shawl over the same dress that I wore the day I was sold. On my feet, I wore slave cloth wrapped and tied.

"You won't make it through the winter with those rags on your feet," he said. "Have you been misbehaving?"

"I do everything I'm told. Please tell Mau Mau that I do everything she taught me. I do the laundry just like she showed me and I keep my voice down and I am learning English words. And tell her I say my prayers every night."

"Yah, yah girl. You come from good slave people. There is no better than Mau Mau Bett. You go tell the missus that I got rags, good rags for sale today and that I won't be back until after the snow melts."

Then he taught me to say "the tinker man is here" in English. He made me say it again and again until I got it right. Then I ran around to the kitchen and said, "Da tinker man is here." I saw her smile, showing the recent gap produced by her husband. She covered her mouth when she remembered. Usually with me, she didn't care.

She bought hemp rope and rags and kept her hand over her mouth the whole time. She hurried back to the house.

"The English man, he is stern with you?" asked Mr. Clauson.

I thought of Mau Mau hearing that I needed to be beaten and how disappointed and ashamed of me she would be.

"He is fair with me."

He stared at me until I grew shy and turned my eyes to the ground. I was caught between lying and needing for him to know how bad things were. When I thought of Mau Mau's response, I chose lying.

Before he left, he gave me oiled rags and pieces of wool that had been washed and washed, shrunk into a thick warm lining for my feet.

"For your feet, girl, or you won't make it through the winter with your fair master."

My heart sang the whole rest of the day. I thought of words to add into the new sentence. I said, "The baby is here. The soup is here. The water is here. The wood is here."

The missus smiled again. We spent the late afternoon cooking root vegetables and grains over the fire. My new treasure of oiled rags and wool liners awaited me in the shed like a fine beacon. I made myself wait until I was truly cold to use the precious oilcloth and wool.

When winter hit full on, I had mixed feelings about leaving my work in the kitchen for the night. With the hearth blazing, the kitchen was the warmest place in the house. I was permitted to take a burning pine knot if one was to be found, or a small hunk of burning wood, no bigger than my fist, in a stone lined bucket.

My gift from the tinker was in the shed. After my work was done and my bit of burning wood was collected, I left for the night. The sky was clear and promised to be cold. The earth and I had a lot in common on these clear, cold nights; the earth grew cold from lack of a blanket of clouds and I grew cold from a lack of proper clothing. This was the night to try out my gift. The night sky popped with stars. If Peter was outside at this moment, I knew he would look at the stars and think of me and think of Mau Mau and her prayers. God was big and clear on a night like this.

In the shed, the dog and I made our nest in the hay piled thickly near the wall. The bucket with the small embers never lasted long. I usually tried to go to sleep before the embers faltered.

I examined my glorious gift. First I unwrapped the old rags from my feet. Small hard cracks had opened on my heels and the balls of my feet. I hung my feet over the bucket to warm them. Then I used part of the old rags that were the cleanest and I wrapped my feet again. The washed wool came next, then finally the oilcloth. Oh, the wealth and comfort I felt at that moment exceeded anything I had known. In my prayers, I thanked God for Mr. Clauson.

CHAPTER TEN

"God is bigger than us and we should speak to God under the biggest sky," said Mau Mau. I followed in her style. I had been saved from John Neely seeing me on the day he went wild with the missus, which I took as a sign that God could hear me particularly well by that burly oak tree. The tree was next to the road where people walked, or rode their horses or wagons so I often lacked for privacy and it was then necessary for me to find another place for speaking out to God.

Behind the house was the path leading to the privy. Beyond the privy the land dropped off sharp and a saw toothed path led down to a stream bed along the backside of John Neely's land, a place unlikely place for him to frequent. A large boulder faced the southwest and I wedged my back against it to soak up the sun on the coldest of days. This was the perfect place to tell God how Bomefree needed to find another master for me before I was killed here, either by the cold or in a fit of fury by John Neely.

When working in the kitchen, I tried to do what I could to help in my effort to get Bomefree to act for us, God and me. When I was scouring the dishes or the laundry, I looked out the window, picturing Bomefree walking with his stiff bony gait, his white wooly hair poking out under his hat, his pockets bulging with cakes made by Mau Mau. I smelled him too, hoping this added to my vision. Then I heard him crunching in the snow and heard his breath coming out in steamy puffs from his lips that were cracked with the cold. Mau Mau was always after him to keep his lips greased, but no sooner would he grease his lips than the pipe would find its way into his mouth, leaving the pipe stem shiny and Bomefree's lips as split as ever. A tiny crack right in the middle of his bottom lip would have made a deep red gully.

I held this vision of Bomefree every day into the deep of winter when the nights became the longest, past when the Neelys and the townspeople had their celebration of Christmas with their plump, stuffed goose, and hot mulled cider and strong whiskey. I continued seeing my father through the icy months when all the water froze, no matter how fast it tried to run.

The tinker was gone for the duration of the snow season. I don't know why he didn't have a sleigh, as most people did in those parts. After he gave me the oilcloth for my feet and wool to stuff between my feet and the cloth, I was as happy as a princess. The oil cloth kept my feet dry which I thought was the most wonderful advancement possible in my position.

As the winter wore on, and as John Neely found ever more errands for me to run, the oil cloth grew thin in places. The cracks in my feet grew so wide that a quill pen could be laid in the worst ones. I don't know now if the winters were truly colder when I was younger, but it shall always be the coldest winter in my memory.

It was as if he begrudged any betterment of my situation. I had stopped asking Miss Agnes about shoes, as I saw that either she had no power in this way with her husband, or that she could not be bothered by my needs.

The cold did not stop John Neely altogether from his night visits to me, but it did slow him down. But then he came on a new idea. His normal way was to carry a large bucket with burning embers to my shed to keep him warm while he spoke his foul words to me, pointing at my body. When he was done, the grand bucket of warmth went with him, making my little tin of embers seem so small.

One night he came in, lantern in one hand and bucket of hot embers in the other. The lantern part was new but I paid no mind to it and I went to stand up against the wall. He started with his usual talk and he made me look at him, though my spirit took flight. But this time he changed. He yanked up my skirt and my spirit was pulled back with a start. He made me hold up my skirt so that he could see my bare bottom. He poked hard with his fingers and I made the mistake of crying out. The night was without wind. Every footstep crunched on the snow and could be heard for a far distance. My yelp must have made its way into the house. I knew it and so did he.

He did not have enough hands to do what he wanted. He put one hand over my mouth and poked with the other hand but that left his sticking-out-straight manhood untouched. When he took his hand off my mouth to grab himself, I cried out again. He dealt a solid blow to my face to silence me.

Miss Agnes treated me with a new coolness after that. She taught me no more words in English. She stopped looking at me when she gave me orders. She did not offer to apply grease to my split lip or swollen jaw.

John Neely beat me again a few nights later. This time we did not go to the barn and he did not whip me on the back. He had me bare my arms, first one then the other. I had to kneel on the kitchen floor and hold one naked arm on the table. He beat my arm with a simple rawhide whip, not the terrible whip used on my back. He had Miss Agnes and the girls watch from the doorway. I was startled to see the long-lost cameo around her throat. The two girls cried as they saw my skin start to open and bleed. A few sharp words to them squelched their sound to whimpers. I did not cry. I fixed my eyes on the cameo, the black face on the white background.

These were not the deepest wounds that I received at John Neely's home; they healed quicker and the scabs were not as deep and hard. But the scars stayed brighter, angrier, plainer to my eye than any other scars on my body. I was told that the scars on my back were frightful to see and an ugly mass. But I could not see them and was spared the sight of them.

The gashes on my arms had a message for me; tell God to send my message to Bomefree. If God needed to hear my voice again and again then I would speak more often. I increased my visits to the tree, to the large boulder by the stream. I raised my arms to the sky and tried to pull God to me. I wondered if there was something that I had forgotten to do. Was God waiting for me to get the message right?

I stood with the scrub board in the washtub, with my eye to the road, picturing my Father, as I always did, when I saw Bomefree coming. He had my boots tucked under his arm. My hands slowly pulled out of the water and it ran down my skirt. When I saw Bomefree speak to Miss Agnes at the gate and hand her the boots, I knew this was no longer my vision, this was my father. Miss Agnes walked back to the house and tried to pass off the boots to me as I ran past her, but they simply fell to the ground.

I grabbed him round the waist and could not let go. He felt smaller than I remembered, the hardness to his body was gone.

"Girl, you'll squeeze the wind out of me," he said patting my back.

"It took me a long time to find your boots, Isabella. Mrs Hardenbergh took them with her to her daughter's house, and her daughter gave them to the hired girl. Your MauMau and me had to work to buy them back. There is not much left of winter, but now your feet will be dry."

My boots, bought with the sweat of my parents, lay near the stone walk. I immediately retrieved them and held them to my chest, as Bomefree relayed messages from my mother.

"She says to remember your prayers, to work hard, and that she was wrong about you never having to learn English."

I could not stop myself. I poured my heart out to him. I told him as much as I could, without shaming myself too much about John Neely and his dirty talk. I told him about the cold, and the cameo, and the beatings. I kept going until I was completely done then I started back at the beginning again. I couldn't stop.

"Stop. I understand, you don't need to keep going round and round. Your mother is going to fret from morning til night when I tell her how you are treated."

"I did not steal the cameo. I worked hard. I am learning English. Please don't leave me here again."

I did not mean to beg, which was wrong and I was ashamed, but I had to let him know the gravity of the situation. He had to know before he started the long walk back to the old Hardenburgh farm, a full day's walk for him. Miss Agnes called to me from the house.

"The laundry, Isabella."

"You must go back to your work now. I will see what I can do," said my father in his stern voice. Then his voice went higher and tears ran from his eyes.

"Children are meant to be with their old parents."

"Yah, Yah. Father, I cannot stay here!"

Miss Agnes called again and I held my father fiercely. Then he turned and walked his painfully bent and crooked walk. He did not turn around and I could not have kept from running to him if he had. My nose was filled with his scent as I slept that night with my boots held to my chest. God and Bomefree sent Martin Schryver in the spring.

* * *

When Martin Schryver rode up to the Neelys' house, the buds were close to popping on the trees, winter was behind us, pulling back to her northern cave to sleep until she was called by the winds of autumn again. Mr. Schryver had red hair, his front teeth crossed each other and he had a countenance that I did not at first recognize. My time with John Neely had beat out my ability to recognize happiness and Schryver was a happy man. Even his horse stepped smartly and did not begrudge him on her back.

"John, sell me this colored girl today and I will give you this purse of $105."

He did not even get off his horse. His eyes were filled with rich brown and his skin covered in freckles. He had a beard of darker hair, red all the same. His horse danced him in a circle.

I had just returned from delivering the nightly contents of the chamber pots to the privy. When I heard his Dutch words, I nearly dropped the porcelain pot, which was in bad need of washing.

John Neely answered him in English. He was fresh from shaving his face in the kitchen and blood clotted on his chin where the razor nicked him. His white shirt flapped loose over his pants.

"I'll speak Dutch or anything I like to you. I know what you paid for this girl and the sheep. Take this purse for payment and you've got a better bargain than you'll ever offer the townspeople from your English blooded store."

He tossed the purse to John Neely. The money clung to Neely's hands like burrs on a dog. Martin Shryver laughed.

"Do you need anything, girl, is anything in the house yours?"

Dear God, I was leaving this place, Bomefree had done it, I was about to walk away from John Neely. My legs froze. I feared he would grab me one more time, throw down the money, and rage at Schryver. I looked from one man to the other. My precious boots were on my feet.

"I have nothing in the house, sir."

"Then come with me. Your name is Isabella, or so your father tells me. He is a good man, Bomefree."

I set down the chamber pot as near to John Neely as I dared to go. I looked back at the house where I had first come last summer.

"Come on, girl," said Schryver.

I turned toward him and walked out the gate, never looking back.

"It's not so far a walk, but we'll make better time with

you on the horse."

As I came near his horse, he reached down and pulled me up with a powerful arm, my feet doing an ungainly flutter in midair until finally made contact with his stirrup, which gave me leverage to push.

I didn't look back at John Neely, though I was tempted mightily to see the look on his pinched face as I rode behind this laughing, red-haired man.

"My back, my back," I thought in the powers of my Dutch mind. "Let the scars on my back show through my clothes like lightning." I let my lightning covered back scream to John Neely. I never looked at him again.

CHAPTER ELEVEN

Martin Schryver spoke to me in Dutch. He was as good at Dutch as he was in English. He passed between the two languages, flitting from one to another like a June fly.

"Is it proper for me to speak to you in Dutch?" I asked him. My voice sounded slow from lack of use.

"Why how else will you speak, wilden?" He called me by the name that some used for coloreds. Wilden, wild animal.

As we rode, he unwrapped a parcel and gave it to me, handing it back across his shoulder. He said it was from Bomefree. I opened it and inside was my father's clay pipe. I held it to my face and smelled his lips and mixed it with my tears so I could smell it more.

"Here now," said Martin. "There's no use in crying over a pipe. We've pipes where we're going too. Twalfskill is where I live, where Rond Out Creek meets the Hudson. We'll not ask so much of you Isabella, as you have paid with John Neely. Wipe your face."

The Schryvers were known as rough and crude people. They had no fine china with sky blue flowers or lace curtains. They were a singing lot, cursed awful and taught me to swear in both Dutch and English, but they did not beat me. They said I was a child with the jitters and they left me to settle down.

"Let her smoke her pipe," said the missus. "The tobacco settles her."

I took to smoking the pipe with tiny bits of tobacco early on. The smoke never choked me the way that I have seen it do to some people on their first puff. My body loved tobacco and never had one bit of trouble with it. If I scrubbed my teeth with birch twigs, I got the stain off my teeth. Mistress Schryver taught me that.I smoked it before sleeping. They asked that I not burn down the barn, that I must smoke outside, far away from the hay. I readily agreed to their request; it was well known that if a colored person was accused of burning a building, they were killed by hanging. I settled into a ritual with the pipe. First I unwrapped it from the same cloth Bomefree wrapped it in, a cloth from Mau Mau. Then I cleaned out the bowl with stick. I pinched a little bit of the tobacco from a leather pouch I kept in my skirt pocket and lit it from a stick that I took from the kitchen fire. I liked to sit down after I lit it and I made a great ceremony of sitting, sighing and sinking slowly into a seated position. For a slave, sitting down was something to be savored. Then I tapped the bowl of the pipe four times; one for me, one for Peter, my mother, and my father. I closed my eyes and let the smoke run down my throat and back out my nose. When I had no tobacco, I just sucked on the stem like Bomefree did.

Eliza and Martin Schryver owned a bawdy tavern in Twalfskill. Martin knew how to laugh and people were drawn to him so they could laugh as well. He was good at remembering the important details of each man's life, the names of their children, the crops that had failed or thrived in the past years, and all the ailments of family members, deaths and births as well. He had a way of letting a person know that he was informed about the calamities of their life, and then he'd have them laughing or distracted or swilling whiskey or rum before they knew it.

He glowed like he was on fire and everyone sidled up close to get the heat. His red hair was more like mine in texture, though more managable by a long ways. Of course he was more free to let his hair go wild, being a man and being white.

Martin and Eliza told me it was fine with them if I slept in the pantry room off the kitchen or in the tavern itself. I chose the barn, with the steaming animals and safe hayloft in part because I had a choice, and partly because I was not ready to be so close to other people. I wanted the full range of the barn. Eliza brought a quilt and a wool blanket to the barn the first night.

"We won't hurt you, Isabella. You've no need to fear us," she said.

She spoke Dutch and English with equal strength. She saw that Dutch was the language to speak to me if she wanted my full understanding.

"You'll be a fine help to us. Bomefree says you can handle a scythe and a hoe. Your mother says you can launder."

My heart was soothed to hear mention of my family. I didn't know if John Neely spoke badly of me to others or if others knew how he had shamed me. Over time, I learned that more than a few people knew that he had gone over the limit in whipping me senseless.

"If you learn to work in the tavern with Martin, you'll need another dress to wear. You can keep this one for gardening and delivering fish. Did you have another dress at Neely's?"

"I came away with everything that is mine," I told her.

"I'm not surprised that Neely saved money by keeping you in clothes worse than rags. He's a scum throated, bottom sucking fish who should be used as bait."

My heart stopped. I'd never heard a woman swear before and she did so with fine form. I practiced the cursing description of John Neely at night when I smoked. I cursed mainly to the trees and as I got better at it, I cursed the milk cows.

Miss Eliza told me she had extra cotton on a bolt of fabric and that I could have a dress or a skirt, not both, but that I should decide which because she was in a sewing mood. Before I knew why, I picked a dress. The sack she made me was striped blue and white, had long sleeves, and pockets in the side seams. "Make it last," she said.

She and her husband Martin took life in large gulps and were like big overgrown, children in some ways. Eliza was round everywhere, face and breasts, her hands also where two happy pads of flesh rested on top, pink and soft. She talked and gestured throughout the days, sending her bigger children this way or that, hauled the baby on her hip letting him suckle as she sat near the window to keep an eye on the toddling children. She whirled through the house and tavern like a ball of light.

After weeks of living with them, she caught me smiling at one of her bawdy jokes about the wood slats on their bed and how they were worn out from over use.

"Well Isabella, your ears do work after all. I thought they were filled with potatoes. Didn't you think so about her ears?" she asked her husband.

I froze when the attention was brought to me, especially from Martin.

"Her ears work fine. She's only trying to save herself from wearing them out from so much talk in this house," he said.

* * *

Eliza did the reading and the writing in the family. Martin said his eyes crossed too much for him to decipher reading. I managed a peek into Eliza's hand mirror one day to see if my eyes appeared to cross like Martin's. After seeing so many white faces day in and day out, my black face startled me. My teeth looked too big for my face. My nose was wider than everyone else's. My darkness startled me. "Wilden," I said to my reflection.

In the time that I was owned by the Schryvers I got a better picture of Twalfskill. The fishing part of their business was as important as the tavern. It was my job to deliver fish to people in town. Sometimes people paid me, handing me coins that I kept in a cloth sack tied around my waist. Most often, they told me to put it on their bill. The missus said not to question them either way. If they could write, I asked them to write down how many fish they took. If they couldn't write, I had to keep straight the number of fish delivered, to who, who paid, and who said to put it on the bill. I had my own way of figuring this in my head. I kept a picture of each person in my mind along with their fish. If they paid, I pictured the coins sitting over the fish eyes. If they didn't pay, I pictured the fish eyes looking up at me with their dead blank stare.

I was also set to gathering herbs for Eliza. At first, she went with me, hiking through meadows and woods. Then she sent me off on my own. I'll admit that I rambled on these errands and I hardly remember all that I did on my long searches for mint, borage, and wild onions. In the end, I'd return with bunches of herbs wrapped in wet leaves to keep them fresh and not know if I was gone the whole day or just the smallest piece of a day. I gardened for the Schryvers too, although they were not much for gardening, as I could see from the overgrown and choked plots that they called their garden.

My smoking grew to a steady habit there. It soothed me. My first pipe and most precious pipe was Bomefree's. My second pipe was one that was left behind in the tavern. By a drunken traveler. Martin kept it up on the shelf for a good long time. I wanted a second pipe to use so that I could save Bomefree's for a long time. In a bold moment, I asked if I could have it. Martin teased me for a moment, turning the pipe over in his hands, giving it a close examination, speculating on its worth. Then he tossed it to me. "We get a fair sized pile of pipes left here by men too filled with drink to remember the Lord's name. It's worth nothing to me, Wilden," he said.

I learned to brew beer with Martin, learned to drink it as well. He grew his own hops, but bought the grain from farmers south of us. I helped him gather great clumps of honey from the forest to sweeten his beer. It was on a full day trip to gather honey that I first started to bleed. Martin was the first to notice.

"You've nicked yourself," he said as I climbed from the lower branches of the tree. "Eliza will fix you up when we get home."

I went to a stream and examined the source of the blood. I was not cut. I was bleeding from where John Neely had poked me with his fingers. We returned to the house with a barrel filled with sticky honeycombs. I headed straight for the barn and packed some wool between my legs and bound it with a cloth. My first blood was not a heavy flow. I assured Eliza that the nick I suffered in the tree was of no matter; it had closed up on its own. If this blood was from John Neely, I wanted no one to know of my shame. If it was a natural start to my own bleeding, then something told me to keep this part of me a secret. I smoked hard on this new development after all my work was done in the evening. I needed to speak with my mother and I resolved to ask Eliza, when the time was right, to give me permission to visit my parents.

Every morning Eliza put a spoonful of whiskey into the left shoe of her newest baby. The baby had not yet worn the tiny leather shoes, as she was still wrapped in swaddling clothes. This kept crib spirits from harming the baby. She did this with every one of her babies, all five of them. Not one of her children had shriveled limbs, blindness, clubfeet, or sour breath. It was true, this family was in a fit of good health and Eliza believed that the great strength of her children was due to chasing off crib spirits from the very start. She put the spoonful of whiskey in the newly made baby shoe each morning, and every afternoon Martin turned the baby shoe to his lips and let the leather soaked whiskey pour down his throat. He saw me watching him once.

"It's a fine family tradition, one that I give my loyal and dutiful support to," he said, giving me a wink.

Eliza taught me about several plants that helped me in years to come. My pipe smoking had not escaped her notice.

I did not always have tobacco available to me and Eliza taught me to find Kinnikinik leaves. Some people called it bear berry, but I liked to say Kinnikinik. She showed me how to dry the leaves, which cured much faster than the sticky tobacco leaves. She said that a person who smoked Kinnikinik smelled better than those who smoked tobacco.

She also gave me a far greater understanding of cattails. Depending on the season, she had more ways to eat cattails than I thought possible. In the spring, she pulled the shoots from the root stock. Those were eaten raw or cooked like asparagas. A bit later in the season, young stalks could be eaten in the same way. In early summer, the flower spikes grew heavy with bright yellow pollen. By shaking the pollen loaded heads into a bag, we collected enough to add to our ordinary flour, turning breads or biscuits rich yellow. She ended the cat tail season by making a sturdy flour from the dried roots in the fall.

This was my favorite part of working for the Schryvers, learning Eliza's way with plants and babies.I saw little bits of the same stock in both Eliza and Mau Mau; the way they had with plants and trees, the way they knew people, and the way people felt good being around them.

I took my moment in the morning, when Eliza was fresher, to ask about going to visit my parents.

"You don't know how long a walk that is child. Your visit would be all walking and not much visiting."

"I could leave on Saturday night after my work is done. And I would return by the next evening," I said.

Eliza sighed and spooned mush into the baby's mouth.

"Let me fix it up with Martin and I'll tell you when you can go."

My two visits with my parents took place when my Saturday supper work was done. Eliza let me go on nights when the moon was full and the sky was clear so that I could see my way. She packed me with fish and tobacco, gifts for Mau Mau and Bomefree. I took particular care to clean my tobacco stained teeth with birch sticks before the long walk to the old Hardenburg farm. If I left Eliza's sight after my evening chores, then I arrived at my parent's cellar home when the stars had moved across the sky midway to morning.

Old age crawled up Bomefree like poison ivy, its bearded vines grew thick around him and sucked any remnant of youth from him. On my first visit, I whispered to Mau Mau, "He looks so old."

"There's no need to whisper. He's also hard of hearing," said my mother.

He had three wives, all chosen for him by his owners. From Mau Mau alone he had sired twelve children, each sold. My father had created a fortune in slaves.

I filled his pouch with the tobacco, saving a pinch for myself back at the gate which I retrieved on my return trip. I had all of Sunday to spend with them.

Now that my parents were out of bondage, Bomefree was too feeble to work. My mother hired herself out for spinning and dressmaking. She was known for her spinning, for the evenness of the thread and yarn. Bomefree, who could no longer cut wood, traveled the fields and forests, staff in hand to steady his bent frame, looking for downed branches to drag home. On my visits, I cut as much wood for them as I could.

Mau Mau and I did not speak of John Neely nor of the damage he did to me. It would be unlike her to strengthen his spirit by saying his name. She told me that I had a better chance now with the Schryvers. She cried when I asked about Peter, who had stayed with local people for a short time, and was then sold to a boat builder near Albany. Even Bomefree who was most diligent about finding information about his children, could find no further word of Peter. I could not picture Peter older. He would be nearly nine by then. He stayed one age in my mind and grew no older. I did not ask about Peter on my second visit. But I had no doubt that Bomefree continued to ask travelers, the Tinker, certainly every black faced person, if they had word of little Peter. When he did not tell us, we knew that even Bomefree's long reach was not long enough to find Peter. I began to picture Peter on a large sailing ship, learning to be a skilled Black Jack. Bomefree said that no Negro man could do better than becoming a Black Jack, a skilled tradesman who both built ships and traveled the rivers and oceans.

CHAPTER TWELVE

I was born with a certain hum in my throat, a deep growl that sounded like the wind. My voice fell away from me after living with John Neely and it only came back bit by bit. Talking came the slowest but my songs were not so damaged. Maybe because I never once tried to sing at his house, he didn't have the power to steal my singing voice.

Songs came easy to me. I needed only to hear a song once and the song moved under my ribs forever. There was no lack of singing at the home and tavern of the Schryvers. Near to everything was different at Martin and Eliza's, except for me. I kept on as if I was expecting to be beat every day. I kept Martin in my sight at all times. I listened for him to come into the barn at night. He never came. That's the trouble with the likes of Neely; he left a bad stink on me and I smelled it long after I was gone from him.

But the one place I let myself change was with singing. I let the sounds roll out my throat, croaking at first, then once they got started, I let them churn up my gizzard, picking up deep flavors at they went, and building up steam like the new ships out on the Hudson.

The Schryvers had a summer dance in the long nights of July on a wide dock built out on the river. People sang and danced until the rose ribbons of dawn streaked across the Hudson River. Women's dresses were starched to a shine. I saw my face reflected in the bodice of women whose cheeks flushed pink from beer and dancing. I heard a song that night about George Washington and it stayed with me. I never had to try and remember the words, they just were, like my fingers or toes.

Toward the end of the party, I drew myself a beer and felt my stomach heat up. I drank another. Martin's eyes were shot through with yellow and red and I knew from Eliza that this meant he was close to sleeping and far from remembering. I saw that the guests needed for nothing and I stepped boldly to the end of the dock and sang the song just as I heard it. They grew silent as I sang and I paid no mind to anything except the story within the song and the spirit that carried the story out of me. The guests stayed silent for moments after I finished. The only sound was the lapping of the water against the piers and the birds who were waking. I turned and faced the partiers who seemed to see me for the first time. One man rubbed his eyes. "Martin's got himself a trained monkey, like I saw in New York City," he bellowed.

There was drunken laughter and a great swishing of gowns as the women turned back to each other. My head felt like it had grown bigger. I did not mind the comment about the monkey, but the tone was filled with mockery. I wondered only if it were true. And never having seen a monkey, I could not decide if it were true or not.

* * *

I observed Martin and Eliza, far more than they imagined. I had seen men and women together, my parents Mau Mau and Bomefree certainly. But like any child I saw them not as man and woman but as burning lights for me. They were to teach me and guide me, restrict me, warn, scold, scuff, reward, and watch. All life went from them to me and me to them. Even those moments of tenderness I saw passing between them, Mau Mau's caress of Bomefree's twisted knuckles, all seemed as regular as the sun rising. It just was.

* * *

From watching Martin and Eliza I learned this; they had a great joy in each other. He loved her bountiful body, the jiggle of her arm as she hoisted a baby on her hip. I followed his eyes as they rested on the rise of her backside bouncing her dress as she made a smart dash to catch a knee high child from crashing headlong into the wood stashed by the fireplace. Martin's eyes crossed slightly, and pulled up at the outer edge, pushed up by his smiling moustache. He was a man filled to the brim with life. I knew this because he told everyone so.

I knew all this about them but still I kept my distance, spoke little to them, did my job. Mau Mau was right of course, by being silent, it was possible to learn a great deal. But the Schryvers eventually took my long silences for dumbness. From my loft perch in the barn, I overheard bits of conversation about me. "Martin, she works well enough, but I'm afraid she's a slow one. She'll do as I tell her but no more. If I send her to the woods collecting herbs, she'll stay half the day. If I ask her where she's been, she tells me she doesn't know."

Martin was well known for taking in stray animals, feeding travelers who had no money and extending a line of credit to his fish customers. As I hoped, he was in sympathy with me. "The wilden comes from good slaves. If you'd spent a year with John Neely you'd look daft too. And you can't expect her to be as quick in the mind as we are. She's a wilden and that's how they are, wild and forever as a child," said Martin. I hoped that Martin was convincing. I did not want to risk another sale.

In my second visit to my parents, my mother seemed to know that it was time to tell me about bleeding. I had not told her about the blood that had come the day Martin and I were searching for honey, but I think she knew my time had come.

She walked with me down to the gristmill. "You're going to start your monthly bleeding. Keep the knowledge of your blood away from your master as long as you can. This bleeding means you're old enough to have children and you're not but a child yourself. Having a baby this young leaves nothing but a dead mother and a dead baby."

"But Mama, they know everything," I said.

"You'd be surprised at all the white people don't know," she said. And she showed me how to keep from being noticed while bleeding. "Take two pieces of cloth. I've got some for you to take back to Schryvers. In the center of the cloth, add another piece of cloth and sew it on top like it was quilting only leave one edge open."

Mau Mau was quiet then and looked at me. Maybe I looked confused. "You learn by doing, daughter. We're going back to the house and I'll show you."

Back in the cellar, she sent my father on an errand. Then she demonstrated how a piece of cloth was tied on diaper like, and between her legs was a pocket for dried grass. She explained that the whole point was not to get blood on my skirts and to keep the blood from smelling bad.

"Blood is a sweet smelling liquid, not so much different from tree sap, or honey. The trouble with blood is that left out in the open, it starts to smell and that particular smell on a woman means only one thing. The less your master knows about this, the better off you'll be," said Mau Mau.

She showed me how to let the dried grass soak up the blood in the pocket between my legs, and how to bury it deep in the ground so dogs don't dig it up, or to dump it down the outhouse hole. "Keep yourself washed well too," she said.

Mau Mau remembered few things about her homeland of Africa, or her mother who survived the long journey aboard ship, only to die shortly after setting shore. But one of the lessons taught to Mau Mau that stayed in her young mind, was the lesson of cleanliness. Somehow, grandmother convinced even the slavemasters on the big ship to provide her with water for washing herself and her daughter. Keeping the body and clothes clean stayed with my mother and she passed it on to me. She often told me to pay no mind to the white people who didn't know to wash as often as they should. "Let them do it their way. But try not to stand down wind of them on a hot day," she said.

She said white people had a peculiar smell that took some getting used to. She didn't know if the smell was natural to them or if it was a result of the extraordinarily long periods between washing.

Inspired by my mother's wise words I was determined to let Eliza and Martin know that I was not dumb, as they suspected. I tried hard to think of an idea to present to Eliza, to let her know that I was thinking about working. Fall was on us, turning the air crisp and the top leaves of the maples gold and yellow and red. My mind was on apples and the task of turning the apple press when Eliza came walking up to me from the house. I was pressing the apples for cider near the barn. She looked stern and I guessed that I had done something wrong.

"Isabella, I just heard news of your family. Stop cranking the handle for a moment," she said. I stopped, doing exactly as she said to show my quickness in thought.

"Your mother is dead."

The bottom fell out of my stomach. My knees gave out and I commenced to holler and cry at the same time. "No no no no no no no no no mama mama mama mama mama."

"Martin! Martin! Get out here!" said Eliza. "Here now, get up. Come on." She was circling me the way you do if an animal has been injured and you want to help it but you also don't want to get bit or kicked, and I was kicking. Part of me was bucking and kicking on the ground and part of me was watching off to the side. I threw up and kept heaving even after there was nothing left to throw up, barking to Mau Mau all the while. Then Martin was there saying, "Oh Lord, oh Lord, she's having a fit. They get this way."

I could not stop thrashing on the ground. I had been hit full force with a wagon and a team of horses, except the horses were still stomping me and I couldn't make them stop. And more than anything I wanted my mother. "She's not dead. What did they do with her? She's not dead. Where is she? I've got to find her," I said to the collected group of

Eliza, Martin, and several of the children. I tried to get up but my body was still thrashing despite my mind wanting to get up and find my mother. Martin picked up a bucket of water and threw it on me. I sat back on my arse with my legs spread out in front of me.

Eliza hauled me into the house, pulled my wet and filthy dress over my head and wrapped a blanket around me. She washed the dress for me. No one except Mau Mau had ever washed anything for me and this made me cry harder. Everything was connected to my mother and she was gone. I was cut loose from the world.
"You need to sleep in the house tonight. We'll fix you up a pallet in the kitchen," said Eliza. Someone brought me my pipe and tobacco but I could not smoke, knowing that it was something that my mother would not have agreed with. But I did suck on the long stem of the unlit pipe as I lay curled on the pallet, unsleeping.

* * *

My mother was days buried before I was allowed to go to Bomefree's cellar home to sit with him. My body was so stored up with going yet waiting, waiting for the permission, the word that let me go, the sucking spiral sound of the world without Mau Mau, that I found a pace somewhere between walking and running to carry me the ten miles north, to even out the hills with the welcome flats. This became my traveling pace ever after. I measured in enough air to fill my lungs to carry me long. I could have gone far longer than I needed at this gait. I could have walked to Albany.

* * *

I found Bomefree in a slump, his back pressed against the crabapple tree, his knees pulled up. In my flight home, I pictured the safety of his arms, strong, pulling me in to let my tears run without stopping. When I saw my father, it was I who held him, my arms were the strong ones. The passing of Mau Mau's spirit severed a cord that fed Bomefree both food and light, drink and sleep. His shrunken form shook and sobbed letting loose a high trilling sound that made me think I held a captured hawk, not a man. My body sent forth steam from my running, and from the vapors of my body, the scream of the hawk, and the shaking that we caused the earth, we honored the changing of Mau Mau's spirit. Elizabeth, daughter of a woman stolen from Africa, Elizabeth, the namer and the un-namer, Elizabeth, keeper of her childrens' stories. Mau Mau Bett. Mama.

"What happened?" I asked my father. He told me how it went. She made bread one morning and asked Bomefree to take it to Mrs. Simmons who she knew would be baking that day. Bomefree did so, then spent a long morning and afternoon collecting fallen apples, some for himself to keep, others to sell or barter. He returned late in the afternoon, expecting the rich smell of bread to greet him knowing that Mau Mau would collect the baked loaf. Instead, he entered a cold cellar, no fire going in the tiny fire pit, no light from any source. His feet collided with something near the door and he tumbled over. It was Mau Mau still alive, spittle on her chin, one side of her body limp and still, the other side able only to jerk to commands still issued from a most stubborn part of her. He put her on their sleeping pallet. He went for the midwife, who could not return with him until the next morning. A hard birth delayed her. He said a flicker still stayed in her, felt by both he and the midwife. She died within the day.

I looked in our old cellar home for something of my mother's. They buried her in the clothes that she wore every day. She owned nothing. Anything that was there, like the few dishes, the blankets for the sleeping pallet, the iron kettle, all these things were Bomefree's. I pulled their blanket to my face, and I sorted out my mother's scent from my father's, drinking her into me. I did not want to live without her.

91

CHAPTER THIRTEEN

"The whole thing is a matter of money," Martin told me. "I bought you and I bought a fishing boat at the same time. I've got to keep the boat." He left me to gather the conclusion.

"Who am I sold to?"

"To John Dumont in New Paltz. I would only sell selectively, Isabella. Do you know what that means? I wouldn't sell you to a man going south, and I only spoke to men in our church."

Martin Schryver went to a Dutch church in Kingston. They took all their children with them on Sunday. Eliza said that Sunday was a day of rest. Martin swore that the Dumont man was not at all like John Neely.

"John Dumont is a wealthy man and he's given me a good price for you. He'll treat you fair."

I kept the white clay pipe that Martin gave me with the long stem to cool the smoke. Sometime after my mother died, I went back to smoking. Eliza said to keep the dress she made for me. I had the shoes that my mother and father had worked so hard to get for me.

"Are there any more colored people at the Dumont farm?" I asked Martin.

"I wouldn't know," he said. I was lonely for another dark face. I missed my brother Peter. I missed the days when all I had to understand was how to take care of the sheep and avoid Mr. Daniels.

Martin loaded up his wagon and drove me to the Dumont place. We went south the best part of the day. He pulled the reins this way and that with the hope of keeping the wheels out of the worst of the ruts. Our talking time was over. I spent the journey thinking about the worth of me and the boat. The work that I did, cleaning, laundering, gathering food and herbs, delivering fish, chopping, and cooking was less than the value of the boat that brought in the shad. There was me and the boat on either side of a weighing scale. I saw the boat side pull hard on the scale while my side bobbed as light as a twig on water. I could not force my side down to be heavier. I could not stop my sale to another master. But I swore that I would not be sold again.

Mr. Dumont stood wide legged with his arms across his chest, giving me a good look as Martin drove away. There was nothing special about his looks and none that would have mattered to me back then. I was without Mau Mau, and without God, because I had stopped speaking with him. I could only half see what was around me. I remember that in the beginning, Sally Dumont, the mistress, was stiff to me, but not cruel. When she first saw me standing out front with her husband, she walked over and said, "Can she understand what I say?"

"Martin said she spoke more Dutch than English, but she'll learn."

"Should we get her a drink of water?"

"I expect so. Show her where she'll sleep tonight. There's an extra pallet in the cellar. Then send her out to me. It will be time to milk the cows."

Sally Dumont was a small woman. I was already her height if not taller. She hand motioned me to follow her into the kitchen where she filled a cup of water for me. I already knew by then that she did not grow up with slaves. She didn't know that I should get my own water.

"Aren't you a tall girl," she said. Her mouth twitched into a smile. "Can you say water?" she asked me slowly.

"Yes."

We paused, me looking at my feet, Sally waiting for something else to say. "Well then, best get out to Mr.Dumont. He has work for you." She pointed to the door.

If Eliza believed I was jittery, I expect the Dumonts thought the same, at least in the beginning. I did not want to be sold again for fear that another sale would take me too far from my father, who was in a miserable state without Mau Mau. He was allowed to stay for a time in the old cellar home. In the first year or so at Dumonts, I was not allowed to visit him, so Bomefree made several long walking visits to me. It looked to me as if walking was all he had left. I asked him if walking so far didn't hurt him but he said walking was better than not walking. As hard as life was for Bomefree, he did not have the faith that Mau Mau had about death releasing us from pain and sorrow. Bomefree wanted to live and if he got to the point where he had to crawl, why I believed he would do so rather than give up and die.

He continued to ask about Peter and after I had been at the Dumonts for a few years, he finally learned that Peter was sold again to work on a ship. He was pleased with the news that Peter was an apprentice Black Jack, as we had hoped. Being a Black Jack offered Peter the best chance that he could have as a Negro. For Bomefree, life itself was the glory, not death, and he fought hard to stay alive and keeping his children alive was a joy to him.

In the early times of living with the Dumonts, I got on well with the eldest daughter, Gertrude. She was close to my age, although she was finer boned and small. Nothing seemed able to either slow my growth or fill my stomach. This was one of Sally Dumont's first complaints of me; I ate too much.

"This colored girl will leave us with no food by February if you let her," she told her husband. "She eats like a man."

"She works like a man and has a much finer disposition than most," said Mr. Dumont.

I later asked Gertrude what disposition meant. She told me it was how I didn't complain and appeared to like to work. I was amazed that so much could be contained in one word. I remembered disposition after that and let it have room inside me. I practiced the word often to let Mr. Dumont know that I was not daft as the Schryvers had thought.

"Your horse has a fine disposition, Mr. Dumont. She could ride from today until tomorrow without so much as slowing down," I said.

"She's not as fine as all that, Bell. All creatures need a slowing down time."

Mr. Dumont shortened my name to Bell. He said a slave girl did not need a name as long as Isabella and he wouldn't have time to say it every day.

Gertrude and I talked nearly whenever we could. She explained her mother to me. Sally DuMont had never had slaves before. No one in her family had ever owned slaves except for the Gedneys who were cousins or such, while Mr. DuMont's family had slaves from as long as anyone could remember. They argued about the worth of colored people and slavery. Gertrude said her father believed colored people needed guidance and looking after because God had arranged it so. Gertrude said it was like if all creatures were on a tree or a ladder, and snakes and turtles and lizards were on the bottom and white men were on the top. "What about fish?" I asked. "Would you rather eat a fish or a lizard?"

"Well then, fish should go up beyond lizards, because I won't eat a lizard," she said. Then came wild animals, mountain lions, bears, deer, and turkeys. Then came the farm animals, cows, sheep, and chickens. "Where should dogs go?" I asked. "They think much harder than chickens."

"Dogs go up the ladder from chickens," said Gertrude.

Then came colored people and Indians. On top of the ladder were white people. And white people had to work the hardest to keep all the rest of us in control and to take care of us. She said that's what God said. "Does God talk to you?" I asked.

"No. God only talks to a few of the men in church. Only the elders."

If it had not been for Gertrude explaining everything to me, there was no telling how long it would have taken me to get an understanding. Fortunately for all of us, Mr. DuMont was a church elder, so God spoke directly to him. Since I was done talking to God, I was relieved that Mr. Dumont did the talking. I suppose it was sulking on my part, but I could not bring myself to speak to God after he tricked Bomefree and me by stealing Mau Mau when we still needed her.

I was so skinny everywhere that I knew Mau Mau would have been ashamed to see me. Sally was right about how much I ate. I could not eat enough food to spread out any sort of difference on my body. When I sat down, out of nervousness I took to outlining my kneecaps with my thumb and forefinger. My kneecaps stuck out noticably and were square like my father's. I'd anchor my thumb at the top of a knee cap and run my pointer finger around and around my knee, feeling the bone covered with the thinnest layer of skin.

I had an aching in my bones that could not be explained by illness. When I told Gertrude about the pains in my bones, she told her mother, who said any fool knew these were growing pains. Bones grew in fits and starts, particularly with girls of this age and they ache from too much bone stretching. She said that girls grew at night while they slept. "Don't you carry on like you have growing pains, copying Gertrude. You don't have the same feelings," said the missus when she found Gertrude and I comparing growing pains one day. Gertrude told me her mother had asked her cousin Mrs.Gedney how to talk to slaves and she was learning fast.

Something was paining me and if they weren't growing pains, I didn't know what they were. Gertrude said she had them, I said I had them, the missus said I couldn't have them. Well if growing pains were so precious, then I didn't want them. I called them my stretching out pains, making them something only for me, not to be confused with white girl's growing pains.

My breasts had started to bud out before I came to the Dumonts. All of the growing business was hard and uncomfortable. My chest went from plain and flat, sleek as a fish, to hard river rocks directly under my nipples which was the most sensitive place on my breasts. I couldn't sleep on my stomach when my new breasts were sharp and jagged. I said nothing about my breasts to anyone. I imagined that the missus would say my breasts weren't really growing or I couldn't really feel what I was feeling so I knew there was no point.

My first summer convinced me of several facts. First, Sally Dumont's thinking about me was different than the way I felt in my own skin. She modeled herself not on her husband, who had an easy way with slaves, but on Mrs. Gedney. She came calling every so often and gave Sally lessons on how to take care of slaves. "You must watch them constantly. They don't know right from wrong and never will," said Mrs. Gedney as they sat in the parlor.

Next, I knew I was only partly bad which meant that I knew some things that she did not know. But what I did to the cat left me stamped as bad, clear enough. What she did when I was stung by wasps warned me that she had a mean streak in her that ran deep. And the wasps were only the beginning. Maybe we were both bad.

I'll start with the wasps. I arrived at the Dumonts' late one fall after my mother died. A grey blanket fell across me after her death so that I have difficulty remembering much until summer burst on the farm. I remember heaviness, moving slow, not hearing words that were said to me, forgetting much of the English that I had learned, wanting only to sleep, or to work in the fields. Fieldwork forced thoughts out of my head; the harder the work, the emptier my head felt, like a bowl washed clean with fresh water. My eagerness for fieldwork is what made Mr. Dumont speak highly of me. He didn't know that I was working my hands raw to forget.

After the supper chores one night, Gertrude and I took a walk to watch the lightning bugs. Gertrude's face was marked by a few remains of the pox she had as a baby. The small circles looked as if a wood carver had chiseled exact hollows in her cheeks and a few along her jaw. She explained what she would do about the holes in her face when she became a fancy lady.

"I'll fill the holes with warm beeswax. Then I'll cover my face with powder. That's what my mother said I should do for dances and parties and for when I get married. Of course, I won't be able to stand too near the fireplace in the winter. Mattie said she's seen wax dripping down the cheeks of ladies at winter balls and they had to run outside to firm up the wax again. What do colored people do?" Mattie is the name she called her mother.

"Well, we wouldn't put white powder all over our faces. We'd look foolish. My mother never told me about what to do in case I had pox scars on my face. Do you want to see some scars that will scare you into always being good?" I asked her.

"I don't see any. Where are they."

"Right here." I pulled up the sleeves on the sack dress Eliza Schryver made for me.

Gert sucked in a fast breath. "You are a wonder, Bell. What did you do that was so frightful? You must have been terribly bad."

If she was impressed with the scars on my arms, then I knew to save the deeper scars on my back for another occasion. Gert touched my scars as if they were fine china. She ran her fingers over the knotted skin and I thought she wanted some of those scars for her own.

"John Neely whipped me for stealing a cameo when the truth of the matter is that his wife misplaced it. Then he whipped me for crying when he hurt me with his fingers down here." I pointed to my crotch with my hand. Gertrude's eyes grew wide, then she looked away.

"You must never tell my mother or my father about this. My mother will think you are the devil for sure. She will say you are lying, Bell. If you are questioned about your scars, say that you broke their best dishes through your nervousness. That will be reason enough for Mattie."

I trusted that Gert knew her mother better than I did and I never spoke of my scars again. I almost made myself think that all that beating never happened. I didn't forget it, but I put it in a box in my mind that I rarely entered.

Other than the pox marks on her face, Gert's skin was cream white. Her teeth were a jumble in the front. I thought it was because her jaw was too small for all her teeth. Since everything on me was big, I had room aplenty for all my teeth with space in between. All the space made it easy to keep them clean, which I tried to show to Gert but she thought it was too much trouble. Her jaw swelled up awful one day and the butcher was sent for, who also tended to people's rotten teeth. He pulled out three of her teeth in the back of her mouth. Two of Gert's uncles had to hold her down on the kitchen table while the butcher, with his knee braced on the table, tugged until the rotten teeth were extracted. I felt so sorry for Gert and I wanted to tell her so after the butcher left, but Sally wouldn't let me near her. When her mouth started to heal, she showed me the red and ragged holes in her gums.

Gert and I let the lightning bugs land on our arms and light us up like we were the night sky and the bugs were the stars. "I know where there's a bees nest," said Gert. "They sleep at night. You can do anything to them at night because they go to sleep."

"No, they're not sleeping. Bees are like colored people; someone is always awake and working."

"I'll show you that they're sleeping."

Gert picked up a stick and headed for the north side of the barn, around the corner from where we sat with the lightning bugs. I protested, having learned about bees from both Bomefree and Martin Schryver. "If they're asleep, they've only just gone to sleep and they won't like it if you wake them."

She paid me no mind. I had seen the nest before and had given it a wide distance. They were paper wasps. Their nest hung heavy from the joist of the barn sticking out like a big hanging lantern. When the sun was full on them, they flew around it in a fury. Now, all was quiet.

"Watch this," said Gert. And she gave the nest a tentative nudge with the stick. "See, they're sound asleep. They're snoring like Poppa." She did an exaggerated imitation of her father's house rattling snore. Then we both started snoring and laughing, each one trying to snore louder than the other, pretending that it was the bees who were snoring.

Gert probably meant to give the nest another small nudge. I don't know. I can't believe that she meant to slash a hole through the nest with her stick, but that is exactly what she did. As soon as I saw the dark gash in the nest, my feet turned the opposite direction from the nest and moved fast. I was around the corner of the barn and streaking for the house when I heard Gert screaming. I was immediately mad at her for smashing the nest and then not running, mostly for not running. I was mad that I had to go back and get her, which I didn't hesitate to do, but I was still mad. Gert was a whirl of arms and screaming and hair whirling in the moonlight. But her feet weren't moving. It took me forever to grab one of her arms because she was crazy by then and acted like she didn't even know it was me. I finally latched onto one of her arms and hauled her with me. The wasps were on me by then, hitting me with jolts of angry fire all over. Wasps are demons when they get worked up.

We must have had the entire nest after us and they had declared war. Gert was still screaming and I let loose with a holler at each sting. People came running from the house. I heard Mr. Dumont yell, "Get to the river!" At the sound of her father's voice, Gert must have come to her senses a bit more because I didn't have to drag her so; she was running on her own. We ran side by side. The river was full and fast in early summer. We aimed for the shallows near a sand bar that offered protection from the strong current. Mr. Dumont appeared with a torch. "Go under, stay under!" he shouted at us. We crouched in the water, taking big gulps of air each time we came up. When we were under the water, he made stabbing motions with the torch, killing the wasps that circled above us. The remaining wasps attacked Mr. Dumont.

When it was all over, Sally Dumont blamed me. She said I was leading Gertrude straight to hell and was likely to get her killed with my evil ways. She said her daughter was covering up my wickedness by taking the blame. Gert tried endlessly to tell her mother that she had poked the wasp's nest, that I had dragged her out of there, but her mother did not have ears for it.

Sally put mud packs on Gert's bee stings. She said the wet mud drew out the poison. Gert's eye lids were swollen, and her lips were bloated up like an animal that is newly dead and filled with air and worms. She was bit in so many places that her mother would no sooner finish putting mud packs on her ankles, than the mud packs on her face would be dry and she'd have to start all over again. It was my job to bring the mud and cool water to the sick room. Mr. Dumont had far fewer bites but he refused his wife's attentions with mud.

As for my condition, I had as many wasp stings as Gert and was as swollen. My left arm was more swollen than my right and was reluctant to bend. It throbbed with hot pain. The wasps had concentrated on my upper body, taking the most liberty with my face, neck and arms. If I was a wasp and someone started smashing my house, I still don't know if I would poke holes in their bodies and fill them with poison.

The only place where I was completely spared bites was on my scalp. The wasps could not extend their cursed stingers through the thick wad of my hair. Gert's hair offered them little resistance and they mercilessly attacked her on the top of her head. Despite her protests, her mother insisted on putting cool mud on her head as well. Although my eyes were near swollen shut, I was tempted to laugh at the sight of

Gert, covered with mud packs, naked except for a sheet that was draped over her. Knowing that Sally considered me the cause of the disaster, I muffled my laugh into a cough. My injuries from the wasps were a source of dispute between the Dumonts.

"Sally, at least put a mud pack on Bell. She is suffering as much as Gertrude," said Mr. Dumont.

"She has not suffered as greatly as our daughter, anyone can see that she is looking for sympathy. Bell's skin is so tough that the bees couldn't sting her. You're the one who told me that niggers' skin is different. Our poor Gert most certainly got stung because the wasps grew frustrated with Bell."

"I find it unlikely that wasps grow frustrated," said Mr. Dumont.

I was standing outside the door, with yet another pail of river mud.

"You told me that I had to learn to handle the slaves, which is what I am trying to do. Yet every time I try to discipline Bell, you interfere. You are spoiling her and embarrassing me."

The master of the house sighed. "At least let her rest a bit. She is as swollen as our daughter. The poison can make a person sick for days and can kill a person if they are sensitive to bees. I can't have her dying just so that you can make a point."

"You have already taken her off field work for the day. Helping me take care of Gertrude will impress on her what her mischief leads to."

I was deciding if I should go in or step outside again so they wouldn't know that I had heard them talking about me, when Mr. Dumont pulled open the sick room door. He had a fair sized welt on his jaw. He looked directly at me with his grey eyes, then he looked at my arms and my neck. "Let's hope we have no more wasp nests this summer, Bell. I don't know if we'd all survive it."

I took myself to the river and sank my arms into the cold

waters of the Hudson River and would have had a long talk with God about wasps if God and I had been speaking. I went to sleep with mud on my face and neck and woke early to wash it off so that Sally wouldn't think I was trying to best her.

The remainder of the summer was spent in hard work, which I didn't mind. Mr. Dumont admired my work and he was free with his praise. Summer work kept me out of the house and in the field, which is where I preferred to be. If I could have stayed working in the fields and stayed a young girl, I might be there still, but that is not the way life goes. And Sally, despite her dislike of me, was responsible in more ways than one for forcing me to eventually change and see the world in a different light. Changing me for the better was the last thing that Sally intended, and if she knew the result of what she was doing, she would have stopped.

Sally was fair enough to her own children. They were of her making so of course they had to be fine. She was also partial to two of the barn cats. She let them wind around her ankles and mew up at her until her stiff face finally broke out in a smile of sorts. She saved table scraps for them every day and the cats made her think that they loved her. Life at Dumonts went downhill for me after I messed with one of Sally's cats.

The two main cats, both females, had a constant supply of kittens so that the number of cats in the barn was ever changing. When too many threatened to over run the barn, Mr. Dumont would give the order to have them drowned before their eyes opened. He also let other farmers have their pick of the kittens to use as mousers.

Of the main cats, one was black with a cluster of white hairs on her chest. Her name was Nig. Another was grey and black striped. Her name was Old Stripe. They danced around the edges of the pigs when slop was given to them and most always got a tin plate of milk from the hired man milking the cows.

I was at Dumonts more than a year although my

reckoning of time back then was strictly limited to seasons, which if you aren't paying the strictest attention can become confusing after a number of seasons accumulate. So perhaps I was there a year, working my hardest to please Mr. Dumont to avoid another sale, and failing constantly to please Sally Dumont who held me in a highly suspicious state.

I worked up to the thought of the cats slow, picturing first Nig, then Old Stripe, then I settled back on Nig. I waited until a Sunday when the Dumonts were at church. I took a slice of cold ham and carried it to the barn.

"Here Nig, come here Nig." I rattled the tin where they drank their milk, although this was the wrong time of day, so Nig had a puzzled look, her head tilted and her back legs braced and ready to run. I had the smallest hemp rope I could find in my skirt pocket. I set the ham on the ground and squatted nearby. Both Nig and Old Stripe came running from a sunny ledge in the barn. I put my hand on Nig and ran my hand across the ridge of her back the way I had seen Sally do and she pushed against my hand until her tail and hind quarters nearly rose from the ground. With my other hand, I took the rope, with its ready noose, and slipped it around her neck and held tight. She went wild quick.

I had to drag her to the center beam of the barn where I intended to lash her up. It was easy to tie her to the beam, but she was still thrashing and her eyes looked wild and crazed so that I almost let her go but I had to go on. She needed to be beat and I had to do it. I wanted to tie her legs because I was afraid she was going to hang herself or break her neck but I couldn't get hold of her legs. I poked beneath the hay with a pitch fork to get the saplings that I had prepared for this. I hefted the saplings that I had stripped and bound together at the handle, the way I had seen at Neely's. I raised my arm. If she had stopped throwing her body and trying to tug herself out of the rope, this would have gone faster. As it was, I had to whip her many more times than I intended.

I did not count on the minister being suddenly feverish that day and all the church people leaving early. I did not count on the Dumonts driving their wagon into the yard and hearing the yowling of one of Sally's most favored cats. I did not count on the rage of Dumont when he saw me whipping the cat and the cat leaking streaks of blood on the hay. I did not count on the ferocity of the beating that he gave to me with the switch of my own making, for he had not laid a hand on me since the day he bought me. I could not have imagined the way his shoulders would sag as he threw the switch to the ground and walked from the barn. When he asked what came over me, I couldn't answer, because it had nothing to do with thinking, it had everything to do with having beatings stored up in my body.

Sally Dumont nursed her Nig back to health but she became a skitterish cat after I beat her. Sally's opinion of me plummeted like a rock tossed from a ravine. Mr. Dumont was able to get over it in a season or two. He was like that. I had a bit more posion to get out of my system but I figured it best to do so in private. I killed a fat grandfather frog not long after beating Nig. I put the frog on a boulder, held him tight, and smashed him to death with a fist sized rock. Then I was done.

CHAPTER FOURTEEN

Sally was a fair looking woman; dark haired with the first hints of grey around her temples, remarkably thick eye lashes, coffee colored eyes, and a good full shape to her body. If I did not know her I would have said she was handsome. As I got to know her, I saw far less of her outer countenance and more of her rage toward me which turned her fair looks to a shame.

If Sally could have stopped me from growing, she would have. As it was, I grew taller than most of the men at Dumonts and Sally couldn't see the top of my shoulders unless I was sitting down. Her mission was to learn how to discipline slaves and I was her target. Slavery was a curse for both of us.

Was she so different from me that what applied to her did not apply to me? Would she have been shamed by what she did to me if she had done it to her own children? By the time I was fifteen, Sally and I entered into our worst times together. When she learned that my blood came every month, she said she had to see it, because she couldn't trust me. "Show me your rags," she said. Sally said I was a black devil, the worst sort of niggers, lazy and dishonest, addled in the mind. This is the same woman who made me show her when the blood came. I would not willingly show this to a husband, to my child, even to my mother. I would keep it for myself.

These were the years when I was no longer talking to God, or I would have asked God to soften the hard places in Sally or to make me stronger where I was too soft. I would have asked God to make me work harder, make me stronger in my arms and legs, toughen up my callused hands, help me to know what Mr. Dumont wanted, help me not to sleep at all so that he would value me above any other slave from the beginning of time. But I wasn't talking to God, not since Mau Mau died and Martin Schryver sold me. I was stubborn. I wanted God to notice that I was good and mad.

For some years after going to Dumont's, I could not bear to be touched. I leaped like a rabbit if someone came up from behind and touched me. Back when I first arrived and when Sally was simply irritated by my presence, she set me to bring a tray of soup to her youngest son, who was sick in bed with the fever. I ladled a bowl of potato soup from the cauldron while my mind traveled as it often did, to places beyond my duties. Why she choose at that moment to reach out her hand to put it on my shoulder, I don't know. Perhaps she had a moment of forgetting how strange I was to her, how my black skin frightened her, as Gertrude had already confided to.

The touch of her hand felt like a cannon going off in my body, like being shot. I yelped and threw my hands over my head, and tossed the ladle and soup into the air. I fled to a corner of the kitchen and crouched low, turning my body into a ball.

She looked at the shattered pieces of the blue bowl. "What's wrong with you?" shouted Sally, her voice shaking.

I tried to answer but my voice was tangled and I said words that made no sense.

"You threw the soup all over! You've broken my bowl! Get out, get out!" Her face was red with anger.

"I had a fright. I won't do that again. I had a terrible fright," I said. My words started to make more sense, at least to me.

I then felt a tingling sensation on my neck and realized that the boiling soup had landed on my neck and shoulder. As I stumbled out of the kitchen, I headed for the well and pumped out handfuls of water that I splashed on my neck and the hot fabric of my bodice.

"You're not hurt and don't pretend you are or I'll give you something that will hurt you." She was after me like a June fly. I wanted to shake her loose and get away, hide behind the barn, until I could quiet the fire on my neck.

"Get inside and clean up your mess. If you were a white servant, I'd take the bowl out of your wages. But you're useless, Bell. I can't understand what my husband sees in you. I can't even make you pay for your mistakes."

But Sally was able to find ways to work off my mistakes. For this error of breaking the bowl, I was denied any meat from Sunday to Sunday and given no supper at all the first night. It was not harvest season or Mr. Dumont would not have allowed it. He always said that niggers and servants alike needed meat during the harvest season.

Mr. Dumont never beat me again. When Sally punished me, Mr. Dumont was not likely to be around but I believed him to be so powerful, so filled with knowledge that he knew every wrong turn I took as well as all the punishments that Sally handed out. It was not until Gertrude interceded once on my behalf that I learned that Mr. Dumont did not know everything.

* * *

It was my job in the morning to have the potatoes cooked for breakfast. I worked in the kitchen with Katie, the white servant girl. She was Sally's favorite and tried to lord it over me. Katie accused me of being a filthy girl, saying I left dirt on the potatoes. And oddly enough, we did have dirt in the cooked potatoes for nearly a week. I was not sleeping much those days and I sometimes slept sitting up in a kitchen chair because I was furious to show the Dumonts that I was worth more than a boat. I truly did not want to be sold again. I was sure that no one could be held accountable but Katie and me. And the fact that I washed and peeled the potatoes myself while it was still dark confused me even more. Not one black speck remained on the potatoes when I cut them up and placed them in the pot. Yet each morning for a week, the end result was a gritty mess that made everyone spit out their breakfast.

"Who is responsible for this breakfast?" asked Mr. Dumont on the first morning. All eyes went to me where I stood near the kettle.

"It's Bell's job to cook the potatoes," said Katie.

My protest was immediate and loud. "I know how to cook potatoes. I wash them once before I peel them and then I wash them again before I chop them. The water is fresh from the well each morning." My loud voice boomed out.

"There is no need for yelling," said Sally with a patient smile. Her long dark eyelashes rested for the briefest moment on her high cheekbones. "I'm sure it is clear to everyone here that not only are you not clean but you are unable to tell the truth." She turned her face toward her husband. "We didn't have this problem when it was just Katie in the kitchen."

"Katie, please show Bell how to prepare the potatoes," said Mr. Dumont.

"Of course, sir."

I started to protest but a look from Mr. Dumont turned the words to stone.

"John, I know that you've worked with niggers for a long time, but it does seem like it takes longer to train them than they are worth. Now Katie must spend more time looking over Bell's shoulder so that we don't eat dirt first thing in the morning."

The next morning was a repeat of the same unsavory disaster. If you want to send people off into a hateful mood for the day, feed them dirt in their breakfast. But it wasn't me who was the culprit. My protests were again unheeded.

Katie sighed and said, "I'm trying to show her how to clean the food, but she is so slow to learn that it takes most of my day."

Now this was an outright lie and both Gertrude and I knew it. Katie spent no more time with me than she had to and the previous day had been no different than the days before. Katie did the smallest amount of work possible and spent the rest of the day giving Sally Dumont a sympathetic ear that clearly lacked sincerity.

Gertrude was not so fond of Katie and she could see through Katie's methods quicker than I could. The next night I slept not one moment. I stood the whole night, pacing the kitchen, to be sure that I would not fall asleep. Once again, I washed the potatoes, peeled them, rinsed them again, and cut them into the large kettle. Katie told me to get more firewood as the morning was slated for making preserves and we would need a hot fire. I brought one armload into the kitchen and three more piled outside the kitchen door. I bristled at Katie's command, as I always knew when to bring in firewood, but I imagined my irritation to be a result of nearly one week without sleep. My hands quivered and I pressed them to my legs to keep them from shaking.

I returned from my last load and the family was seated, waiting for Katie to serve them the potatoes. She ladled only one scoop, for Mr. Dumont, when he stood up so abruptly that his chair fell over.

"Have you lost your mind Bell? I do not have the patience of Job...I will not eat this slop!"

Gertrude stood up as well and spoke to her father. "Poppie, it was Katie, I saw her. I have been hiding behind the kitchen door since I first heard Bell go out this morning. It was Katie herself who scooped ashes from the fireplace and put them in the pot."

"I have never known you to tell me a lie, Gert." He looked first at Katie then at his wife. "It appears Katie has been spending her time learning all the wrong things. Katie, I will not have Bell take the time to do again what she has been doing correctly all week. You will cook us breakfast again which we shall all eat at noon. Bell, I need you outside with me today." He looked at Sally, who stared hard at the wall.

Now where would Katie get the idea to make me look bad, especially in front of Mr. Dumont? I looked at Sally for the briefest moment. There was a look of great disappointment on her face. She was anxious for me to do wrong, so anxious that a plot with Katie had been her course.

I would have hugged Gert if her mother were not there. My heart soared the whole day knowing that Gert stood up for me, even at the risk of exposing her mother's involvement in Katie's trickery, which was as plain to my eyes as the sun. Mr. Dumont instructed me in splitting rails for a fence. I caught on to the swing of the axe naturally. In work like this, I could lose myself and forget about Sally for the best part of the day. I wondered if Sally had work that allowed her the same freedom of thought.

* * *

I was beating the rugs one spring day, with all the dust and dirt settling directly on me after it left the rugs, when I heard a familiar sound. It was the sound of metal tinkling, creaking wood wagon slates, with the accompaniment of slow and steady horse hooves thudding on the clay road. I had already lived a lifetime since the last time I saw the tinker. I ran to the road and saw him coming from the south, his long, yellow and white hair catching sunlight and sky. I ran to meet him.

"Mr. Clauson! You are so far from home," I said. As soon as I said it, I realized that I didn't really know where his home was, only where I had seen him the last time.

"Isabella. Aren't you the image of Bomefree and Mau Mau. I am sorry to hear of your mother passing." He pulled up the reins on his horse. "You can't grow any taller or we won't have ceilings high enough for you. What in the world

111

JACQUELINE SHEEHAN

are they feeding you here?"

"I eat fine here at the Dumont farm and I have shoes in the cold weather," I said, remembering the last time I saw him with my feet bleeding in the snow.

He wrapped the leather reins around the post on his wagon seat. "You couldn't help but do better than be a slave to John Neely. That man is a blight on all of us."

"Let me look at you, Isabella. You are still as skinny as a sapling but most young girls are. And look at this." He took off his hat and stood shoulder to shoulder with me. He was right. My bony shoulder rose higher than his.

"You'll be having another slave here soon. A sad story. Tom, a run away. He's been caught in New York City by a slave catcher that John Dumont hired."

I had heard mention of a slave named Tom. Gert said that three years before one of the slaves ran away and her father was fit to be tied considering how much money he lost and how much work had to be done on the farm. Losing an adult male slave was worse, according to Gert, than losing several horses and oxen.

"What I've heard about Tom you could put in one eye," I said to the tinker, hoping that he had more news.

"I don't know him well, but I remember him as a hard worker, good with animals. But Tom hired himself out on Sundays to save enough money to buy his freedom from Mr. Dumont, but between you and me, he'd be as old as Methuselah before he had that much money. Tom ran away and probably thought he was done with slavery. You can be captured and sold south or to one of the islands. Or a hired slave catcher can bring you right back to your old owner."

"How does a runaway slave know where to go?" This was the big question for me, and one that I would only ask someone like the Tinker, who clearly had a peculiar view on slavery.

"There are white people who don't abide with slavery, like the Quakers, and they are likely to help negroes. The wind is starting to turn. Slavery in New York will one day be a thing of the past. It's happening in other states. New York is a slow one to change."

Within days a colored man more than twice my age was brought back to John Dumont. He was shackled by a chain so that he couldn't take a full length step and yet he had to walk beside the slave catcher's horse. He took fast small steps. He had a rope around his neck held tight by man called Mr. Van Meter. I had never seen a slave catcher before and I was scared to even glance at him. The strange thing is, he looked just like any other white person, yet I knew he was the worst sort of human. I suppose it was around this time that the seeds were planted for me to hate all white people for the reason that I had no way to judge the kind of heart from the wicked. I looked on Gert as a queer exception. And I looked on Mr. Dumont as beyond my reckoning; his power was too much for me to understand.

When it became clear to me that Sally despised me and wanted me to have nothing of my own, I changed my pipe smoking practices. I smoked late at night, long after I could hear her sleep filled breathing come through the bedroom door. In the first several years, I slept on the kitchen floor with a blanket. I took my pipe outside and sat under the stars with a good thick shawl wrapped around me, sucking down the sting of hot tobacco smoke. The smoke soothed me when nothing else would and let me sleep, still tasting the rich stain in my mouth.

Or if Sally was gone for a blessed day, visiting friends, then I smoked out in the open when my work was done. Mr. Dumont brought me little bags of tobacco when he came back from Albany or New York City. He slipped it to me when we were working on the fences, or when we were loading hay before the rains. "Here," he'd say, "I know you can put this to some use."

He never said, "Now don't tell the missus." He didn't have to. We both knew if Sally got wind of Mr. Dumont giving me such extravagant gifts, I'd be the one to suffer.

When Tom was brought back, Sally did an unusual thing.

She normally didn't speak to the male slaves. But when Tom arrived, she put him on a carving project while his back healed up from the slave catcher. She said she needed a form to darn socks, that she wanted it made of maple so that it would be firm. When he was done carving and shaving on the piece of maple, it looked more like a fat frog and I laughed out loud when he was working on it.

Sally's first occasion to use her darning egg came quickly. I burned the supper meat beyond recognition one day, left it searing over the spit and forgot it while I watched one of the steam powered boats along the river. I admit to this wandering and dreaming. The farm was so close to the river that all of us were prone to stop our work and gaze out, even Sally. Mr. Dumont had been gone for some time, and was not expected back on the day I burned our supper.

Sally was furious as I expected she would be. But Mr. Dumont's absence permitted her rage to burn like a house fire. She picked up a broom and made to strike me. I could not stand for it. I moved quickly and Sally was not prepared. She fell on the floor in an ungainly position.

"You are a danger to all of us here," she hissed from the floor. She righted herself and said, "Come with me or I'll make sure you are sold. Follow me to the smoke house."

As we crossed the yard, she yelled for Tom to come as well. He had advanced from whittling to weeding the kitchen garden. He stood up and fell in line with Sally and me. The smoke house was the building farthest from the main house. It was up on stilts to keep the animals out. The three of us entered the building. Inside, smoked ham and beef hung, covered in cloth to keep the insects from laying eggs. Stout beams crossed over our heads.

"Tie her hands and hoist the rope over the beam." I turned my head to her in surprise. "For burning the meat?" I was more shocked by her judgement than by the circumstances.

Tom did as she said. I suppose his back was too raw to say no. He tied my wrists and threw the rope over the beam until only the tips of my toes skimmed the floorboards. I tried to get him to look at me but he wouldn't.

"That's too high," I said.

"What?" said Sally. "Are you telling me how to punish you? Did poor Nig have a chance to say how she wanted to be whipped by you? Do I have a choice that you must live among us? I don't want to hear your foul voice."

And with that, she pulled the maple darning egg from her pocket and pushed it into my mouth. She pushed and shoved until my jaws were wide open, ready to unhinge like snakes do when they eat a rabbit. Then she told Tom tie my feet with a wide board between them so that they were held far apart. My dress came down and we were long in the smoke house.

Sally stepped near me and looked at my body. Then she reached up and pulled hard on my breasts. Her breath came faster. "How is that, favorite slave? How is it to be without the protection of my poor husband?" All my thoughts went to my jaw muscles that spasmed and shuddered from being forced open so long and from my tongue pressed flat and low and from the sound that could not escape my mouth. I dared not cry because if my nose filled I would suffocate.

There are injuries that can be inflicted without causing welts or bruising. Sally picked up another piece of wood and brought it between my legs. "I am learning to be wise, Bell. Unless I am firm with you, you can not be taught." And with that, she brought the small log up hard between my legs as if I was riding it. I jerked in the air. She heaved the wood a second time and sharp light seared through me. Would she kill me like this? My eyes went to Tom and pleaded him. His own jaw muscles clenched.

"She will not be able to walk if you strike again. Mr. Dumont will ask for her to work in the pasture when he comes home," said Tom.

My heart pounded until I thought the force of it would cause me to die. Tom had a voice. Sally paused and looked at him with a wild eyed stare. He walked toward her and took the wood from her hand.

"Take this switch to her. Make sure nothing shows." He did as he was told. I rode the waves of tremors in my jaws, grabbing on to the shout of pain that only I heard in my head, and hung on.

CHAPTER FIFTEEN

Sally found more occasions to take me to the smoke house and Tom was called to help. Each time, Mr. Dumont was absent from the farm. I feared his leaving and if I knew he was planning a trip down river or up to Albany, I boldly suggested to him that I could be of service to him on his trips. I could not, of course, tell him what his wife did to me, how my dress was taken from me, how I was bound and how my mouth was filled with the hard maple until my jaws soared past screaming. To tell Mr. Dumont meant incurring a wrath from Sally that would be worse. When I suggested to Mr. Dumont that I go with him, he tilted his head as if he was considering the prospect. But he always said that I was needed here on the farm; Sally couldn't do without my help.

There are only three people on this earth who knew what happened in the smokehouse, and I am now the only one left alive. There is no one else to say the words, to tell of the shameful deeds and I will not say the words. I chose not to name those times.

Bomefree was too old and too weak to intercede on my behalf. After Mau Mau's death, he was allowed to live in the old cellar home for a time, then was shuffled from one Hardenberg family to another, and was finally offered a wind blown shack in the woods, far from the sight of anyone who might have to see him cold and starving. He came once to the Dumont farm after moving to the shack. A kindly man and woman drove their carriage miles out of their way to deliver him to the farm. He and I sat by the river, watching the boats. Or I watched the boats and told my father about them; his eyesight was so poor by then that I'm not sure he could pick my face out from another colored girl.

"How does it go for you here, girl?"

"Not so good as the Schryver's but not so bad as the Neely's," I said.

I could not burden him with the details of my shame with Sally Dumont. Knowing that I was protecting him from the pain of my life gave me some comfort. If I couldn't care for him every day as I longed for, I could spare him the pain of hearing my trials. I rubbed his twisted knuckles the way Mau Mau had done. I held his cold hands in my sweated palms and let my heat sink in. He smelled more spoiled than I remembered, but underneath was the good smell of wood and leaves. We smoked together.

"I hear a lot of talk about all the slaves in New York going free. You'd be free to come take care of me."

"If I could leave this moment, I would keep a fire going for you, steam apples, get us good pot cheese. I have strength for the both of us. When is the freedom supposed to start?" We spoke in our own Dutch language that comforted me.

"I don't know. There is more talking up in Albany and more arguing and more wailing on the part of men like the Hardenbergs and your Dumont. I don't think it will happen soon enough for you and me."

I noticed that Bomefree's concerns drifted mostly to his own pressing need to stay warm and fed. He dreaded being alone. I longed to be with him and care for him. This was an idea that white people missed entirely, that with our dying breath, colored people wanted to be with the people we loved.

With my help, he stood up and adjusted himself, letting his bones fall into place. He could not stand straight and it pained me to watch him walk.

"I best be moving again. My bones don't like it if I stay

in one place too long."

I was allowed to give him my supper to take with him and to drive him as far as the grist mill, where he could hopefully pick up another ride from a farmer hauling freshly ground flour back to his home. I cried my way back to the farm, letting the horse guide me. Neither the horse nor I knew any other place to go.

When I returned, Gert was excited to hear me tell of my father. Where did he live? How was it that he could walk so far and be such an old man? How old was he? What did he eat? What did we talk about? Gert bounced her questions off me and my sorrow went unseen.

"I can't speak now of my father. I am too sad. You are a lucky girl to live with your parents, to see them at the breakfast table, to hear their voices, to have your mother place her hand on your brow when you have the fevers," I said.

"Mattie says slaves don't need to have their mothers and fathers with them to grow up. It's better for them to be taken away and taught to work and then the white people can take care of them," she said, explaining her mother's vast knowledge about negroes.

"Mau Mau told me that children are meant to stay with their mothers and fathers until they are old enough to go off on their own," I told her.

"Your mama couldn't have taken care of so many children as you said she had. Papa says nigger children die unless white people take them in. He says you should have been taken from your Mama sooner, that's why you don't get on so well with Mattie."

Gert was sounding more and more like a grown white person. She and I were in our sixteenth summer. She picked up a yellow buttercup flower and held it to her neck. She tilted her chin to the sky. "Tell me if I like butter or not. If my neck has a yellow glow to it, well that means I like butter."

"You must like it because your neck looks yellow to me," I said without looking at her skinny neck. I was still thinking about negro children being taken away from their Mamas.

"Now you do it, Bell. Here, hold this buttercup up to your neck and let me see if you like butter." She picked another buttercup and handed it to me. "Go ahead, tilt your chin up and let me see."

"I like butter well enough when I can get it," I said. I was ready for the confirmation from the flower.

"You don't like butter. I don't think any niggers like butter. And here's the proof, there's no yellow on your neck."

It is hard to say how I could have forgotten that she could hold all the buttercups in the world up to my neck and no yellow glow would shine on my dark skin.

* * *

Gert was courted by several young men, all eager to join the Dumont family. As soon as the courting started, we drew farther apart. We no longer knew how to end each others sentences, no longer shared glances across the room. She spent more time with her mother. If I entered the room as the two of them were talking, her mother looked at me while she placed one hand on Gert. Then she turned to Gert and placed one finger to her lips and smiled her thin smile to hush. I longed for a road back to Gert but I could not find it with word or deed and we could not speak of it.

"Are you going to marry one of those two boys?" I asked her.

She threw the buttercups down. "Mattie says so. She says I can't court forever, that eventually I'll have to marry one and let go of the other." She ran her fingers over her hair that was firmly pulled back and knotted at the back of her neck. She no longer wore her hair long and loose like a child.

I patted my hair. It was braided as best I could and covered with a scarf to keep out the dirt.

"Will you move away or do you expect you and your young man will live here at the farm?"

"Here first, until Father gives us a parcel of land to build on." She looked off to one side, away from me. "I couldn't bear to be away from Mattie, so we'll build close to the farm."

Could she bear to be far away from me, hadn't I been the one to save her from the wasps? Hadn't she saved me from Katie's trickery? Had she forgotten all this?

I stood up and slapped the dirt from my dress. "The sooner the better, I say." I headed back to the house.

CHAPTER SIXTEEN

If I could have said what I longed for, it would not have mattered. If Sally knew what I longed for she would have let me get within a hair's breath to it and then snatched it out of my hands. That's the way she was. But even I did not know exactly what I longed for, I could not see it.

The longing grabbed me down my throat and pulled my stomach up in a knot. I heard the longing call to me when I walked the fields in the autumn, when all the wheat was in, the apples were pressed or dried, the potatoes and squash sat idle in the root cellar, and all of us paused waiting for the sign of how the winter would go. I looked everywhere for a sign; I picked up rocks and held them to my ear waiting for some whisper to come out. I stood in the midst of three white birch trees, grown from the same root. I sat in the middle of them, pushed hard with my back on one tree, pushed hard with each foot on the other two. I said to the tree, "You tell me right now, Birch Tree, what is pulling on me making me want to fly like a red tailed hawk over the long Hudson."

I demanded, I implored of tree, wind, stream, fish, and rock. I still refused to speak to God, but my resolve was weakening. When I thought of how long since I had spoken not one word to God, I wanted only to cry. I wanted to let God know why I stopped speaking. I was ready to explain it all to God and I felt foolish pouting for so long. Did God hold it against you if you held something against Him?

Perhaps God could tell me about this longing that felt like a river in me, that kept me wild awake at night listening to the owl. I needed to work up to talking to God again. Right there, knowing I was getting ready to talk to God ended the loneliest part of my life. It did not end my trials by a long sight, but I was never so alone again.

I worked up the courage to speak to God out loud when the longing in me was too great. God is more available around water and so I waited until the Dumont family rode off in their carriage to church. It was spring and the milk was running off the cows, heavy for the calves. We made thick cheeses, buttermilk, and on Sunday I churned butter, filled the butter crock and put it in the ice house all packed with hay. When I was done with the butter, I pulled a shawl around my shoulders and prepared to travel to God.

I headed due west, as if I was reaching for the Catskills themselves and stopped near the creek. The creek was wide and slow and a sand bar sat in the middle of it. On the sand bar, two willow trees grew long, waving tassles. I picked one tree and stepped under the umbrella of its branches that hung to the ground. I swept the ground clear with my hands and I made it the God House.

I had never been in a church before and did not know what people did in church, so I continued to rely on Mau Mau's old ways. I stood at the outer edge of the circle made by the soft branches, letting them run across my back. I looked up toward the middle of the tree as if God sat on the uppermost part of the tree.

"God, I haven't talked to you since Mau Mau died and I'm not proud of why I have stayed closed mouthed. I was furious about losing my mother. Her death was too soon for me and she had just been given her freedom and I was trying to get back to her and Bomefree, thinking I could take care of them, get sold to a master nearby. You might as well know I thought the whole thing was your fault, or that you were sleeping the day she died, or you let someone else run the world on that day."

I paused to take a breath, not from so much talking, but from pacing in a tight circle and waving my arms. I tried to hold still. I was worried that I had forgotten how to talk to God. "Mau Mau made me promise to talk to you and this was one time I didn't mind her. This has gone on for a long stretch. Years. That's the whole story in the shortest way I can tell you. Yes, I know this is mostly about my anger getting the better of me. My anger makes me act the fool. I've gotten older since I last talked to you. I should mention to you that I don't need to grow any bigger now. I'm taller than all the women here and most of the men. You can stop that part now. I'm not telling you how to run the world, but I thought you might not have noticed that I kept growing while you and I weren't speaking."

I was out of practice. Should I tell God what to do? I thought he saw everything, was part of everything. What was I supposed to say to God?

"I would very much like to see my father again. I've seen him only twice since Mau Mau died. He is a pitiful sight. He needs me to take care of him and I want more than anything to take care of my father. Isn't that the way things should be? You should see him now God. He is no longer straight and tall like you first meant him to be, but bent over and crooked everywhere. His hair is snow white and he can't see for the thick clouds that have grown over his eyes. You will understand that he needs me. He is no longer a slave, you'll be glad to hear that. Or have you already heard? I honestly don't know what you know or don't know about what's going on down here. Bomefree has been set free in the most terrible way, left in his crippled state without a soul to take care of him. Please God, I worry night and day about my father. Please do what you can."

Then, I had to tell him the worst part. "I need to tell you about an evil thing that I did here at Dumonts. I beat Sally's cat, Nig. The cat didn't do anything wrong, there was no deserving on the part of the cat. I thought I needed something to beat. That's the truth. I know I was wrong about being cruel to the cat. I killed a big, fat frog too while I was on my rampage, but you might not pay as much attention to frogs. I didn't want you to think I was leaving anything out."

I held up my arms to the sky. "I'm back now God and I won't ever go away again."

Later when Robert came to me, I took him as a gift from God.

CHAPTER SEVENTEEN

Robert lived on an Englishman's farm, a man by the name of Catlin. My only experience with the English was bad and I wondered if all English were wild dogs like John Neely. Robert was a slave to Mr. Catlin and had been with him since he was a small boy, purchased away from his mother in New York City. I learned all of this from Robert who started to take a notice to me all of a sudden, as if we were looking at each other and could see for the first time.

Mr. Catlin had a debt to pay Mr. Dumont and Robert was sent to work it off. He did everything we did, raked the hay after we cut it, some of it to the barn, hauled the rest for sale, butchered hogs with us, rendered the lard so that I could make soap. I came to enjoy the debt between our two masters. Tom was loaned out frequently, once Mr. Dumont had determined that Tom was done running away.

I held my body in a certain way when I knew Robert was looking, like I had eyes and mouths all over my body, on my back, down my legs, winking from my backside. I knew without looking if Robert paused with the hay rake, his shirt soaked through with sweat as his eyes rested in the angles of my body. I wanted him to know that my body had soft spots, even if I was long and hard, bone pressing out on skin. I wanted to be seen by Robert.

My Robert glowed warm, smelled rich and salty. Full summer was ending and he and I wore no shoes, which is how I liked it in the summer. I liked the cool, smooth dirt beneath my feet, liked how the soles of my feet toughened up by June so that I could walk over nearly anything.

At the end of the day that we'd worn thin with our looking, he prepared to return home in Catlin's wagon. He sat high on the seat of the wagon, holding the reins to the worn looking horse. I stood by the wagon, my chest even with his feet. His feet were easy for me to look at, and I let my eyes travel down the thin bones from his ankles to his toes where a couple of dark hairs stood rangled up. I wanted to stroke those fines bones that spoke to me.

My longing for him made me daring. "It's good Mr. Catlin owes Mr. Dumont. I hope he owes him so much that you keep coming here," I said. I suppose I should have moved in easier, but I couldn't, the quiver moving through me wouldn't let me heed caution.

"Let the two of them work out their debts. When I come here and look at you, I'm close to heaven," said Robert. He released the brake and as the old horse started to move forward, I stole one last glance at his beautiful feet.

I thought of Robert far into the nights, when I twitched awake, waiting for the dawn birds. I thought of him when I cut down the rye, when I cooked the morning potatoes, when I emptied the night jars. I let thoughts of Robert crawl up and down me. We continued our sweet agonies of looking and longing through the fall and into the winter.

He laughed the first time he saw me smoke my pipe. He drove a wagon back at night to deliver pork for a Christmas party, a gift from Mr. Catlin. It was dark out, past our evening meal. I stood out by the well, smoking to soothe my nerves. He must have seen the red fire when I lit the bowl. "Who's smoking over there?" he asked, knowing that Dumont was inside the house and that it had to be one of the servants or one of the slaves.

"It's me, Bell," I said.

He walked to me with swift steps, pulled by a cord. "You're a girl smoking a man's pipe, but oh, how it looks good on you. Everything looks good on you."

My blood was set on fire, sent scurrying, colliding in all parts of my body. What was he telling me, what had he said?

Robert was near eye level tall with me, a knuckle's width shorter. He wore a knit cap over his closely cropped hair. His wool coat was a moonless, midnight blue. Something bigger than me told me to press my body against his, to match our bodies at the hips, the shoulders, press our belly buttons together, and let our toes kiss.

"Let me taste your pipe," he said and his words drove me into the ground. His steady gaze from his rich brown eyes held me up and kept me from falling in a heap. He reached out and touched my hand, let his fingers rest on mine as he relieved me of my father's pipe. Hadn't anybody but me touched that pipe since it was delivered to me by Martin Schryver, so long ago. Something shot from his skin to mine, got inside me and struck me with lightning.

He held my pipe in his hand, still looking at me the whole time, and slowly moved the pipe to his mouth, let the long white stem rest easy on his bottom lip. Then he closed the top of his mouth down on the stem and drew in from the hot bowl of tobacco. "Ummm," he said, "I can taste your lips."

He ran his tongue over the stem. "Your lips taste like honey suckle and clover, but they look better than clover. They look like columbines. Those are my favorite flowers. You know the ones I mean? They grow along the creek between the road and the last hayfield."

I liked to faint. My head grew lighter and lighter.

He passed the pipe back to me. "Here. Now taste me. What do I taste like?"

My hand would not raise up to meet the pipe and my voice was hid somewhere behind my head.

"I didn't mean to say the wrong thing." He bowed his head. The first snow flakes of the year fell on his head. The flakes melted in steam before they hit me. I feared that Robert would see the steam rising from my head and know my secret that I was burning from his touch.

He said, "When I try to go to sleep at night, I hear your voice. Then when I go to sleep, I dream about you. Last night, I dreamt we were swimming like beavers and we had a house underwater and couldn't nobody get in except the two of us. What do you dream about?"

"I dream about what it would feel like to touch your face," I said. Robert's head tipped back up again. I put my hand on his cheek and that was all it took to get us started, just a touch of my palm to his face. We pulled in together. I had never kissed anyone before and Robert said he hadn't either. From that night on, we grew skilled at kissing.

Taking pleasure in Robert helped me move five paces beyond Mau Mau's death. Until the shock of his touch ran its course through my body, my veins had been filled with silt from flooded rivers. Robert started to flush out my veins and make them run sweet with clean blood. I woke one morning to a complete racket of noise. It was the birds singing and calling. My eyes had been plugged with misery and I had been left deaf to the life going on around me.

We spent the winter stealing moments, putting time together in little bundles until we had bigger bundles. Winter blew past us without causing so much as a chill us. Spring made our desire for each other grow. When Robert placed his hand on the small of my back, resting on the long muscles on either side of my spine and just above where my rump started to jut out, my eyes lost the glaze of gray cloth that had hung across them. I saw colors that shocked me into a drunken state. I saw a blue bird that looked like heaven. I saw goldenrod that took color directly from the sun and made me drop to my knees in thanks. When Robert placed his hand on the small of my back, I felt fire shoot out from his hand, down my legs, straight up my back and out my arms. I know if someone had seen me, they would have seen star lights coming out the top of my head and my finger tips. To his touch, I felt fluid, hot, cold like icicles, bent over like a sapling.

Life went wide open for me. I was talking to God again

129

and God was so glad to see me back. I wondered if Mau Mau didn't have something to do with all this. Was she whispering in God's ear that I needed to be rescued from my too long sorrow? I could feel Mau Mau at every turn where before it had been a stone cold silence.

I got back my sense of touch also. When I ran my hand over the soft skin of my inner arm, I felt like Robert was touching me all over again. If I ran my tongue over my lips, I was in clear danger of fainting. I stopped needing food; I was fed by air and water, by the rich colors of butterflies in the field. I longed to tell someone of this discovery. But how could anyone believe me if they never knew for themselves what Robert and I had? It was likely that we were the first and only people to burn so bright with love. For the first time, I felt sorry for Sally Dumont because it was clear that she had never known this.

Tom was still with us and when he was not rented out, which could be for weeks at a time, I saw him everyday. But he mattered so little to me during my time of wearing the mantle of love for Robert. As it turned out, even sleeping in the same cellar with Tom did not make me notice him anymore than I'd notice a toad.

The Dumont farm had a cellar that stayed mostly dry. The house was set on a bluff immediately overlooking the river. This is where I slept after the first few years of sleeping on the floor of the kitchen. I moved into the cellar right along with the two colored boys who were not but youngsters with high voices. Then when Tom was brought back, he was told to sleep in the cellar as well. I arranged for my sleeping pallet to be held off the ground, and I taught the boys to do the same. This prevented fevers and chilblains, and later, rheumatisms. One layer of boards was laid down, another few slats to separate the first layer of boards from the second, then our straw pallets were spread on top. I had spoken long with Mr. Dumont about the need for us to stay off the dirt floor.

"If the boys get the bone chills, then the fevers, I will

have to take care of them and this will leave you short handed," I said. Mr. Dumont wanted more, not fewer slaves and he wanted more not less work from us.

"Take the wood that you need," he said. "Sick niggers are of no use to me." I knew that I could appeal to his thinking in this area. He was uniform in his treatment of animals and slaves.

I was pleased with our sleeping arrangements. I know that some slaves slept in the attics and that was fine for the winter when the heat of the house rose up. But in the summer the heat in an attic was enough to choke the breath away. Given the choice of the two, I'd choose a dry cellar any day. I didn't have a choice, but if I did, my choice was below and not above.

The boys, Arnold and Tobias, slept under the stairway. I slept by the far wall, near a short window that offered some of our only light. I told the boys stories at night if I had any left in me at the end of the day. I told them about Mau Mau and all the stories I learned from her about my brothers and sisters, and about her trip across the ocean with her mother. I told them about Bomefree, who was once a man so tall that he was called a tree. I told them about the fancy dances at the Schryvers' tavern and how I stopped them all with my songs. I bragged about drinking ale when all the other party goers were too dizzy to tell the difference. I told them if they were fortunate, they could grow up to be as strong and handsome as Robert. The boys didn't like it so much when I talked about Robert, because my mind wandered off and I started to hum and often left the boys in mid thought.

When Tom was first brought back, I left him to find his own sleeping place. We had not spoken of how Sally used him to punish me. I saw no point. We gave each other a far distance. I was glad when Tom was loaned out to work on other farms. He was a sour person, filled with grief and anger. And I had no time for him with my heart filled with Robert.

The smoke house cruelty stopped as strangely as it began,

131

although the filth of it stayed with me. I don't know how many trips were made to the smoke house over a year's time; I chose not to keep track. In my conversations with God, I said if this was punishment for anything I truly did, then I would take my punishment. If this was Sally's addled mind at work, reaching out to strangle my spirit, then I would choose to take flight in my mind, to keep my spirit far from her. I chose the latter path. I never told Robert of those times. I expect there were also things that he never told me. But he was my confidante in all other ways. He knew how I spoke to God, where my God house was, and how I could read signs from God in the water, the tree, the bird. He knew how I longed to care for Bomefree.

Our moments together were finer than any of the thin boned china in Sally's cupboards, finer than blue satin, sweeter than apple pie, greater than all the wealth sought by John Dumont. Robert said I was a wonder, that if I truly wanted to be more of a house slave, I could. I could muster reasons in the mind of Mr. Dumont for keeping me warm indoors in the winter, cool in the summer. Once he put his ear right on the middle of my forehead, and held the sides of my head with his hands. "Let me press my ear next to your mind so that I can hear all your beautiful thoughts hard at work in there. Oh, there is a mob of thinking going on in there! And songs. And now you're thinking of me holding your head just so." Then he turned his head and kissed me and ran his hands the length of my belly.

We learned that Mr. Catlin, Robert's owner, owed a far larger debt to Mr. Dumont than we first realized. "Do you think Dumont could buy me outright from Catlin? Or that Catlin could turn me over to Dumont completely?" asked Robert. We had no idea of figures and sums of money past easy numbers. It was clear to me that my master admired the work that Robert did and he found his countenance pleasant.

"I don't know what he can or can't do, but he doesn't seem to lack for much. He has two carriages. We'll butcher six lambs this spring. And if he gets any more cows, I won't be done milking till past breakfast." This was my best estimation of Dumont's wealth.

"Bell, if I was bought by him, you and I could be married. We could work every Sunday and buy ourselves from him."

I didn't personally know any negroes who purchased their freedom at a young age, but I was starting to hear more about it, from the tinker, and from old Tom, although I didn't know if I should believe his wild stories or not. And as much as Mr. Dumont was against it, a time was coming when slaves were going to be free, but I could not fathom how far away that time was. The tinker said there were states where colored people lived without owners and without starving. Tom told of colored people in New York City working and putting their own pay in their pockets. I doubted what I couldn't see except with God. "If we didn't live here, where would we live?" I asked.

"We'd hire ourselves out and be paid in money or barter. You could launder and cook, keep house as Katie did." Katie had recently taken her leave of the Dumonts without so much as a goodbye to Sally, who swore she would never offer a recommendation for Katie. I was glad to be rid of her.

Our plan to buy our freedom grew every day of the spring, and into the summer. I pictured Bomefree living with us, free at last from the fear of loneliness and starvation. I saw myself tending to him as my mother had done, easing his knotted spine, rubbing lard scented with herbs into his skin, filling his belly with hot soup. I pictured the warmth of Robert's body next to mine, crunching the husk filled mattress, all the rest of our days.

We planned as best we could, certain of our success. Some days when I woke and discovered that I was still sleeping in Dumont's cellar with a nest of nasty smelling boys and snores of old Tom in the far corner, I was shocked back to the task of reality. I needed time and careful words to present the idea to Mr. Dumont.

Tom was the first to notice that Robert and I were

sweethearts. He said, "Just because you're a white man's nigger, don't think you'll get what you want in love. You'll never get that." Tom didn't know that my mother had been called a white folks' nigger so it held no sway with me.

I heard the word sweethearts from Gert, who was quickly admonished by her mother not to speak in such a vulgar way. I loved the word, sweetheart, because that is just the way I felt; my heart was filled with sweet liquid. I double checked with Gert, who was just sane enough from her own romancing to be able to speak to me. I asked her if sweetheart meant what I thought it meant, and she whispered back yes, it did. If two people were courting, you could say they were sweethearts. So that's what Robert and I were doing, courting. And we were sweethearts. I knew if Sally found out before I could get things squared away with Mr. Dumont, she would try to ruin everything.

With the full heat of summer, we became bold in our passions. My eyes soaked up every part of him that I could see, the soft curves of his ears, the strong black hairs of his eyebrows, the unfortunate way that his bottom lip cracked open both in the dry cold of the winter, and from too much sun in the summer. My knees grew weak, felt like they would collapse when he brushed up against me. When Robert stayed over for a long stretch, he had to sleep in the barn. I was never so glad to be the first person awake, the one to milk the cows. I took to waking Robert by lying full out beside him in the hayloft, bringing him a cup of milk fresh from the best cow. We figured we were as good as married and we did as the married ones do. Our fingers could not fly fast enough to unbutton our clothes. Every touch from Robert was new and soft. He licked the scars on my back just like that bear had done in my dream long ago. I tangled my arms and legs around him and pulled him into me. There was no stopping us.

CHAPTER EIGHTEEN

I picked my time to speak to Mr. Dumont. The summer season was going as well as any farmer could hope. The frost did not come late in the spring, no blossoms were torn off by late blizzards, the fields dried out enough for planting, and soft rain kept the young plants from drying out. These things made a farmer happy. Mr. Dumont and I looked at his herd of cows, admiring the strength and the color of the calves.

"It would be grand to have another pair of hands to help around here," I said. I had already said this a number of times and was getting no response. "Robert is the best worker I've ever seen." I pictured his shoulders and thought I caught a scent of him, which I did in the strangest of places.

"The full story is this," I said to him leaning my garden hoe against the fence. "Robert and I are thinking about the time when slaves are to be freed and we want to be ready. If you buy Robert from Catlin, he and I can work every Sunday, hire ourselves out and we will pay you back for the both us. Until then, you'll get the same hard work from me that you've always had."

I stole a glance at him. Dumont drummed his fingers on the fence post. "There's no way to explain how complicated our arrangement has gotten with Catlin and how difficult it is to work with a man who knows nothing about farming. He should have stayed back in England painting portraits of ladies. I have of course been thinking about the worth of buying Robert. And I have been waiting to find a strong mate for you. You could increase my holdings Bell, if you have children as strong and healthy as you are. The rest is nonsense; you and Robert would be better off staying right where you are as slaves."

"So, you're going to try and buy Robert?" I could hardly believe my ears. Out of everything that he said, all I heard was the part about buying Robert.

"Yes. But you are not to say a word about this to anyone, not even Robert. I don't want Catlin to think that he is getting the lesser deal. Lord save me from artists who become farmers."

I exploded with joy. I danced a little jig and Mr. Dumont laughed. "I want lots of babies from this Bell, lots of good stock."

I didn't even tell Robert, which took most of my strength because all he had to do was look at me with his sweet brown eyes, and a halo of sweat around his forehead and I was ready to tell him anything. But I didn't. I trusted Mr. Dumont to take care of us. I told Robert to wait, and there was no need to worry.

We worked ourselves into a frenzy that summer. I didn't handle the heat as well as past summers. I was hot all the time and more tired when I should have been full of go. No matter, I preferred the hard work of the summer to being trapped in the house with Sally. I pulled out the weeds that threatened to choke out what we planted. The sun beat down hard on me. Sally refused me a straw hat to work in the sun. All the hired hands had straw hats. The hat shaded their eyes, cooled their heads, and saved their skin from burning. Even the younger slave boys were allowed hats.

"Bell, your skin won't burn, you're as black as a devil and your true color comes out more with the sun," she said. She often repeated this in front of her women friends when they came to visit. "She's so black, she doesn't need a hat in full sun." All the white women shielded themselves from any

136

exposure to the sun.

Mr. Dumont stopped hearing a lot of what his wife said. It was well into the summer before he noticed I was without a hat.

"Bell, you're a fool to not cover your head in this sun. You'll grow so black that I won't be able to see you in the night."

I cautioned myself. I could not speak against his wife. I could not upset him and spoil any of the chances for him buying Robert.

"Do you think I should? I would like to try a hat but only I don't have one and I don't want to bother the missus. If you'll get me one, I'll wear it," I said.

He brought me a hat and I kept it in the barn. I wore it only in the fields. I never wore it while working in the kitchen garden, only my head scarf which kept the dirt out of my hair. I don't think I could have made it through that hot summer without a hat. As it was, I took to vomiting in the morning and felt light headed during the day. Gert said that she didn't plan to get whatever I had; nothing was going to spoil her wedding that was to take place in the winter.

One Sunday I truly could not rise from my bed. It was closing in on harvest season and I normally would have helped out and perhaps earned a bit of extra cloth or food. The cellar door opened and Mr. Dumont's heavy feet pounded down the stone stairway. "Is Robert with you?"

The alarm in his voice made my sick belly spasm even tighter. "Robert has never been here in the cellar, sir. Are you looking for him?" Robert spent the last week back at Catlins. I was hoping for a visit from him but my swooshing stomach dampened my enthusiasm even for Robert.

"If you see him, tell him to look sharp and beware. Catlin and his son are here looking for him and threatening to flog him. They say he's run away with a plan to come and get you."

I stood on a box and looked out the cellar window in time to see the Catlin men converging on Robert who was covered in sweat, his shirt flying open. I could see that he had run all the way, that he was trying to get to me. Robert was coming to see me all right, but somehow Catlin had learned too much about us, learned that Robert was hoping to be purchased by Mr. Dumont and that no slaves would be sired that Catlin could claim. I saw all of this in the red face of Catlin who was growling with anger.

I climbed down from the box and climbed the stairs to the kitchen, steadying myself with my hands on the cool stones of the wall. Mr. Dumont was just leaving the house heading for the tangle of angry bodies in his farmyard. He turned back to me. "For God's sake Bell, do not come out. I'll do what I can for Robert."

I went as far as the door and saw both of the men beating Robert with their walking sticks. They took deliberate aim at his head, his beautiful black eyebrows, his soft ears. They bloodied all of it. Robert was knocked so senseless that he did not put his hands up to ward off the blows. Mr. Dumont jumped in the mix. "They'll be no niggers killed on my farm!" he yelled.

I fell to my knees in the doorway. Sally stood next to me, her blue skirt brushing my shoulders.

Mr. Dumont made a dash for Catlin's walking stick and put his heavy hand on it as the man raised it for yet another blow. "He's no good to you dead. You'd not kill a plow horse would you?"

Catlin's goitered neck was covered with sweat and dust. The large mass on his neck caused him to turn his whole body to look at Dumont. "I'm not losing a slave that I paid dearly for. Our business deal is over. I'll pay you every dollar I owe you, but this slave is not leaving my farm," he said.

His anger matched that of his son's, who waited only for a word from his father to smash in Robert's head completely. Catlin shook off Mr. Dumont's hold and he lowered his stick. The son lowered his after a challenging glare from his father convinced him. They hoisted Robert up to a groggy stand and tied his hands behind him in miserable tightness. Even Sally flinched at this.

"Loosen the rope on this fellow or you'll break his arms at the shoulders," yelled Mr. Dumont. He had the power to slow down Catlin although he couldn't stop him entirely. As the father and son proceeded to march Robert homeward, Mr. Dumont got on his horse. "I'll see them to their farm," he called to us. Robert's head was covered with blood and I wasn't sure that he could see. As the men passed from view, I once again threw up, making it only to the stone steps leading from the kitchen.

I waited at the end of the lane for Dumont's return. By late afternoon, I heard the sound of his horse and I ran to meet him. "They cooled down by the time they reached home," he said. "I don't think they'll beat him more this day."

"He'll be well enough to work in a few days. He's stronger than I am. We should be expecting him back, shouldn't we?" I asked. I shaded my eyes to the late day sun.

"Don't count on him coming back Bell. The Catlins don't know how to run a farm and they don't know how to manage slaves. I was wet nursed by a colored woman, a family slave. I understand slaves. People like them feel they have to whip everything from horses to niggers to get work out of them."

I didn't care who wet nursed Mr. Dumont and I didn't care about Catlin's lack of good sense or general human kindness. I heard only that Robert wasn't coming back. "What do you mean he's not coming back?"

He gave his horse a squeeze with his thigh and headed slowly into the farm. "Part of what made him so mad was that he just bought a young wench for a rich price to marry off to Robert. He's planning on increasing his stock of slaves."

I fell backward. I felt a solid weight, as big as a sack of grain, crash against my ribs. My breath flew out of me and I could not regain it. Everything in me came apart and as I hit the ground, I heard the horse's hooves continuing on to the Dumont home.

CHAPTER NINETEEN

The Copperhead is a much maligned snake. The fact that she has poison in her fangs makes her honest and purely defensive, when she isn't looking for a meal. Copperhead came to mean something different when the full out battle against slavery grabbed us all by the throat. Then it meant a northerner who was in favor of slavery. They picked too honest a creature to describe such a vile person.

I watched the world of animals and I learned most of what I needed to know about people, with some exceptions. I found no animal that enslaved another animal and forced it to do its bidding. Nor did I ever see one animal beat another animal except to protect its young, to defend itself, or to chase away other males in the mating season

Here is what I learned from the snake, and the one I happened to learn the most from was the Copperhead. When the sun warms the earth and wakes up all the sleeping ones from their winter grogginess, when the snow is another year's memory, and when the rocks are warm to the touch, then the snake takes notice and with her boundless wisdom, she emerges. I truly don't know where snakes go in the winter. It must be deep because they would freeze and shatter if left exposed to one of our winters. But come mid-spring, when the bulb plants have burst through the earth, the snakes wake up.

I liked to find them on logs near a creek, sunning

themselves, staying still for so long. John Dumont had no patience for snakes and killed them if they had the misfortune to cross his path. The snake was unfairly hated. I knew what it was like to be hated on sight, to have lies said about me by people who knew nothing of my thoughts or actions. I gave snakes a chance until they proved themselves untrustworthy, which they never did. If you understood them, you could trust them to be perfectly honest.

Their changing was what I most admired. At some point, their outer self grew tired, too tight and had to be abandoned. They shed their old outer self, like a full length scab that must be scraped off. I had occasion to watch a snake or two leave her old self behind and emerge fresh and bright, aglow with colors begging for hope. It looked like birthing, hard groaning work, and that the emerging body was too unprotected. Then the old tube of skin hooked on a stickery bush and the copperhead with her dangerous eyes and honest fangs was born different from before

I wanted to be sister to the copperhead, I wanted to shed my old outer self and emerge scarless, fresh, full of hope and coil my body round a warm rock and flick my tongue for the whole sunny part of the day. I did not want to be who I was, where I was.

Robert wasn't coming for me. Goiter-necked Catlin had married him to one of his own slaves and would not send him to our farm ever again I did not begrudge Robert another woman, a warm body to hold him; if nothing else, I wished him whatever comfort he could gain. I knew he had no choice, and that the beating had been as bad for his spirit as his body. My dreams of being with Robert, loving him, were not torn to shreds by the lash of his master, but by the crush of his spirit. I could not bear to think of Robert without his passionate heart, his glorious vision of our future as freed slaves, as a man and woman together.

In the days after Robert's beating, I remained ill, and the master let me be. I did not step out of the cellar except to relieve myself when my chamber pot grew too full. I heard him tell his wife that she had to let me gain my strength as harvest season was fast on us.

What no one knew except me was that I was with child. They say that with the first pregnancy, you might not understand what's happening. I don't see how that could be. I had not told Robert about the baby because by the time I was sure, Catlin stopped him from coming back to the Dumont farm. Because I was as skinny as a stick, I was like a room with only one chair and table in it. When I got pregnant, all of sudden I had four chairs and a dish cupboard in a room. My belly did not poke directly out because my body is so long, giving the tiny babe lots of up and down room. Layers of aprons, skirts, and underskirts helped as well.

For several years, Sally thought it prudent for me to show evidence of my monthly bleeding, so she made me show her my bloody rags each month. She said she had to know. She told me that she learned from other white women that this was how she could be sure that I wasn't stealing her husband away. I didn't know where Sally was getting her lessons about colored people women, but to imagine me stealing a white man was unthinkable. If she had not had such a solemn look on her face when she told me this, I would have laughed out loud.

To keep up the fiction for as long as possible, I nicked a spot on my scalp with the edge of a hatchet. The scalp bleeds like a river and I sopped up the blood with my monthly rags. I cut myself just inside my hairline, let the blood spill, then squeezed the cut hard together. I was pretty near half way done with the pregnancy before Sally walked past me one day, as we headed full force into winter. I squatted in front of the fire to tend it. Something must have caught her eye, I don't know what to this day. Probably it was the way a woman's face changes when she carries a baby, the eyes grow bigger, the skin fills out a bit, even on sharp cheek bones like mine. Maybe it was the way I held my knees apart when I squatted to give my hard middle some room. She saw it all in an instant. She placed her hand on the walnut sideboard. "You're a lying nigger girl. How long have you been with child?"

I didn't have the power to care about Sally at that moment. Losing Robert took almost all my strength away and turned me quiet on the outside. I stared at the fire, letting my knees spread more with the truth.

"Right before they beat Robert and dragged him off, right then," I said. I was relieved really; I would no longer need to slice my scalp. And I never lied outright, I never spoke a lie to her.

She sat down at the table and folded her hands. She had a changed look on her face. "Now you'll be making babies. More slaves. My husband will be pleased."

She was right, her husband was pleased, with one exception. I was not present when she told her husband, but I imagined her satisfaction at telling him something about me that he didn't know. He fancied himself the lord of the slaves and took offense when his wife took an upper hand.

"You must be married Bell. Colored or not, I'll not have you carrying a child without a husband," said Mr. Dumont the following day.

Me being with child had more to do with his feud with Catlin. If Catlin found out that I was carrying Robert's child, he might make a fuss, thinking that property was being taken away from him. The truth was, the newborn child of a slave was the property of the slave owner, and any child born of a slave, was immediately a slave the moment it took its first breath. Slavery passed from the mother, not the father.

"Bell, you've shown yourself to be old enough to be married. Tom is as good a husband as you'll find here," said Mr. Dumont.

A sick feeling came over me. "I don't want him! He's too old for me. I'll be eighteen years old when this baby is born in the spring. I don't know how old Tom is but he probably already had a wife before I was born."

"This is not a matter where you have a choice. You don't know what's best for you and you certainly don't know what

143

is best for me. Now, I want this done before Gertrude's wedding or there will be bitterness to pay in my house."

I knew what he meant. Sally did not want any distraction from her daughter's wedding, which was to take place after the Christmas holiday. Sally saw no need for me to be married and already objected to any comparison that might be made between me getting married and Gert getting married. The two events could not have been more different. Sally said that marriage did not fully apply to slaves, and Sally's tutors on the subject let her know that slaves did not have the full ability to marry in the same way that white people did. Mr. Dumont said slaves should be married, and if Sally kept up on the laws changing, she would have seen that slaves in New York could indeed marry. He had the last word on the subject.

I dug my heels into the ground in the only way I could. I waited until the boys were asleep in our cellar. Tom wasn't snoring yet so I knew he was still awake. I slid off my pallet with the blanket wrapped around me and walked to his side of the room, standing over his bed. "I know you're awake, old man." He rolled over and looked up at me.

"They're bringing Soan and her husband here on Sunday for us to get married." Soan was a slave from Poughkeepsie. She was midwife to all the colored people and some of the white ones. Her husband, by association, was assigned the power to marry colored people. Or that's what the white people thought. We all knew it was Soan who said the final words that made it real.

"Then that's the way it will be, won't it girl," said Tom.

"Not until we talk about the smokehouse. I won't marry a man that aided in the unnatural things that happened to me."

He rose up on one elbow. "You're so damn young, you don't know the half of anything. You haven't seen a bit of what I've seen in this world. You don't know what freedom is, don't know what it tastes like. You were born from white folks' niggers and that's what you are too. And don't tell me what I need to talk to you about."

144

"How could you go along with her? There's plenty of ways of slowing down white people. You call me a white man's nigger. I call you mean and ignorant if you don't know how to talk to white people to show them a way to go easier on a slave. My parents taught me to deal with the white man, not make matters worse."

"You don't think it could have gone worse for you? Look at my arms! You don't think I could have done more damage to you than was done? I held back my strength, made it look like I was beating the daylights out of you. And I won't ever speak of the business she did to you. Now if we got to be married, then you best know that I'd sooner tangle up with a porcupine than end up with the likes of you. You're tall and skinny and hard to look at."

I didn't know he had that many words in him. I didn't know Tom and he didn't know me. He let me know not to make him angry, not to endanger him. I stepped out of his reach.

I was taller than Tom but he was thick armed and broad shouldered like men are when they get older. That's why young men are cautious of the older ones; they know that if an older man gets a hold of them, they're done for. I was fast but if his thick veined hands got a grip on me, I couldn't shake him loose.

"Let them marry us then. Don't expect nothing from me until this baby is born. Don't come crawling to my bed," I said. I turned from him and heard the rustle of his blankets as he slid down into his blanket. "Do one thing before they marry us. Burn that cursed thing."

Tom sat up. "Burn what thing?"

"You carved it for her. The darning egg."

He slid back down without answering me. I went to my pallet and lay on my side, pulling my knees up to make a shell around the baby and me. I cried without making a sound. I hunted for a scent of Robert, ran my tongue over my arm looking for a forgotten spot of him, and failing that, I sent my spirit out to him, to find him at Catlin's farm and wrap myself around him. The first storm of the season hit the house sounding like broken glass. It was the worst sort of storm; freezing rain. The winter was merciless from that point on.

Soan and her husband Luke came across the river from Poukeepsie on the ferry one week before Christmas to marry us. Sally said she was too busy in the house to be bothered with us so we did the ceremony in the barn with Mr. Dumont and Gert standing on either side of the doorway. Tom and I had no interest in each other and we were both shamed by the marriage, being that it was put upon us, instead of us choosing it. I already told Soan I was not going to touch that man even if I did have to marry him. Soan was a grandmother many times over and had the good fortune to know where most of her children had been sold. She told me to hush.

Luke told us to stand side by side. The Dumont's Sunday best carriage took up most of the open space in the barn, so we were all forced to stand close to the big doors near the entrance. We all wore coats and mittens against the bitter cold. The wind shook the doors keeping the horses stirred up, huffing and snorting, blowing steamed breath. Luke placed a broomstick on the ground in front of Tom and me.

"On one side of the broomstick, you are two people trying to get through this life. You are alone and without help from anyone except God. When you cross over the broomstick, you will be together, helping each other work through the sorrows and the joys. Hold hands and jump over the stick!" He was old and white-haired. He raised his arm and closed his eyes, as if he expected us to do just as he said.

Soan leaned over and whispered in his ear, loud enough for me to hear, "I told you to leave out the part about holding hands. Now say it like I told you."

Luke lowered his arm and opened his eyes, peering first at Soan, then at Tom and me. "All right, each one of you, step over the broomstick."

My arms were crossed tight over my chest. I looked

straight ahead and stepped over the stick. I heard no movement from Tom. I looked back. He didn't want this any more than I did. I had a moment of pity for him.

"Come on and let's get this over with. I can't do this by myself," I said.

Mr. Dumont laughed and so did Gert. "Let's hope your wedding has more willing parties," he said to his daughter. I could have killed Gert for laughing.

Tom stepped over and Luke said we were married. Mr. Dumont slapped Tom on the back, telling him how happy this made him. Gert and I looked at each other and there was nothing to say; she kicked her boots around in the hay for a few minutes then excused herself to the house, followed by her father.

Soan closed the doors after them and turned to us. "Now you two stand right here in front of me and drop those vinegar faces. Isabella, you are bringing a baby into this world. Tom, you are about to be blessed with a family once again. Each time a child is born, we have hope anew. This child may live with fewer years of slavery. This child may have hope. And your job is to have hope together. You stand before me and God and promise to be kind to each other, to take care of each other and to protect each other from as much harm as you can. I ask you, in God's name, to agree to take each other in spirit and in body."

I was stunned by the transformation in Soan. Suddenly, her long white hair was loose, her cape fell off her and her eyes were on fire. Her voice filled the barn and I could not speak.

"This is not about a slave master!" she roared. I feared that all the people from the house would come running. "In God's name, will you bind to each other?" she demanded.

Tom stepped into her light. "I have had two wives before this. One from choosing and one from the will of a slave master. They were both sold from me. I will bind to Bell if she will have an old man like me, but this cannot be a marriage."

I looked over at him. He stood tall and straight and he spoke directly to Soan. I couldn't believe this was the same evil eyed man who had scowled at me since he arrived. Soan turned to me. "Now you have a choice, and none but the four of us will know of it."

I was getting something that Robert didn't have, I was about to choose. But I was not about to tell a lie. "If I could truly choose my husband, every one of you knows who that would be. And Robert would choose me."

Soan stepped closer to me. She reached her hands out to me; they looked like brown paper stretched over her bones. "Don't let them take every choice away from you, child. I ask you again if you will choose to bind to this man in God's name."

I didn't know that this marriage was going to have anything to do with God, so I wasn't prepared. I thought it was just the same as being bought by a white man, sold with a herd of sheep, taken away from one more person who I loved. If we were going to talk to God, then I needed to go to my God house and speak directly with him.

"I will say yes for now. But I will speak my own piece to God about this. God and I haven't spoken of this and I don't want to surprise him," I said.

Soan sighed. "Then in the name of God, I bind this man and this woman to each other."

I delivered the news to God later, letting him know that I took Tom as my husband. I asked him to tell Robert. Tom delivered the ashes of the maple darning egg to me.

* * *

That winter tried to tear my skin off. Not a single person could get warm long enough to remember it. Soon after words were said over me and old Tom to make us married, it was the Christmas holiday. For slaves, this was no small holiday, even in foul ice storms as we had. We were given the full week off, Sunday to Sunday, offered bottles of St. Croix rum, and given food that was denied us the rest of the year. Because we were so scattered out among the white families, one colored face here, another two on a farm ten miles upriver, we liked to get together in one place if we could, if we had permission to travel. It was best when we could fill up an obliging farmer's barn and sing and drink and dance. We could catch up on news about babies born and died, the ailments of the old ones, and any slip of news about slavery ending in New York.

Of course, a slave owner didn't have to permit us this holiday, but it was generally agreed on by the old families, those who had owned slaves for years before me, that the Christmas week was a rightful gift to the colored people and that it gave us something to look forward to. John Dumont offered his barn every year to the local slaves, and each year I had been at Dumonts, I went to the long party, to be with other dark faces, to catch a feeling of family.

This year, I half hoped Robert would be allowed to attend, that his thin brained master would have the sense to ease up on him. Catlin knew by now that Dumont had married me off to Tom, knew he was in no danger of Robert running off. Since his beating, Robert had not come near the Dumont farm. If he had come, I'd have sensed him miles before he set foot in the barn, I would have heard the crunch of snow under his boots the moment he started out.

I sat, with my bulging belly, a blanket wrapped around me, and watched the revelers. I soaked up the music from the violin, soaked up the heat of rich voices telling tales. Tom paid little attention to me, which is how I liked it. This was the first year that I didn't join in with the dancing and the singing. I did not have the heart for it.

Robert never came and I was glad when the holiday was over, glad to be back to work. Work was a well worn path for me and I did not have to think as hard. I had no expectations about work, no hopes to be dashed.

Gert was married in the coldest month of the year. She was married in a church, and I hoped to attend. I heard Gert arguing with her mother over letting me go to the wedding.

"I would like Bell to be at my wedding," said Gert. She was in her mother's bedroom trying on her wedding gown. I was at the foot of the stairs.

"Let's not spoil a special day for our family. She's not a fit sight for a church," said Sally.

"You know that's not why you don't want her to come. I've seen other niggers at the back of church. She doesn't look any different. I could fix her up some, give her a shawl to wear and a hat.."

"Don't start giving her good things to wear. She doesn't know how to take care of them."

"She washes our clothes every week better than Katie did. If anyone knows how to take care of clothes, it's Bell."

"Well, it wouldn't look right, let's put it that way. Please do this for me Gert, do this for your mother?"

I heard silence from the upstairs room. Gert had spoken up for me on many occasions but her mother had been slowly fencing her in, wrapping her up in fine silks and lace, folding quilts in her marriage trunk, telling her secrets about the duties of a white woman, how to talk to servants and slaves. I never knew when the old Gert would run into a room, squeeze my hand and say, "Bell, I must tell you the most clever thing I read in my book!" or if she would suddenly pull herself tightly back.

I stood at the bottom of the stairs, my hand on the walnut post waiting to see which Gert would answer her mother. She must have nodded yes, as her mother said. "You're learning to be a proper lady."

CHAPTER TWENTY

I was alone with the labors of my first birthing until my screams split open the night. Then Sally came to the cellar and said that my pains could not be that bad and she was agitated by my noise. She came only that once while I was laboring, standing in the dark with a candle lighting up her face.

My mind was wrapped around my belly tightening and threatening to crush me. The pain started in my spine, then spun around to my middle, feeling like the baby was desperate to get out and that it was being crushed by the grip. Every woman I knew went into birthing accepting the possibility that death could take her and the baby. When the next hard pain struck me, I squeezed my eyes shut from the onslaught. Sally was gone when next I looked.

I heard the scrape of Tom's boots on the stone steps. He asked me how I was. And I said if I could get up, I'd kill him. I don't know why I said this to him. I cursed him and tried to rise.

"You're close to birthing, Bell. I've seen women before they bear babies and they all cursed me right before the baby came out," he said, still staying beyond my reach.

"You come closer to me and I'll show you something," I screamed at him.

Midwives came for slaves only if the midwife was within shouting distance, or if the midwife herself was a colored

151

woman. Our closest was Soan and she was across the ice-choked river. Mr. Dumont had been gone since morning with the sleigh and he was not expected back for two more days.

If I closed my eyes again, I figured I was lost. I did not want to accept death, I wanted to live and I wanted my baby to live. I could no longer speak words, but I kept my eyes open to keep from being broken apart, my arms and legs shattered, the rest of me split up the middle. I kept my eyes on Tom. He came closer.

"You have to push the baby out," he said, coming closer still and putting his hand on my forehead. He put another hand on my leg and I was anchored. I wanted to tell him, do not take your hand off my leg what ever you do, if you expect me to stay in one piece, but the words would not come out.

We both feared the baby was stuck. I pushed for so long that thin rays of daylight came through the one small window. Tom said, "If you can't push this baby out, you'll die, Bell."

With the next pain, I pushed from everywhere and this time I was ready to die trying.

"The head is out! You're near to done. Do that again."

Tom was more midwife than I could have imagined and I was as grateful to him in that moment as I would have been to my own mother. He had not pleased me in one small way since I had been married off to him, nor I suppose had I pleased him. I heard something like caring in his voice, as he coaxed Diana out, like we were working together.

That's how Tom and I took to touching, him squatted between my legs, me spread out and howling, bucking the way a horse does when she's had too much to eat and drink and her insides are bursting. He wrapped the baby in one of his shirts of rough weave. He put her near me. The cord was still attached, poking out the swaddling cloth.

"You're not done yet. The afterbirth has got to come out," he said. This was another place where birthing can go wrong. If I was too weak to make one last push to slide out the after birth, then he'd have to go in to get it. I'd get a fever if anyone went fishing for the afterbirth and would most likely die within the week.

"Sit up some," he said.

I could no more sit up than fly. He ran over to his pallet, folded it up and after pulling me to a near sitting position, propped me up with his pallet behind my back.

"Now let this afterbirth run down stream," he said, once again between my legs. I felt something effortlessly slide out of me.

"That's good, that's good." He put the afterbirth near the baby.

"My first wife, Anne, said the after birth needs to see that the baby is cared for, and breathing, and that she can suckle. She said don't cut the cord before the baby suckles."

With that, he held the baby up to my breast and pushed one nipple near her mouth and she latched on like she'd been doing it for years. I always remember the first time of everything new, and the first time of suckling felt like a flock of butterflies landed on my breast, all tugging in tiny ways. Something tightened up low down in my belly.

"Your Anne was a midwife?" My voice was thick from lack of use.

"Yes. Anne could call a baby from any woman who came to her. And few died. I learned some from watching her, mostly from listening to her when she came back after a birth. She'd be all lit up, needing to talk about it. Anne was sold from me when our own babies weren't older than five years. Our master was offered a price for her that was far greater than he'd ever paid for a slave. She was sold south, to Maryland, to tend to a large slave owner who was looking to increase his numbers. Then I was sold from the babies."

There were four of us on my pallet; me, Tom, the baby, and the afterbirth, which looked like a large liver. "My mother said to bury the afterbirth near the house," I said.

"Ground's still frozen," said Tom.

"I want it buried with the cord. Mau Mau said that

burying the after birth with the cord keeps the baby from losing its breath as it sleeps. I want this baby to live."

He tied the cord in two places with leather strips, then cut through it with his whittling knife. "I'll wrap this and keep it in the ice house until the ground thaws, then we'll bury it."

Tom's calling as a midwife was a secret that he shared only with me. He was a complicated man, and as soon as my daughter was born, he packed away his midwifery self into the far corners, back with his memories of Anne. He became more like his old self, only I knew him better and took more kindly to him.

We had pain in common; Robert had been taken from me, and his Anne had been sold from him, as well as his children. I was Tom's third wife. He said that considering his age, he probably wouldn't be married off again, even if I was sold.

"Not sold," I said, "I won't be sold again. I'll be here at Dumonts' or I'll be a free woman." This was the first time I'd ever said those words and I wondered if God put them in my mouth, or if it was the birth. They tasted light and sweet in my mouth.

* * *

My pallet was soiled with blood and all sorts of wetness, so until it could be replenished, Tom let me and the baby sleep on his mattress. He slept up against Tobias, the youngest boy. Tobias didn't dare say one word about not wanting old Tom sleeping with him. I could tell from his eyes that he was scared to death of him

Tom reported the birth to Sally. She asked who was going to make breakfast the next morning. He told her that breakfast would somehow get made if he had to make it himself. Mr. Dumont was pleased. I had just produced something that would normally cost him one hundred dollars. Like a good yield on a crop, this is the part of slavery that thrilled the slave owner, when slaves produced more slaves.

154

CHAPTER TWENTY-ONE

I had heard of slaves or servants spitting in the master's soup. I have more sense than to spit in my master's soup and then slide the bowl under his nose and get revenge knowing that he was drinking my spit. I knew Mr. Dumont could read my mind like he read his books. I never saw anyone as learned as Mr. Dumont and I was humbled before him. He was lord of the land as far as the eye could see. The other Dumonts who lived within a day's ride took their troubles to him and came to him for advice

I took his praise as the greatest gift on this earth. His words also meant I would not be sold to another. I burned up my hands on carding and spinning to hear him say, "There's no one who works as fine as you do, Bell. What would we do without you?"

I was awkward at first with spinning and wondered if my fingers were too large for the job. Most of my learning came from Sally. She and I were not well matched for teacher and student, but when I was too heavy with child to work quickly outside Sally decided that I needed to learn new work. She offered no encouragement and I thought it best, for the both of us, if I learned with all due haste to put an end to lessons between us.

In the months after Diana's birth, before the fields dried out enough to plant, I practiced spinning at every opportunity. The first sounds that Diana heard were the swooshing rhythm of me peddling the wheel as the wool became yarn. As I became more skilled, I could pull the wool finer and finer. Sally had to create faults with me and mentioned none of my improvements while Mr. Dumont sang my praises. I wished he wouldn't carry on so about me in front of Sally; it was the only thing he couldn't see, how she grew hot with rage when he favored me.

"She is responsible for all discord between us," said Sally to her husband as they sat in front of the fire in the sitting room. I was in the kitchen, putting away the work from supper and getting a start on the next day's work.

"I cannot bear the way she displays herself to you, showing her arms, her neck, her ankles! Oh, for the sake of God! I am daily stricken to see you rest your eyes on her."

I stopped wiping the bowls. Had Mr. Dumont let his eyes rest on me? If he had, I was too busy working to notice. I padded silently to the doorway. Her profile was framed by the glow of the fire, one of the last of the season before a reluctant summer beat back the winter. She was darning, the sight of which made me clench up with fear, remembering the old days of her fury.

Sally spoke with her lips pulled tight across her gray teeth. She wanted more than anything to have her husband to send all the slaves away. We were the worst souls on earth, or to hear her tell it, we were creatures without souls. If we were to disappear, life would become heaven for Sally. She had no desire to see us free, just gone.

"And I wish that you had not wasted good money sending a slave catcher after that black rascal Tom. My sleep is ruined. You snore beside me and Tom snores loud enough in the cellar to rock the floorboards," she told her husband. She was on to a new point of discussion and I was glad to have the problem be with Tom and not me for a change. I returned to my dish cleaning.

Mr. Dumont said, "Neither Tom nor I can help it. And perhaps you are too delicate a sleeper. Yes, that is likely to be the problem. Bell! Come in here."

There was no way to predict when I would get pulled into their dickering. I dreaded it because there was no safe position for me to take. If I agreed with one, it meant nay saying the other. I set down my dishcloth and went into the sitting room.

"Bell, do you hear Tom snore?"

As I formed my answer, I wondered why white people thought negroes were deaf unless we stood directly in front of them. They'd talk and talk, say all kinds of things that I wouldn't want folks to know about me and figure if a colored person was more than ten feet away, that we couldn't hear them. I heard more than I wanted to most of the time. I will admit, it was sometimes to my advantage, but this moment was not one of them.

"Yes, he snores and I hear him."

Sally turned a knowing look to her husband, as if to say that she was correct.

Not to be beaten, Mr. Dumont said, "If you had not mentioned the snoring, Bell would never have complained. She is not the sort to complain."

I knew that Sally counted up one more fault of mine; I did not complain of snoring when she did. My faults kept Sally exhausted, to hear her tell the story.

As I said, I was not one to spit in the master's soup, nor did I come from people who took to such tricks. But I found, quite by accident, that I derived satisfaction from a reaction that I could draw out of Sally. It was an indulgence on my part.

Sally was frightened of me, and by rights, she should have been. Once a person does something wicked to another, they expect revenge and fear the day it will come.

She needed to be a body length away at most for this to take hold; perhaps her eyesight was less than keen. If she was close to me, I would stretch out my long arm and extend my hand, fingers spread wide and act for the smallest moment if my reach was traveling to Sally. Then suddenly, my reach would change course slightly and I would pick up a child, or

157

a chunk of wood, or scratch my leg or support myself on the arm of the chair as I stood. Always, when I stretched out my arm, I would pause one moment longer than I should, yet not long enough for Sally to shout that I threatened her or meant harm. No, it was a balance of time that grew longer as I grew bolder, knowing that Sally was frightened of my size and knowing that anyone else would see nothing but a colored woman stretching a bit before work.

I reveled in the stutter of her backwards walk from me, her quick glance to see how far she stood from the door, the quick pull back with her head. When I grew boldest, I let my fingers rise one by one, showing her the full size of my palm. I told no one of this trespass on Sally except God and I told him that if I didn't make Sally twitch on rare occasions then I would burst, so He best not be so hard on me.

* * *

Diana grew strong and healthy, which is the greatest blessing one could hope for a slave baby. She had the colic in the beginning and she was a fright to listen to, but then her belly settled when all of us thought we couldn't stand another day of her howls. There were no other babies that demanded my attention, so Diana had full nursing from my breast, on which she grew fat and round.

I wanted Robert to see our fine child, not to cause grief in his heart, but to give him reason to hope.I could not go to Catlin's farm and Robert's chain was tighter and shorter than my own. I dared not even get a message to Robert for the chance of someone less than a friend intercepting the message was too great. I was aided by the strangest angel, Sally.

"I admire the firm hand of Catlin. He's not had one bit of trouble with his nigger since he showed him who was the boss," said Sally as she entertained her aunt Mrs. Gedney one midsummer's day. I brought them cool mint tea in the parlor.

"He's fresh to slavery and does not have such an

attachment as your husband does to niggers. For all his fine points, I dare say your husband spoils your slaves," said Mrs. Gedney.

"Thank goodness I had you to teach me to manage slaves or I never would have understood the peculiar strictness that one must use. Take Mr. Catlin again; that black rascal Robert is as meek as a kitten now. He drives with Mr. Catlin to the grist mill. I've seen him on the past several Fridays taking in the hard wheat and he's lost all his sauce and swagger."

I heard no more. I knew immediately what I would do. That night, I stole into the kitchen and took most of our last sack of flour and ran with it down to the river. I threw it in, making a white cloud on the river till it sank. The next day I exclaimed at our lack of flour and offered straight away to go to the gristmill. I took Diana with me. The work wagon was hitched up. I set Diana in a box, wedged in tight with three sacks of grain.

Half way to the gristmill, I pulled off the lane to fetch water for myself before I started to nurse the baby who squalled in a fierce manner. The moment she started to suckle, my own thirst was great. I sat briefly on a fallen tree and tended to her. Diana's eyes closed before she finished with my breast.

I heard the wagon approach along the rutted lane. I stood along the sideboard and waited for the wagon to pass before starting along my way again. I took the moment to enjoy the weight of Diana in my arms, her contented face tucked in near my breast. Since my plan was to be at the gristmill before young Catlin and Robert arrived, it did not immediately occur to me that the wagon coming in the opposite direction would be my love. I thought I would always know if Robert was on his way to me; I was wrong.

The approaching wagon held a black man and a white man seated next to each other on the bench. I stood frozen by the side of the road, my baby in my arms, not knowing what to do. Young Catlin was on my side of the lane, Robert was farthest from me. I had not seen him since the end of last summer, yet my heart pounded with fresh yearning.

It was young Catlin at the reins and I saw no design on his part to slow down or to make conversations with me. As they came closer, Robert starred straight ahead. I detected a change in his face, as if the parts had been reassigned locations. I pressed my back against the side boards to let them pass. They came even with me and young Catlin gave me a glance and quickly looked forward again. Robert finally turned his head, and I pulled the cotton cloth from Diana's face so that he could see her. He turned his head no longer than it would take me to count from one to three, but in those moments I saw that Robert had lost an eye in the terrible beating that he received in Dumonts yard or in beatings since that time. With his one right eye remaining, he looked at Diana then at me, then back forward again. For one searing moment our eyes met and he tried to tell me everything and then he was gone. The wagon rumbled on with the two men swaying with the uneven lane.

My fine and beautiful Robert, who loved me and said he could not sleep at night for thinking of me, had lost the powerful flicker of life that I had known in him. I set the baby back in the grain box and shouted at God to give Robert back his spirit, to send it to him, take some of mine if He needed to.

"Give it back to him, God! Don't let him go around like that, one eyed and lacking in his spirit. I'll stop my fussing about Sally, I'll work till I drop, I'll never curse again if you will give Robert back his spirit."

I shouted to God until my voice was hoarse. Then I said the Lord's prayer in the soft tongue of the Dutch. When I was done talking to God, I asked the wind and the sun to carry a whisper to Robert that was so quiet, no one but him would hear it.

CHAPTER TWENTY-TWO

I picked up the newly ground flour at the grist mill one day. As I tossed the bags into the wagon, I overheard two white men talking. "There's one old nigger who just won't die. It's sort of sad, don't you think, when they get so they can't work."

My stomach tightened. I said, "Excuse me sir. Which colored man are you talking about?"

"I think he was Hardenberg's old slave, Bomefree."

"Is he sick?" I asked, already knowing the answer.

"Oh, he's worse than sick."

When I heard about my father, I wailed and could not work and so bemoaned this terrible grievance that Mr. Dumont said I could go visit Bomefree on the next Sunday. "You can go, Bell, but only if you return to your work. I cannot bear to hear you wailing. I'll try to get word to Soan to tend to the old man until you can get there."

I could not have walked to the old Hardenberg area and back in one day, so Mr. Dumont agreed to drive me to Kingston, which took a good many miles off the trip, but I would have to walk home again. I took Diana with me.

I stopped at the Kingston black smith and asked if he knew where Bomefree lived. I had not earned permission to visit him in too long and his traveling days had passed.

"On the Hardenberg land. There's some shack that's more fallen down than standing up. There's no road in there and the trees are thick. Follow the stream along the footpath, he's about a mile or so up stream."

The sun was at the high point of the day when I found him. Even though the day was cold with the first true stirrings of winter, and the nights had been freezing for a good while, no smoke came from the small building. I thought the worst and I ran to the shack and pulled open the door that hung on one leather hinge.

Bomefree lay curled against the cold on his pallet. He jumped from my noise of struggling with the door.

"Who is it?" he croaked. He sounded afraid and small.

"It's me, Isabella, come to take care of you."

The smell from Bomefree was putrid, like he had messed in the cabin, plus something was clearly rotting. Despite the cold, I already wanted fresh air. My father stared past me.

"Can't you see me?"

"I can see some, mostly light and dark," he said.

I brought baby Diana up close to his face. She was ready to suckle again even though she should have been filled up from the last time.

"Here's your granddaughter, Diana," I said.

He reached out a dirty hand and poked at her face. His fingernails were too long and filth was packed underneath them. His attention quickly left the baby.

"Did you bring anything to eat, daughter? I can't remember when I last ate."

I gave him all that I brought; smoked pork, dried apples and bread. Then I hauled water for him, first for him to drink and then for me to wash him. I dared not put the baby down once I saw the vermin in his hair and in his clothes.

"Is there no one to stay with you, no other slaves who are freed?" I asked him.

"Caesar was here with me for awhile, then he took sick and died."

Caesar was a freed slave who was younger than Bomefree but not as stubborn about staying alive beyond hope and reason as was my father. "When Caesar was here we kept each other encouraged."

He was so weak that he could not sit up without me holding him up. But his voice grew stronger from the water and food I gave him. "If you can hang on, I know that the slaves are going to be set free and not just the old negroes but all of us," I said to him as I held him with one arm, my baby in the other.

Mr. Dumont could hardly talk of anything else these days, how the world was going to hell because a hoard of colored people was going to be set loose on New York. When, when, that was my question.

I tried to reassure my father, but even in his famished, fevered state, he understood far better than I did. He coughed a bloody mass into a tin plate.

"Another ten years! White people figured out a way to let the slaves go free and yet hang on to them for another ten years. I won't last another ten days, never mind ten years, waiting for you to go free."

I would not allow the brutal truth to lodge within me. I shushed it away like I do the chickens when I walk through the yard. I chased it from my legs, from my milk filled breasts.

"I'm going to get someone to come and take care of you. But you know that I have to walk back to Dumont's farm. There's a good moon tonight and I'll walk fast. Mr. Dumont will have to let you live in his woods so that I can come take care of you every evening. I'll work for extra on Sunday to earn food for you."

I gathered my baby closer to me. Here I was, in the same room with my helpless hungry baby, tied on to me, and with my father, just as helpless, wishing he could be tied on to me as well.

"I'll stop in Kingston and get you a colored woman to tend to you. You've lived so long Poppa, I know you can keep going."

I think if he was stronger in body, he wouldn't have cried, but in his weakened state his body let him down and he couldn't stop from crying when I made ready to leave. "I'll be back. You hang on now, I'll be back."

I ran the mile or so back to the road, then I skimmed the road all the way back into Kingston. It was well into the night and I knew I was in trouble with Mr. Dumont. I got a woman to say she'd bring my father food, make a fire for him if she could. She remembered Mau Mau and said it was a shame that once all the work was squeezed out of a good man, then he was tossed aside and left for the birds to pick. She gave me a fresh cloth to diaper Diana and I could only trade her the sodden one.

"Why don't you stay the night, you're already in a swamp of trouble."

We both knew I couldn't stay.

So I walked in the moonlight, sang songs to let animals know I was coming and by midmorning the next day, I opened the kitchen door. I told Dumont straight away that my father needed tending to and gave him my idea of moving Bomefree closer.

"Must I have the weight of every nigger on my shoulders? This is exactly what happens when you turn them loose; they can't tend to themselves and they create a burden. I'll think about it Bell, give me time to think about it." He pushed back his chair to leave the room.

The urgency of my need was lost on him. This was my father! I spoke to him as I had never done before. "If your father was frozen and starving, would you stop to think about it?" He looked puzzled and his mind worked over what I said. If Sally had heard us, she would have flown into a fury about me comparing Bomefree to Mr. Dumont's father. We stared at each for a long time and I held my bottom lip tight with my teeth to keep from crying. Finally, he bobbed his head and grunted. I took this as a yes.

I pictured the improvements in my father's condition when he would be situated nearby. I went and talked to God later that day and thanked him for making Dumont a generous man. He told me I could go fetch my father in two weeks.

I heard of my father's death when the full moon that guided me home was but half its size. Soan found my father, frozen and curled up like a baby. The woman in Kingston never went out to the shack as I had asked her. Soan said it would not have mattered; my father must have died shortly after I left.

When one of the Hardenburg grandsons heard of his death, he got all drunk and announced to a tavern full of men that Bomefree had been a good nigger, deserving of more than a shallow grave in the woods. He bought him a white casket and buried him with a bottle of whiskey, which was a sacrifice to a man who loves the drink.

My grief was deep. I did not sleep well or long. I moved like heavy rocks filled all my pockets. My only relief was crying, which was all I could do in my God house. I was too sad to talk to God, yet I still went there to see if I could get a message to Bomefree. My message was always the same. "Tell him I'm sorry, sorry. I had to leave him."

The winter passed and a heavy snow season left the ground mud soaked. Soan arrived one day with her boots soiled up past her ankles. "Bomefree needs a proper burial," she said.

My father was months dead. "Bomefree is buried. The Hardenburg's did the burying."

"And you'll need burying yourself unless you let the man go. Let me speak to Dumont." There was little that I could hide from her.

Colored and whites alike respected Soan. Whatever she said to Mr. Dumont worked in my favor. In a few weeks, when the mud had dried enough, Soan drove me and Diana to Bomefree's grave. Soan borrowed a carriage.

The colored cemetery in Hurley was set off with a rough wood rail fence. The earth was still raw where he was buried; spring grass hadn't yet taken hold. The Hardenburgs had not to buried Bomefree next to Mau Mau. Her grave, marked with a wooden head piece, was far from his.

If Mau Mau had been there, she'd say Bomefree was at rest, that he'd spent a long life working and toiling for masters and now he was free. She'd say that was how freedom came. The world was buzzing with talk of negroes going free and not through dying. I could finally see a time when free didn't mean the same thing as dead.

Soan brought a shovel and began to dig. "How far down do we need to go?" I asked her. I was doing the digging. Soan was the elder and she had more experience with helping people pass to the other side.

"We don't need to go all the way to the casket. Something about this size." She carved a shape of a big pumpkin with her hands. "Right here, over where his heart is."

We each had things to put in the hole for Bomefree. Soan started. "This is straw to keep you warm. This is from your daughter's own bed, which she would have gladly given to you when you were alive if she was able." She filled the bottom of the hole with hay. Next she took a bowl from her cloth bag. Into the bowl she placed bread.

"This is the bread that all men should be able to eat when they are old and creaking." In went the bowl and the brown bread. I had made the bread the day before just the way that Mau Mau had done for so long.

I pulled his pipe from my pocket. I had kept it near to eight, since Bomefree had sent it to me as a sign of hope. I filled it with tobacco, sparked a light and pulled in the flame to fire the tobacco. "This is to give you comfort." I passed the pipe to Soan but she said she didn't smoke and wouldn't do so even for Bomefree. With the pipe still lit, I placed it into the bowl. "That's all he needs," I said. "He didn't ever need much."

Then I said the Lord's prayer in Dutch because I thought he could hear it better that way. Soan held out her arms, and talked directly to God.

"God, if you haven't already, then take this man home. Take him up into your arms because he was so weary down

166

here. His daughter and his granddaughter are here to send him along to you." She picked up a handful of dirt and tossed it in the hole. I helped baby Diana to throw in some dirt too. Then I crouched down on the ground and picked up the pile of dirt by the handfuls and buried my father the right way. I smoothed the dirt over the hole.

"There," said Soan. "He's got warmth from a daughter who loves him, food made by your own hand, and a good pipe to smoke. That keeps most men happy."

I wished anew that these small gifts had been granted to my father while he lived.

CHAPTER TWENTY-THREE

It's true what they say; you mostly remember the bad times and the first times. Most of ordinary life drifts by us as if we are asleep. When Diana was grown, she'd say to me, "Don't you remember the time you left me with baby brother by the edge of the field and he cried and cried and I was so scared that he would choke to death? Don't you remember that? You left me all day with him and then you got after me with the switch for letting him cry." And I had to say no, I didn't remember that time. It was either one of the bad times for Diana or one of the firsts, maybe the first time she was really terrified about a crying baby. I was used to my babies crying while I worked.

Robert dying was not one of the worst times for me. Seeing him half dead, a man walking and talking and breathing without his spirit was far worse. Mr. Dumont came to tell me of Robert when he heard. He took care that I was alone and away from the house. I didn't know if he took this trouble because he feared my wailing grief would disturb the household or if he had respect for my need in this case. I chose to think the latter. I was sewing up a torn shoulder on a lamb and had done a clean job of it when I heard him approach. He told me straight out. "Robert is dead."

I finished with the lamb and sent it back wild-eyed to her mother. I sat down on the milk stool with my knees spread wide. My bones were suddenly too soft for me to stand. I looked at the place where Robert and I had been together in the early mornings, when our clothes fell around. I didn't want the people I loved the most to keep leaving me. I didn't know what to say, and Mr. Dumont still waited.

"Do you think Mr. Catlin will ever paint again after this?" I asked. His reputation as a once famous portrait artist was legend in our part of the Hudson Valley. Back when Robert and I were courting, back when his spirit glowed honey warm, he saw some of Catlin's paintings and said that he finally understood him better. He figured every ounce of his kindness and compassion came out in his paintings, leaving him completely drained of these in all other parts of his life.

Dumont raised his eyebrows. I repeated my question. "Why do you ask Bell?"

"I think if you steal a person's spirit, your own spirit shrinks up like wool in boiled water. It turns hard and dense, not good for much. How could a man like that paint?"

"Do you think Catlin stole Robert's spirit? Robert was never baptized. He did not have a soul such as Christians have. But you wouldn't know that."

For the first time, I understood the limits of what Mr. Dumont knew. This is what Mau Mau meant; you'd be surprised at what white people don't know. "Do you think I am without spirit?" I whispered. He did not answer me but I saw his face fight to keep from twitching and his eyes turned red. I shouted, "Do you think I am without spirit?" He turned and left the barn.

Dumont had no answer for me, but after he told me of Robert's death, I noticed he treated me differently. He'd ask for my opinion, if no one else was present. He'd say, "What do you think about the way the blight is hitting the turnips this year?" Or,"Gert has been married for several years now, do you think she is barren?" There are moments that change people and our talk in the barn when Robert died was one of them. The change was in Dumont not me. Robert's death was a relief to me.

I went on, knowing that my time as a slave was counting down every day. In the year 1817, New York passed a law that said I was to go free in ten years. My babies would have to stay until they were twenty-five for the girls, twenty-eight for the boys.

Diana was six years old when another child was born who lived. I'd had one born with the caul still on him, which Soan said gave him the power of sight, seeing what will happen before it happens. But my baby boy did not live the night. We called him Tom because Tom wanted a child named after him. He said all his babies with his wife Anne had been girls.

Soan snipped the caul with her teeth and ripped it open to let the baby out, but he didn't want to breathe in this life. Maybe he did have the sight after all and he didn't like what he saw coming his way.

Sally caught me right before my milk started to dry up. One day after the baby was dead and she saw that my bodice was soaked from milk, she handed me her baby boy who was near to half a year old.

"Bell, you wet nurse this baby. It's time for me to fit back into my old dresses again." White women were a mixed bunch when it came to nursing their own babies. Some thought it was below them to suckle their own babies, while others claimed it was old fashioned to have a wet nurse. Sally was of the persuasion that babies need only have her teats for a short time.

Her baby saw no difference between his mother's breasts and mine. I watched as he drank up all of my dead baby's milk and in a strange way this helped with my sadness. I was not being asked to deny milk to one of my own babies, I was being asked to feed Sally's baby simply because I had milk. I begrudged no child. Soan said nursing the Dumont baby was a blessing in disguise. She said if I kept the milk coming good and hard, I would not have another baby as soon.

When Soan's master died, he left a will that said she was to be set free. She moved to our side of the river to New Paltz Landing and got a job as a cook and a housekeeper and was paid regular for her efforts.

Soan became my confidante and I hers. She never tired of me asking about babies or herbs. She listened to my stories that Mau Mau taught me about all my brothers and sisters, she held me when I cried about my brother Peter and how I never saw him after we were sold. I tested her with my lesser secrets, I told her about Neely and his wickedness with me.

"I think we should poison him," she said when I told her of his cruelty.

"Have you lost your senses? I haven't seen Neely since the day Martin Schryver bought me and rode away on his horse. Let God take care of Neely."

"God doesn't act quick enough on some people. I like to help God out and let people receive their just rewards in this lifetime."

Soan made me gasp. I shivered with delight as she told me of the earthly revenge that she doled out to her owner.

"I spent twenty years with my last master. He was not a man of generous spirit in word or deed. I was worked hard by him and was unfairly punished on his whims. I once saw him kill a black baby when he was a young man. Picked it up by its feet and smashed its head into a tree. When he grew old and sick, I was left to tend to him. His wife was daft with old age and too weak to take care of him. I'd lift him up to change his bedding, put my arms around him and squeeze hard until he could not take a breath and then I'd squeeze a second longer. Then I'd drop him hard on the bed. He lost his speech with an attack that left him paralyzed on one side. Once he understood that I was going to deliver some of what he dealt out, his eyes burned black at me. His wife said, "Is everything alright in there?" I'd smile down at his frowning face. Spittle hung off the corner of his mouth. "We're just fine in here," I said back to her. One day I wrote up a will that said I was to go free after his death. I learned to write long before he bought me. He signed it with a scratchy X. After that, I went a little easier on him."

I don't know if Soan added to his death or simply scared him into dying.

CHAPTER TWENTY-FOUR

I had five children in all, counting baby Tom. I followed Soan's advice about suckling Sally's baby; I gave that child my breast and I did so eagerly to soothe myself and to stave off another pregnancy. I nursed him solid for another year and a half. It was Mr. Dumont who put an end to my suckling of his son.

"I can't have you running back to the house so often when I need you in the field. Ignatius is old enough to fill his belly with food. Do not give him your breast from this day onward."

During the time that I nursed him, I slept in the child's room, on the floor. When Ignatius learned to walk, he often climbed from his cradle in the middle of the night and slept with me on the floor. Whether it was the hard nursing or the forced separation between Tom and me, I don't know, but I did not get with child until after I moved back to the cellar again with Tom and Diana. Peter was my next baby, named for my brother. He was followed three years later by Elizabeth, named for my mother. Last came Sophia, named for one of my sisters. Mr. Dumont did not impose himself in the naming of the children. I had complete freedom in choosing their names. Mr. Dumont said only that the names be something that he could live with because the children would be with him for a very long time. Each time I named a child, I went to Mr. Dumont and reported the name. He'd nod in approval. He asked where the names came from. In the case of Peter, I told him that Peter was my brother and I still thought about him every day.

"You haven't seen that boy in over fifteen years. Why are you bothering to give thought to him?"

"If one of your brothers was taken away by someone, would you ever stop thinking about him?" I asked him.

"But you must expect that with niggers, being sold off is what life holds for you."

"You may be right about one thing. We did expect that we could be sold. But every time one of my sisters or brothers was sold, my mother's heart broke apart. What we expected out of life and what we felt in our hearts were different creatures. I miss him every day. When I talk to God, I ask that he look after Peter and that we find our way to each other."

He hooked his fingers into his suspenders. "One prays to God. One does not talk to God as if he were a neighbor. If you were able to understand the Bible, you would know how queer an idea you have."

* * *

Soan and Tom were my midwives for the last four births. Tom and I were closest to each other during birthing times. I considered sending Soan away for the births but she wouldn't have left no matter what I told her.

"He's the best man midwife I've ever seen. That still doesn't make him as good as I am," she said. "He doesn't understand what it's like to be with child and feel every part of you split open. But he's good. Don't get me wrong. It's a pure shame he isn't this attentive to you the rest of the time."

* * *

Tom persisted in his belief that he was married to Anne. Soan offered me her wisdom on this matter between Tom and me. Not that I asked her. I figured that's what old people get to do, they get to tell the rest of us what to do.

"Tom is more likely to be a widow, than a married man. His Anne, from what I've heard, had the curse of being born beautiful. Not just handsome to look at, not just pleasing to the eye, but beautiful. Thank the stars above that you are not cursed with being beautiful. Anne had no power over the way men saw her, and worst of all, how white men saw her. Word was that she fetched the largest price of any negro in the valley. Tom was beat senseless when she was sold; nothing else would have stopped him. We never heard, but her life in Maryland must have been filled with the devil. We all knew she was meant for that slave owner himself. If she bore any children to the white master, the white mistress would have hated her and turned her own thinking around until she blamed Anne. Or she might have died in childbirth. If she became disfigured from a cruel master or the vengeful arm of the mistress, then she was sold further south where no one cared how she looked. They could work her to death in the fields."

"What if she's alive and pining away for old Tom like I was for Robert?"

Soan watched me turn over the little patch of garden that was mine and Tom's. She sat on a stump. She was old, but she could still pull her legs up to her chest like a child.

"We won't ever know if she's dead or alive or a shriveled up old woman living with the dogs. In Tom's mind, she's a beautiful young woman who loved him body and soul and he's staying faithful to her in the only way left to him."

I paused in my digging. "I won't begrudge him such affections. We all have to hang on to something. He'll come around to me someday." Once Robert had died I believed myself truly married to Tom.

Soan sighed. She made the rare choice of not having the last word.

Not long after Elizabeth was born, I felt the day of

174

freedom creep up on me, as slow as a box turtle, clawing away at the days. Mr. Dumont looked on it as so much foolishness and probably the end of the world. We heard rumors of farmers selling slaves down south before the freedom came so they could get cash in their pockets before they had to set slaves free. Of course freedom day didn't include the poor negroes born after 1799, which naturally included all of my children. This part of the law made no sense to me. Mr. Dumont didn't have to buy my children; they came from me, right out of my body and didn't have anything to do with him, yet they became his.

Tom and I talked at night in low voices, after the children were asleep, about how our life would be after the freedom.

"Dumont promises us a cabin on his land if we'll stay and work for him. The children could live with us and still work for him, except for Diana who they'll need as a house servant. We can grow our own garden and keep everything in it," he said.

"I don't believe him," said Tom, stroking my arm. He must have forgot himself for a moment. He must have been thinking of Anne. "Nothing goes easy for colored people and this plan sounds too easy for me. Freedom comes and we get a cabin with a garden but we still work for Dumont. I don't believe him Bell."

"He's never lied to us. That doesn't mean I agree with everything he says. I know where I stand with him," I said. In fact, I knew I had a favored status with him. I suffered unending criticisms from other negroes, except from Soan, about being Dumont's white nigger. He bragged about my loyalty, my strength, my ability to breed and giving him slave babies. He gave me small favors when he could; we already had our own garden to tend off the backside of the barn, and Diana wore a dress of new cloth rather than slave cloth which made Sally throw a fit.

Soan's wisdom about suckling hard to keep from getting with child again did not keep me from pregnancy after Elizabeth. Maybe the accident had something to do with it.

In a blink of the eye, my finger was cut off. It was a slip of attention, working with Tom of all people, chiseling out the holes for the fence posts to take railings. A frost still covered the wood; we should have waited until the sun took off the frost. I should have been the one with the axe; he should have been the one holding the post steady, but there was no point in speculating after the act was done. His hold slipped, took off my finger and it skidded across the post that I'd been holding. I didn't feel the pain at first. I looked at the pointer finger of my right hand that landed in the dirt. I wrapped my skirt around my hand to slow the blood. Soan later said that was a mistake. Let a thing bleed for a bit, clean it out. Tom ran to the icehouse and chipped off a hunk of ice and pressed it against my hand.

I got an infection for a time and my whole arm heated up like a stove. Soan came and soaked it in hot water and herbs, then she had to lance it to let out the pus. My hand was wrapped tight with cloth and spider webs to beat back the infection. Late winter is one of the worst times to find spider webs, which may be why the infection took such a hold.

In my fevered state, I was convinced that my finger would grow back and that the fever was cleansing out the infection like a fierce fire. I stayed feverish from the dark of the moon to the next. I remember the time moving slow as if we were all standing still and Diana feeding me soup that tasted of rusted metal. I sat up one day to find that weeks had gone by. For a few days, the fever cleared and the hot pulse that shot up my arm was quiet. Tom came to me in the night and pulled the covers off me and spread my legs apart with urgency.

As he climbed on me, he said, "I thought you were going to die." His chin was puckered and quivering. He was on his hands and knees, his legs pressed my legs further apart, and his hands pushed up my night dress. "If you thought I was dying, then what do you want to do this for?" Tom was a puzzle to me. We could fight all day, spat about the sun rising and setting, but come time to bed down and he was ready to spread my legs and dive into the deepest parts of me.

I had neither the patience nor the interest after being sick. "Get off me old man."

"Don't sass me, Bell. This is mine. No one can stop me."

I tried to sit up and push him off. Both our bodies coiled tight. "You're the one sounds like you have a fever." I couldn't use my right arm and he saw my disadvantage in a second. He yanked down hard on my good arm, jerking me down flat. He put his palm on my chest up near my throat and he pressed hard. I heard him opening his pants, fiddling with his buttons. Then I stopped fighting him. I might have been able to fight him off but I didn't care. I went slack everywhere and let my mind spin off like I did with John Neely.

So that was how Sophia came about. I never told her of course. But she always acted mad at me when she was older. I felt like saying, "Be mad at your father, he's the one who brought you into life in a fit of fright. I'm not the one you should be fussing with." But that's not the sort of thing you say to a child.

CHAPTER TWENTY-FIVE

The next year, the first grasses of spring took my breath away. One minute the earth was brown, stubbled, the trees were silver and gray and the next minute, the earth was covered with thick blankets of sweet green pastures carrying yellow flowers like a river. Everyone's spirits picked up. I could have sworn that I heard Sally whistling a tune, but it was more likely the wind. Right after the grasses came the apple trees. If I'd had the freedom to do so, I would have danced slow through the apple orchard until I'd smelled every last tree and then like a mama sheep, I'd know each one like my own baby, just by sniffing.

Sunday was mine, or at least part of it was mine. I often worked extra on Sunday, but knowing that my time was near up as a slave, I took the full part of a Sunday when the apple blossoms were at their best and gathered my children with me for a day of rest. I was wild with extravagance, anticipating my freedom. According to the arrangements between Mr. Dumont and me, Tom and I were to be set free on the fourth of July, 1826, exactly one year earlier than the law said. That was only months away. Dumont was known for his honest word. He said he'd never seen anyone work the way I did, man or woman. I was to be rewarded for my labors.

Diana was near as old as I was when I was first sold away from my parents, and Peter was seeing his fifth spring.

Elizabeth was not but two years old so it was best if I carried her for most of the walk to the orchard. I gave the new baby, Sophia, to Diana to carry. I took them all to the orchard and brought apple jack, bread, and cold ham. I was not feeling cautious, not with birds making nests, not with rivers of mustard flowers ready to burst, not with jack in the pulpits bobbing in the sun. When freedom was in sight, I allowed one day to not be cautious.

I found the center of the apple orchard, like it was the center of the sun, and I told my children to stop. I took off my shawl and placed it on the grass. The sun held true promise of warmth on my arms. I took the baby from Diana and set her to my breast. This always made the other children come near, they liked to watch her drink. I opened up my kerchief and spread out the food, breaking off bread and meat for each one, and a sip of applejack and water to warm our insides.

I rolled back on the grass and stared straight up at the sky. A breeze grabbed blossoms from the trees and they showered down on us, covering us with white petals. Little Elizabeth ate one. I don't suppose it hurt her. My children, particularly the older two grew uneasy; they were not accustomed to seeing me idling on my back, watching apple blossoms.

I tried to reassure them. "We're taking this whole afternoon, children," I told them as my fingers sank deep into the moist, tender grass.

Diana looked the most restless. "We won't be able to hear the mistress if she needs something. We should move closer to the house." Her eyes searched the horizon for tell tale signs from the house of the Dumonts requiring our help.

"Diana, come sit with me. Stop thinking about Mr. Dumont or the mistress and tell me what thoughts are in your mind." She sat down next to me and kept her eyes flickering back to the lane that led back down to the farm.

"I was thinking how tomorrow is laundry day. You'll want me to haul water so we'll have to put the baby in the basket hammock so she won't holler so much."

I looked at my eldest daughter. She was going to be tall, maybe as tall as me. I saw bits and pieces of Robert in her; thick eyelashes that curled up tight, soft skin around her ears.

"Where do you think God is Diana?"

"You tell me God is everywhere."

"Is he up in this apple tree?"

"Yes ma'am. I expect God is in the apple blossoms."

The best I could do to protect my children was to do as my mother had done. She taught us how to pray. And she told us that God could hear us anywhere. She told us not to lie and not to steal. And to work hard. Lord knows I did enough of that. This is what I tried to teach my children. I always felt that my mother was better at teaching children than I was. My mind wandered to thoughts of freedom, tangling with Sally, making a life in our cabin that Dumont promised us. My mother kept her mind on her children, when she had them.

I recall this day in the orchard because it was a day where I thought I had everything figured out, thought my life was going to be a certain way. I pictured my little cabin with Tom, pictured our children nearby, the reward of hard work paying me in the fairness of Mr. Dumont. My life looked so much improved compared to my parents. By the time Sophia was born, my hand had healed up, and I understood that I was going to travel through life shy one finger. I admit that it slowed me up in my work, but not nearly as much as John Dumont would later claim.

It wasn't but a few days after my moment of idleness in the orchard, that I happened to have a conversation with Mr. Dumont. I saw everything as my last; my last spring as a slave, my last planting as a slave, my last child that I would bear as a slave. I sought to mention this to Mr. Dumont, more in gratitude than anything else.

"I've been meaning to talk to you Bell. I can't let you go early like we talked about. Your accident with your hand cost me dearly. You weren't up to your old way of working. You can go free when all the other coloreds go, not before. Fair is fair."

Here was the trap; all those years with John Dumont and I believed most every word that he said. I believed him when he bragged about me to other men. I believed he understood that I was doing the work of two people. I believed him when he told me about the cabin. I believed him when he said I was a person to be trusted.

So of course I believed him when he told me that I was to go free one year early. If I had to say which moment in slavery was the worst, it was not the beatings, the grief, the despair, the loneliness, it was when John Dumont lied to me. I knew he was wrong. I could feel it.

After the sourness left my throat from choking on his lies, I went to my God house. All these years my little God house was my place of comfort. I pulled the willow branches away and stood beneath the parasol of the tree and let loose with a torrent of words.

"God, I'm in trouble. John Dumont stopped telling me the truth. I need to know what is fair and just because I am clouded by his lies. Didn't I work for him since I was a girl? I've grown to be married, old enough to bear five children, and I've worked sixteen years for him, rising long before the sun to milk the cows, to start the fire, to haul water, plow. I did it all, God. You know I did. You see everything. Tell me what is just and fair?"

I knew Dumont was wrong but I didn't know how to make it right. I spent many nights in my God house, my blanket wrapped around my shoulders, the willow branches dusting my arms, the sound of the creek talking to the rocks. I returned every morning to the cellar and saw my children asleep in a heap.

Tom had long since lost his power to see beyond his nose. When he heard that we weren't going free early like Dumont had promised, he folded up on himself. He was old when I married him and he was that much older when we had the dispute with Dumont. We had talked nightly about our little cabin, with our garden. We both had it pictured in our minds

181

for so long that I knew right where I was going to plant flowers, right where I would sit to smoke my pipe in the evenings. Now the picture burned up like a torch was put to it.

By the time the man came to shear the sheep in June, I had decided that I was leaving. My recovery from the accident took away some of my labor to the farm, that was true. So I formed an arrangement to make it right. I would help with the shearing as I always did, then spin it after it came back from the carding house, and on the day that I was done, I would owe him nothing. I did not share this plan with Dumont; he and I spoke little after he lied to me.

Dumont hired a man to shear the sheep, but as always, I sheared right along with him. A sheep will behave herself with me, not so much because she likes me or I like her, but because I never nicked one with the shears. I wasn't as fast as the man hired to shear; he flew like birds over the wool, keeping it in one neat piece as he clipped. He was good, but he sometimes nicked their legs, and I swear that sheep do not forget.

I wanted only one thing and it started to sound like a prayer. "I will shear the wool from this herd and I will spin it all, every last ounce. On the day I am done, I walk away." The prayer hummed through me as I clipped. I pulled the sheep to me one by one, as an act of leaving. I saw their eyes filled with fright. I put one hand on the neck, one on the rump and guided each one as easy as they were one of my children. Each stroke I offered was my last. My black hands would shear them no more.

No one knew my secret, except for Tom. I asked him once to take leave with me, to take our promised time back from Dumont. Tom had grown too old and I saw it in an instant.

"No use stirring up the hornet's nest when we'll go free next year like all the rest of them," he said.

"I know what's fair and we took Dumont's word. This year is ours," I said.

"If you go, you're going without me," said Tom. He couldn't look at me. Slavery had claimed one more spirit. This sent me straight back to my God house, snug under the willow tree, far from anyone except the crows and the peepers. I sat long with God; I was past caring if my absence caused disharmony in the kitchen. When I heard from God, when the hair stood up on my neck, I didn't blame Tom for not daring to leave with me. We were, as we had always been, out of step with each other. He had done his running away in his younger years and he had nothing left in him now.

I longed to talk to Soan, but she took a job caring for an elderly gentleman in Albany. "Lord help him," I said to her when she prepared to leave.

She said that he was a fine gentleman who had been a doctor in his good years and had helped more than a few negroes in his day make their way to Canada. "Don't you worry. I only thrashed that other fellow because he was cruel to me for many years. This man is a Quaker and has never owned slaves."

I grew silent with the Dumonts. One hundred pounds of wool came back from the carding house. In my mother's day, she had to card the wool as well as spin it, but the world was changing, and the hard work of carding was done by a few men, clanking away at their machines in a mill. I was glad of it. The sooner that I was done with the wool, the sooner I was gone.

The great wheel takes up most of the kitchen, and the kitchen was busy with preserving summer foods, so I asked to take the great wheel to the loft of the barn. Tom helped me carry it. It takes two strong people to haul a great wheel; the small wheel used for spinning flax can be lifted by a child or set on the back of a horse. I could spin longer if I was out of sight of the family. There was no point in them asking why I didn't sleep most nights, why I stood pacing with the great wheel, spinning until I heard the noisy geese and chickens start to murmur with the break of day.

It was said that if you worked steady at the great wheel most of the day, you had walked about twenty miles. That's how it was then, three steps back with the wool in my left hand, pulling steady, turning the wheel with my right hand, then three steps forward again. If I had no other work to do, I could have finished sooner. The summer was blistering hot, forgetting to cool down at night. I stripped down as far as I could to save my dress from being drenched with sweat. I wrapped a cloth around my breasts, and wore an old underskirt. If the moon was bright enough, I did not use a lantern. As it was, I finished spinning the wool by harvest time and the first touch of cool air descended on us at night.

I was filled with hate during all the spinning. I was angry at Dumont and wished that all white people were taken from the earth with no seeds left to grow. They were slave catchers, thieves, and fools. They took children from mothers. The wool that I spun was soured with hate and I wished the wearers misery.

It was during this time that Dumont came to me to say that he found an apprenticeship for Peter, a chance for him to be a cabin boy to a gentleman. Dr. Gedney had a friend in New York City who was looking for a new boy to train. Dumont said this would be a loan, to see if Peter would work out. I thought this was Dumont's way of taking the sting out of breaking his promise to me. This was a good position for Peter although I feared he was a year or so too young. Dumont said that the gentleman knew of Peter's young age and would be mindful and that he would be gone only for a few months to see how things worked out. Peter was not to be sold, but apprenticed and given the same ability to advance that many boys had. Of all the places where a negro boy could apprentice, one of the best places was at sea. Tom told many grand tales about the black seamen in New York City.

Peter's advancement was a relief to me. My mind was filled with my task at hand that my full attention was not on the sadness that Peter felt when his time came to leave. I

184

wrapped a clean cloth around some flat bread and told him not to lie, not to steal and to listen to what his master told him. On the morning that Peter left, he kissed his baby sister goodbye and my throat tightened fast. Peter carried himself like a rooster, and that was my name for him. "Do what the master tells you to do, Little Rooster," I said before Dumont loaded him into the carriage.

I was frightened as each step brought me closer to leaving. My children never looked so dear. I was proud to bursting of Diana, who could handle a kitchen as well as I could. Elizabeth started talking, calling her big sister Dea, Dea. The baby Sophia liked to sit up and watch the others at night, swatting her arms up and down, bumping along on her bottom. What evil sort of monster was I to think of leaving them? Hadn't my own mother fought every day of her life to keep her family together?

Tom would stay at Dumonts and watch over Diana and Elizabeth. The baby had to come with me. I knew what the law said about slave children needing to stay with their masters until they were twenty five, but I was sick to death of Dumont's explanation. "They have to learn to be free first before we can let them go entirely."

I pulled my children to me one evening. Nights were cooler and their bodies close to mine gave each one of us the little extra warmth that we needed. "There will come a day when we will all live in our own home, without serving white people. The time of slavery is coming to an end." Elizabeth liked to sit by my right side and wrap her arms around my ankle. My children sat on the floor and I perched in a chair. "What will our house look like?" asked Diana.

"It should have a porch, so that we can sit outside and do our needlework in the summer," I said. Diana nodded in agreement. "We are a family and no matter what, that won't change. This family will be together in our own home someday, I promise you."

Now that the wool was all spun, I was suddenly fearful of leaving. My courage melted away with the last bits of wool running through my fingers. I had all but decided to stay at Dumonts for the next year. I waited until the children were asleep, and old Tom was snoring, then I slipped out the door to go tell God. I went out behind the barn and started in on my reasons to stay. When I was well into my first reason for staying, God stopped me. My voice fell away and I did not need it. I was filled with the most tender of love and the words, "It is time to leave this place." God had never spoken so clearly to me before, in such crisp words. I was ashamed that I had wavered and that God had been forced to speak to me as one would speak to a child.

I returned to the cellar, picked up Sophia and wrapped her well. She was still on the breast and could not be left. Diana sat up. I went to her, crouched by her sleeping pallet and squeezed her arm hard. "I have to leave. God has spoken and the time to leave is now. You stay here and make Elizabeth mind you. Look after Old Tom as best you can. There will come a day when we can all be together." Diana had tears running down her face but she knew better than to go against me. I could not pause for tears, I could not pause for my husband whose snoring had stopped. I stood beside him and was silent.

I did not run away. I walked. I held up my head, carried my baby and I walked.

CHAPTER TWENTY-SIX

The night covered me as I walked straight down the road and I let my long legs skim the distance. With the first light, my mind chattered with the talk that kept me slaved, how I owed John Dumont because he paid money for me, clothed me, fed me, and how I let him down with the injury to my hand. In the dim light before dawn when thinking is the most muddled, I was sure that I was guilty of thievery. As the sun broke the edge of the horizon, my mind cleared and I realized that if this was stealing then yes, I stole back my legs, my feet, my strong back, my hay baling arms, my breasts, and my breath.

Mau Mau Bett said that the white people expected us to steal and she had rejoiced in never letting them be right. "We are not thieves or liars. We don't have to give everything to the white man. He is wrong and we won't steal to make him right," said Mau Mau. Yet here I was, stealing myself. I felt the pull of the Dumont farm on my body, weighted by my children. I was in a confusion. I walked until the full force of daylight drove me and my fear off the rutted lane.

Even though I had just spoken to God in the hours of darkness, I sought his help again. If I could speak to God, say my peace, and listen to Him, I would get on course. So I walked off the lane, still pocked with puddles by yesterday's rain, and squatted in a grove of white birches.

I let the baby suck and I leaned my cheek up against the birch tree. "Where is my road, the place for me?" I asked out loud "Dumont will soon be after me and I need to find a safe place and I have never known a safe place." I must have dozed awhile because the sun was higher still when I next opened my eyes. Both breasts were sucked dry, and I knew where to go.

I walked first to the home of a Quaker, Levi Roe. Soan once said he would be friendly to any negro seeking freedom. I hadn't told even my confidante Soan of my intended leaving. I was too afraid that I would change my mind and disappoint her.

Levi Roe and his wife lived in Poppletown. I knew the way well, having passed it on my trips to Kingston. I hoisted the baby and set off, with a keen ear to approaching horses. If a rider approached, I ran to the woods and crouched under a snarl of low growth.

Mrs. Roe greeted me at the door and welcomed me. She wore the simple gray dress of Quaker women and her eyes were full with sadness; death hovered somewhere in the house. Levi Roe was sick and dying. "Soan told me once that you helped slaves get to freedom. I have just left John Dumont's." She directed me to Levi's bedside. His skin looked like parchment pulled tight against his skull. The smell of death hit me full force. Although the day was not cold, I could see he was chilled and unable to get warm.

"I will not live long. You must go to the home of Isaac and Maria Van Wagenen. They are not Quakers, but they are firm about their loathing of slavery. They can be trusted to help you," said Levi in a strained voice.

I was bolstered by his words. I had to travel many miles to get to Wahkendall where the Van Wagenens lived and I wanted to get there before nightfall. By early evening, I reached the town of Wahkendall. Lanterns lit the stone house and I was unsure if the yellow light meant a welcome or a threat.

When I knocked at the door, both Isaac and Maria came to the entryway. I explained myself and let them know in most certain terms that I considered myself a free woman and that I would not return to slavery. I asked for their help in sheltering me and in return, I would work for them.

"We'll have no such arrangement," said Isaac. "We will hire you to work for us. We knew your mother and father long ago and they were honorable people. You have no debt to pay us, Isabella. And we have a room for you and the baby, although it is small and simple."

I did not want to cry but I could not help it. He had both welcomed me and made mention of my parents in such a way as to strip off all the brittle parts of me

"Mr. Dumont will come after me," I said.

"Good lord, I will be glad of the day when we are done with the foolishness and evil of slavery. If John comes here to our home, then he will have to answer to me. And I will not send you back."

Maria held out her arms to hold Sophia. "Give her to me for a bit. Your arms must be ready to fall off."

Everything that they said seemed to stun me into silence. Let me hold your child. Come into my home. Are your arms tired? It was if I entered a strange country of people and my entry granted me the privilege of their kindness. Maria asked me if I was weary and she must have thought me dumb because I could not answer her. No one had ever asked me before and she might as well have asked me if I could fly. I was sent in to a spasm of weeping again.

"Well, that's my answer sure enough. Who wouldn't be tired from carrying a baby from one side of creation to another. Let's get you settled in for the night. You're about ready to drop on your feet."

* * *

John Dumont waited several days before he showed up. Word travels fast in the country and he surely knew where I was. But I'd already crossed over the line of freedom and he knew that too. When he came riding after me to the Van Wagenen's house, he had to make a fuss.

189

"Get on back to the house, Bell. I own you for one more year. If you don't come with me, I'll have you put in jail."

"Then you best put me in jail then because that's where I'd rather go before I'd go back with you." A few nights of food and rest amidst new friends emboldened me.

"That baby comes back with me too, you know that." He sort of smiled like he had practiced the words on the ride from New Paltz.

I rearranged the baby in my arms. "She's not weaned. She has to stay with me."

I didn't have to say another word. Mr. Van Wagenen flew off the porch and lit into him, using words like a sword. In the end, Mr. Van Wagenen paid him for the last year of my enslavement, which was twenty dollars, and he threw in a few more for Sophia.

Dumont never did get down off his horse and he never did say good-bye to me. He pulled the reins to the right and rode back the way he came. Mr. Van Wagenen assured me that I was free, that he had paid Dumont out of his belief that one person could not own another.

After I left Dumont's farm, I thought the biggest scare was watching my back, waiting to hear the pounding of hooves as Dumont rode his speckled horse to find me. But it was the bed, in the small room off the kitchen, and not the sound of Dumont's voice when he commanded me to return. The first night, I couldn't sleep in the bed. It looked as high as a table. I rolled Sophia up in a blanket and slept with her on the floor. The second night, I moved closer to the bed, still wrapped in our blankets on the floor. The third night, I worked up my courage and lay on the bed but I woke up throughout the night to make sure I wasn't getting too close to the edge for fear of the baby or me rolling off. By the fourth night, I let the quilt drape over me as I stretched out on my back, and the bed and I made friends.

As long as I stayed working for Isaac and Maria, baby Sophia stayed with me. I was a live-in housekeeper, no longer a slave. The kindly VanWagenens enjoyed Sophia.

The mistress sewed a muslin bonnet for Sophia to keep the sun out of her eyes and the dirt out of her hair. The VanWagenens were unlike nearly all the white people I had known.

"However do you manage this hair on your child?" asked Maria. "It is so difficult to comb."

I had to agree. Sophia's hair was just as tight as mine, which is strange for babies. Usually their hair stays soft for a few years before it firms up. Mau Mau had used everything on my hair from eel grease to lard.

I was not accustomed to my children being treated with such interest simply for themselves, instead of as property to be fed like cattle, or as a nuisance. Isaac made a cornhusk doll for Sophia by tying string around the gathered husk where the neck should be and again where the waist would be. He splayed the cornhusk out at the bottom so it looked like the doll was a girl with a skirt.

He held out the doll and admired his work. "She's too young now. I suppose she'd try to eat it at this age. I made all of our children corn husk dolls." His children were grown, mostly living nearby with children of their own.

I didn't tell them that none of my children had been afforded such a treasure as a cornhusk doll. Nor had I. The doll sat on the shelf in our sleeping room. Sometimes at night when Sophia was sleeping in our bed, I went to the shelf and picked up the doll and looked at her. I was not at all sure that my children back at Dumonts' would know what to do with a doll.

I trusted that Tom would look after Diana and Elizabeth as best he could. It was a relief that Mr. Gedney was apprenticing young Peter to look after a gentleman at sea. I thought that this opportunity would make Peter's chances in life easier, that he might be treated less like a field animal if he had the proper training. He was big for his age and this made him look older than his five years. I worried that people might think him slow, not knowing that he was a small boy inside a bigger than usual body.

During these months of ease, I stopped talking to God in a personal way. I turned my back on the ways I had with God, speaking directly to God, hearing his words land safe in my ears. Sudden comfort in my life for the first time made me forget how hard I had battled to leave slavery and how God had pointed the way. I was with the kindest of people, I slept on a bed, and was paid for my work; I was satisfied. Hadn't God answered every prayer of mine? My youngest child was free along with me, my son was learning to be a gentleman's servant, and my two other daughters had Tom to look after them. There was no longer a need to bother God with my lamentations. I gave Him a rest.

I counted this as my true birth as a free person, the day I found the kindness of the Van Wagenens, the day I walked away from slavery. I was free and being so, I forgot some of the sting of the past as Pinkster approached. That's how it happens; you forget the pain of childbirth, the moment of fear when a finger is cut off, the depths of grief. Forgetting the worst of things lets us go on, but it also makes us foolish.

This would be the last slave Pinkster holiday, after which all slaves in New York were to go free. I'd been free the better part of a year and I longed for the company of colored people, I longed to turn my belly hot with rum, to dance to the fiddler, to sing myself dizzy. I was light headed with my freedom and my thinking became muddled in a way that I now find hard to explain. I found one day that I missed the farm at Dumonts, I missed my children beyond measure, I even missed the smell of Tom. As clear as could be, I knew that Dumont was going to come for me again. We were that close he and I, that I could sense him coming, just as he could sense me softening and wanting to come back.

I stopped my work in the kitchen. We were preparing to whitewash the kitchen walls to freshen them for the summer. I told Maria that I had to get ready to greet Dumont because he was on his way.

"How can you possibly know such a thing?" she asked me as she stacked a neat pile of plates on the table.

I answered her as truly as I could. "I saw him in my mind this morning when I first woke up. He was rigging up the carriage and heading out."

"That sounds more like a dream," she said. I had to agree that it sounded like a dream, but I knew the difference between waking and sleeping. I excused myself to go outside. I stood by the road, still as a tree, until I heard the carriage approach the house.

"I knew you'd come. I was waiting for you," I said.

He shook his head like he always did when he didn't understand me. "I've missed your peculiar sayings. And how does this life suit you, Bell, since running off as you did?"

"I never did run off. I walked."

"No difference. All the rest of the coloreds are going free in the legal way this fourth of July." He got down and ran his hand over the flank of his horse. "Diana took on a lot more work since you left. She keeps Elizabeth with her for the most part. Tom took to bed for a month over the winter. Of course they could have used your help."

It happened in a flash. I wanted to go back. I had proved my point with Dumont. He had owed me a year and I took it. Now most slaves were going free and the younger ones could gradually go free so there was no point in me staying away from my family. I had gone far enough, farther than either of my parents had ever imagined, farther than I had imagined.

"I'm ready to go on back with you," I said.

I could see that I had surprised him. He smiled and said, "I won't take you back Bell." I didn't believe his words with that big smile on his face. I knew he wanted me back but he had to act like he was doing me a favor.

"Wait just a moment while I get Sophia and my things." I turned to walk into the house. He offered me no argument.

As I walked out of the house with my small parcel and with the child on my hip, I heard Maria say, "Well, for heaven's sake!" Dumont was back in his carriage and I was about to hand him Sophia. That's when it happened.

I was thrown off my feet and showered with a shattering

light. I thought that I had been struck by lightning and that my time among the living was over. Then God was displayed to me. God was everywhere in the universe, there was no place that God was not. I was immediately aware of my great sin in abandoning He who had led me to freedom. All my promises to Him rose up in front of my face and my shame was so great that I tried to hide and crawl away, but there was nowhere that God could not see. All else was gone, it was just God and me and for the first time I saw Him and He filled every crevice of earth. God looked into every part of me and saw how I was ready to go back to Dumont, how I craved rum, and how I didn't want to have to go further. I wanted to stop and rest. I wanted only to have God release me from His gaze, because if He looked any longer I would perish in my shame. The next thing I knew, I was sitting up in the road outside the Van Wagenen's house. Dumont was gone. Maria held Sophia in her arms and Isaac had a bucket of water that he appeared ready to douse me with.

I was shaken for the rest of the day. I did not try and explain myself to my fine friends. They had an explanation. "Sometimes people have a fit and they are never again troubled by it. It was the shock of seeing John Dumont again, that's all." But I knew they were wrong. Later that evening, I traveled out to the orchard under the cover of darkness. "If you are God, show yourself to me again," I demanded. I wanted to make sure who I was talking to. I was prepared to be struck down by the full power of the light. Yet I had to know.

I was struck full force, yet not by a destroying force. It was God again, of that much I am sure. Yet this time, God knew I needed someone sweeter so that I could bear it. I saw a friend between me and God, standing there in a space that God made for us. At first I thought it was Soan, because she was my truest friend and because I could not see clearly. Then I willed my heart and soul to see and understand and I knew that if it killed me, I had to know who this friend was. From deep inside me, from a place that I did not know existed, I said, "I am ready to die to know who you are because I know that you have always loved me and that I have always loved you."

The person before me cleared up, like morning mist burning off with the sun. I saw cheek and jaw line, full eyes, gentle mouth. The person never spoke out loud, yet in my heart I heard a voice other than my own say, "It is Jesus." And I knew that this was true.

My heart was changed, the healing of a torn heart began, and I was jubilant. I stayed in the torrent of this love, not sure that my feet were touching the ground, thankful beyond measure for finding the doorway to God, although I was not at all sure how I had done so. By the time the clear presence of God was gone, the first color of dawn touched on the buds of the cherry blossoms.

I had heard of Jesus before this, but I only knew Him as a famous man that people looked up to and read about. In that moment in the orchard, I felt that I was the only person to be so loved. I gave up drinking rum on the spot.

I found a place to talk to God so I didn't disturb the others. I ended up shouting often, to make myself heard and Maria said it was a distraction and could I please have my conversations with God out by the cherry orchard. Of course I agreed. When Maria discovered that I spoke to God, she asked if I went to church. I had to tell her that I had never been allowed. "Well for heaven's sake!" she said. They belonged to the same Dutch Reform Church that Mr. Dumont did, so we didn't think that was a good place to start out. She figured the Methodist Church was the place for me.

I went back to my talks with God, loud as I could and as often as I could. The first time I went to church, I was so afraid that I only stood outside and listened below an open window. I could hardly believe my ears when I heard them sing when the spirit filled them and how they spoke of the love of God. As time went on, I grew brave enough to go inside the church, and by the deep of winter, I felt welcomed there at last.

CHAPTER TWENTY-SEVEN

There were two things that John Dumont did that made it clear to me that either God did not talk to him as I had thought, or that Dumont did not heed the word of God. He went back on his promise to set me free one year early. The further I traveled from him, the more I was sure of the lack of truth in his thinking.

The second thing he did was let my son be sold south. I don't know if he intended to sell Peter when he first loaned him to Dr. Gedney. But the loan was tolerable to me; Peter was going to get a chance to advance himself and learn about the world.

I learned that my son was given away to Solomon Gedney, the doctor's brother, because he performed poorly in the job of looking after a gentleman. Solomon then promptly sold Peter to a brother-in-law in Alabama. At that point, I doubted that John had ever heard a word that God had to say because I was absolutely certain that God would not tell a man to sell a six year old colored boy away from his family to go south where slavery had an iron fist.

The selling part happened in a flash, and it was little surprise that Sally's side of the family was at work in the matter. By the time I heard of it, Peter had been sold off to a Mr. Fowler, a relation to Sally's kin by marriage. It was Diana who got word to me by way of the Quakers in Poppletown.

"This can't be right," I said to Isaac and Maria. "A confusion must have come over Dumont. He's never talked of selling any of my children, not once."

"Once the child was out of Dumont's hands, it is likely that greed took hold of Gedney. People are selling slaves out of state to make the last bit of money off the poor wretches. But they are breaking the law as I understand it. Can't sell slaves across state lines," said Isaac.

I set out like a fox for Dumont's, walking the whole way, I was in too much of a fever to think about a horse or a carriage. Every step of the way, I thought of Peter being in terror, taken away to a strange land where negroes are killed with less thought than it takes to feed the chickens.

Surely any woman would recognize the wound in my belly that meant my child was taken away wrongfully. I went straight to Sally for that reason, plus it was her kin who did the selling. I wanted to touch the place in her that was a mother. I knew that she loved her own children. Whatever discord had passed between us was over in my mind. This wasn't about me so much as it was about a child, and surely a woman would understand that. I was no longer slave and she was no longer my mistress.

"I need your help to get Peter back. You can help me clear up this confusion." I was breathless from the trip and I tasted salt on my lips from sweating. I stood on her stone step to the kitchen.

"Of course he's been sold. I wrote to Solomon and told him not to bring that boy back here. I told him to sell him to Cousin Fowler." Her arms were folded across her chest.

I was taller than she was even with her standing in the doorway and me standing out on the step. "He is my son...," I started to say.

"You can't take care of the children you have. You ran off and left them with no mother to tend to them. Did you think I'd be taking care of a pack of nigger children? Isn't it just like you to make a fuss about a paltry little boy." Sally turned to go back inside her house, the same house that I had known for sixteen years.

I could not bear it. I reached out my arm and pointed my fingers into her face and shouted, "I shall have my child!" I do not know where the words came from, but as soon as I said them, I felt so large within that I might step over the Hudson like a giant. I saw Sally jump and she looked to see if anyone was nearby to help her. She stumbled backward, catching herself at the last minute.

"Don't go running to my husband. He knows about it now. There's nothing that can be done," she said.

I went to the house of Mrs. Gedney, whose very daughter was married to the plantation owner Mr. Fowler. I knew that she favored this daughter Eliza, who had a kind disposition.

"I come to you because you must understand the grief of a mother who longs to be with her child. Do you not long to be near your daughter?" But she would not be a woman with me, would not go to the raw place of each of us giving birth to babes, each of us covered in a mother's love for a child. She stood back and took the upper step.

"You couldn't take care of your children. You ran away and left them. Ran away to Quakers and nigger lovers. Your kind doesn't give one hoot about your children. You wouldn't feel anything if all your children were sold off. That's a fact from God. If your boy had been worth anything, Solomon would have kept him."

"My son is six years old. He is too young for the sort of life on a plantation."

"Get away from my house. You're causing a hallooballoo around here."

I would have begged her, fallen to my knees and promised her my life if I thought it would have helped. But this was the woman who taught Sally how to treat slaves. She was beyond hope.

Sally's heart could not be softened, nor Mrs. Gedney's. To them, I was not a mother and Peter was not a son. I could forgive them for taking the side of their men on some matters. But they went too far when they told me that I could not feel, that I could not grieve the loss of my son. I ran from her wretched sight as the night began to fall. I spent the night at my old God house, sleepless and cold.

* * *

I was advised by the Van Wagenens to go to the Quakers, as they knew laws well and what had happened to Peter was against the law. The Quakers set me straight and helped me to understand what was legal and what wasn't. They drove me to Kingston so that I could go to the courthouse.

It was a warm October and I was accustomed to wearing shoes only when cold weather set in good and solid. Now that I had to supply myself with shoes instead of waiting on the Dumonts to hand out the year's ration of clothes, I had to conserve the only pair of shoes that I had for the worst of the cold months. So my entry into the world of laws and courtrooms was done barefooted. Back then, it didn't matter to me.

I did as the Quakers advised me. They told me to go to the courthouse and present my case to the Grand Jury. I stood outside the courthouse, which was the biggest building I had ever seen. It was three stories tall and wide enough to fit a steamboat. I dusted off my skirt as best I could and entered through a side door. I was too frightened to enter through the front door. I stopped the first man I saw who looked like he was someone of knowledge and stature. I immediately poured out my whole story of Peter being such a young boy and sold wrongfully.

He frowned the whole time I was talking to him. He had white hair and his eyebrows were white and thick, standing out from his brow like a ledge. He looked at me from my feet to my head and back down again. Then he said, "You should come with me."

He led me upstairs, looking back to make sure that I was following him. "It's not me you should be talking to. I'm not but a clerk and you need more help than I can give."

"I was told to find the grand jury and you looked grand enough to me," I said.

As he knocked on a door, he leaned close to me and whispered, "Tell them you wish to make a complaint."

Which is what I did. I stood barefooted before half a dozen white men, dressed in finely tailored coats. I know I must have told them my story true enough, but what I remember most clearly is the way the sun slanted in the windows, lighting up broad stripes on the floor. I ended my complaint by asking, "Is it true that the law says coloreds can't be sold from New York into a slave state?"

The men looked from one to another, turning their heads just enough to allow their eyes to touch the gaze of another. Finally one of them spoke up.

"Yes, the law seeks to protect negroes who live in the state of New York from being sold to a slave state."

His words echoed in my head. There was protection for my son. I could hardly believe it. "The law is clear but the process is complicated. You will need to hire a lawyer."

"I've never met a lawyer but I will look until I find one. My son can't stay in Alabama, he won't last on a plantation," I said.

I thought I would get Peter back the next day or maybe the day after. If I had known how long it would take, I'm not sure that I could have gone on. I spent the next few months talking with lawyers in Kingston, each time walking the five miles back to the Van Wagenens. Bruyn Hasbrouck finally took my case, and I eventually worked as his family servant to pay him back. By the next summer, I moved into his house. Isaac and Maria had helped me beyond measure and I was sad to leave them. Isaac made sure I took little Sophia's cornhusk doll when we left.

Mr. Hasbrock convinced Solomon Gedney to retrieve Peter from Alabama. That was late summer. I was sure I would get Peter back as soon as I heard this, but Mr. Hasbrouck said there was a fresh problem. Soloman Gedney had Peter somewhere in New York but he refused to deliver him to Kingston. He said he was obeying the law just by bringing him back to the state.

"I'm sorry, Isabella. We have come a far way with this matter and yet your son remains out of your reach. We may have to be satisfied with less...the boy is no longer in a slave state and at least that is something."

There were days when it felt like God was carrying me along and I was made strong. There were as many days when I felt that the power to get my son back rested not with me, but with men who I had to constantly convince and beg to help me. Mr. Hasbrouck finally told me he could not spend all of his time getting Peter back.

As much as I was indebted to Hasbrouck for getting Peter out of Alabama, I had to seek out someone to make Gedney bring Peter to the courthouse so that the law could decide where he rightfully belonged. I was sent to one more lawyer, Herman Romeyn. He had a reputation for dealing with scoundrels and that's what Gedney was. I would not rest until Peter was out of Gedney's hands.

"You will need to get me five dollars to hire a strong armed man to persuade Mr. Gedney to bring your son to court."

"I've never had five dollars in my life," I said. I was astonished at the sum.

"The Quakers won't turn you away. Go back to them for the money."

I did as he advised that very day. I walked to Poppletown and within a few days, the industrious Quakers had raised over eight dollars. They said with the extra money, I should buy a pair of shoes. But I didn't need shoes or clothes. I only needed my Peter back. If five dollars were needed to get him back, then eight dollars would get him all the better."

When I traveled the same ten miles back again to Kingston, I went without pause to lawyer Romeyn's door. I opened my hand as soon as I saw him, dropping all of the coins into his hand.

"Gedney is a fool beyond comprehension to make such a

fuss. He will be publicly shamed in court and a spectacle will be made. On top of that, he can be fined a rich sum. I can't imagine why he is delaying in bringing the boy. Come back in twenty four hours and I will have news for you about finding a man to apprehend Gedney."

Now here was something that I had never heard before. "Twenty four hours." I had never had to determine that before. As a slave, I knew when to start the milking, when to make the fire ready for porridge, when to expect the days to shorten, what day of the week the Dumonts went to church. But no one had ever said to me, in twenty four hours, something will happen. Now, if he had said, come back the next day, of course I would have known.

Because I did not know what he meant, I stayed right on his porch, and every so often, I knocked on his door to ask for any news. After the second time of this, he scolded me firmly and said, "Come back late tomorrow." Which I did.

CHAPTER TWENTY-EIGHT

Peter was gone for the better part of a year when I finally got word that Gedney was going to bring Peter to the courthouse in Kingston. When I returned to his office, lawyer Romeyn said to be at the courthouse first thing in the morning. There was a long pause as both of us wondered if we meant the same time.

"The courthouse opens at nine o'clock. I expect you will be there waiting long before any of the rest of us," said Romeyn

I wore my shoes as it was mid November. I wrapped a wool shawl around my shoulders. I walked in the sweetest light I had ever seen on the day that my son was coming back. I sat on the steps of the courthouse waiting for all the rest of the world to catch up with me.

One by one, they filed past me, clerks, lawyers all giving me a glance as they opened the door. Romeyn came at last, still straightening his vest, giving it a tug at the bottom, encouraging the fabric to stay down and not ride up over his belly. "Have you been waiting long?"

"No. This morning was not a long wait. But, this past year was wearisome."

I followed Romeyn into a first floor room and we sat on a bench facing a judge seated behind a thick table. Romeyn whispered to me, "We're in luck. That's Ruggles, and he's as fair as they come." Ruggles pulled a pocket watch from beneath his coat, eyed it, and glanced at Romeyn. Before the question could be asked, Romeyn spoke up. "I have no doubt that Mr. Gedney will appear, Your Honor."

A side doorway opened and I stopped breathing. Gedney stood in the doorway with Peter peeping out from behind his legs. I made to stand up, but Romeyn gripped my arm and held it tight.

Peter had grown. He was longer, more stretched out, and his nose had started to grow a bit. That's how children grow, a nose broadens, the teeth look too big for their head. I saw in an instant one change that stabbed me in the heart. Here was a boy who lived in fear. He clung to Gedney's pant leg as if he were his family instead of me.

The judge wasted no time. "Mr. Gedney, is this the boy who was sold to Mr. Fowler in Alabama?"

"Yes sir he is. I went to a great amount of trouble to bring him back."

"And Mr. Romeyn, is this the boy that you requested be returned to his mother, this colored woman Isabella?"

Romeyn looked at me because he had never seen Peter before that moment. I answered in a voice that came out too loud, "He is my son!"

Peter set up a screech that raised the hair on my neck. "My mother is dead. She's not my mother!"

If not for knowing that Peter's thinking had been damaged, I don't think that I could have borne a worse pain than for him not to know me. In desperation, I grabbed Romeyn's coat sleeve and said, "That is Peter, there is no mistaking my son. I swear to God that child is my son."

Gedney, still trying to save his own neck, tried to discredit me. "She is the worst sort of black devil. She has caused trouble even though no damage has come to her."

Thankfully, the judge paid little heed to Gedney. The judge raised up and came around to where the lawyer and I stood. All three of us attempted to calm the boy. It was plain to see that the child was in a state of agitation and fear and that no clear answer would come from him until he was settled down. The judge had sweets brought from his chamber and gave a candy to Peter. I talked low and soft to Peter, saying the names of his sisters, his father, reminded him of how he walked like a rooster.

The judge stepped closer to Peter and directed Gedney to step back five paces. A scar ran from the outside of Peter's eye to his mouth. The judge looked at me and then Gedney. Then he faced Peter. "How did you get such an injury?" asked the judge.

Peter looked at Gedney. "Mr. Fowler's horse hove me, sir."

"And here, on your neck, what happened here?" asked the judge, pointing to a jagged scar that showed above the collar of his coat.

Again the boy looked at Gedney. "I fell against a wheel spoke, sir. It was my fault."

"It looks like you had a run of mishaps in Alabama." The judge sighed. "Tell me if you think this woman is your mama."

This time Peter looked at me and not Gedney, although Gedney commenced to clear his throat to get the boy's attention. Peter kept his eyes right on me. "Well, she looks like my mama used to look," he said after wiping the candy syrup from his mouth. Finally he let me come near him without screeching like a hawk. Romeyn told Peter to take off his coat. I knew what Judge Ruggles wanted me to do. My son let me lift up his shirt to expose his back. "Oh Lord in Heaven," said Romeyn when he saw Peter's back.

All that we could see of his body was covered in scars as wide as rope, rippling across his back. Bile crept up my throat and I forced it down. "Not a bit of this happened at Dumonts'," I said.

In the end, Gedney was fined a hefty fee and Peter was given back to me. Judge Ruggles also said that Peter was free of any indentured time to Dumont.

* * *

205

In the weeks that followed, Peter told me more and more of life in Alabama with the plantation owner Fowler. His sleep was peppered with nightmares, shattering the night air with his screams. I still lived with the Hasbroucks as their servant. I offered for Peter and me to sleep in the carriage house to save them from the disturbance, which they readily agreed to.

Peter's scars covered his entire body. On the first night that I saw his scars, I covered my face with my hands and cried, "Peter, how did you endure it?"

"Oh, these are much better now. Mr. Gedney said my sores had to heal before going to the court. He also said that a wicked woman was going to take me away and that you were dead." He put his hand to my face as if to make sure that I was real and not a ghost. "If you think my scars are bad, you would scare to see Phyllis."

"Who was Phyllis?" I was on my knees next to him, making myself smaller to shrink his fear of me. I wanted to draw him into to me, wrap my arms around him but his recollection of me was frayed and was only starting to come back. Later, I found out that Fowler not only told him that I was dead, but that I'd been an evil person, filled with the devil and that Fowler had saved him from me. No one would take him in except Fowler, or so Peter believed.

"Phyllis was like me, a slave. She had a baby when I first got there. Fowler tied her up, tore off her dress and whipped her until milk ran down her front. It was milk and blood. She must have done something bad for Fowler to whip her."

In that moment I feared that I'd lost him to the sickness of slavery. I pictured him watching Phyllis, suffering beyond endurance for a crime that may have been as little as smiling at her babe, or for no crime other than being in the presence of Fowler when he woke up particularly mean. I pictured Fowler, the worst of men, keeping little Peter in his vision, building up his power over the boy, breaking his spirit. I did not want to frighten the boy further, but I could not keep the tears from running down my face

I put my hands on either side of his face. "The judge said that Mr. Gedney broke the law by taking you to Fowler. And I'm telling you that any man who treats people with the cruelty of Fowler is wrong. What he did was wrong Peter."

He paused in contemplation, weighing what I had said. "Mrs. Fowler, she cried too. She found me hiding under the porch and rubbed grease into my wounds when the master beat me. She cried all the time. If the master saw her crying, he beat her with his fists."

I could not sleep on the night that Peter told me about Phyllis. I crept outside to talk to God. I shook my fist to the sky. "Let them feel double the pain of my son. For everything they caused to happen to Peter, render double onto them!"

CHAPTER TWENTY-NINE

I got Peter a position with the lock tender along the newly
built D and H Canal. In a fit of what I hoped was regret,
Mr. Dumont offered a recommendation for Peter. I left the
Hasbroucks' household and took other employment as
servant to families in Kingston. I visited my two children at
Dumont's as I was able, and we went to church together as
often as we could. Tom wouldn't come with us, of course. He
acted like an old man who used to be a friend of mine, not
like a husband.

Dumont and I began talking again when I went there to
visit my girls. We started out slow and jagged, both of us
holding back at first. He and I had come a long ways together
and I could see he still wanted to have some say about my
life. When I became a free bondswoman, he and I had to find
a new way to be with each other, and the going was filled
with bumps.

I had just arrived at Dumonts' for a visit with the girls,
when Mr. Dumont saw me walking to the house and came
out to greet me. As we stood talking about the crops, one of
Gedney's cousins rode up. This was one of the men who had
talked bad about me from morning to night when I was trying
to get Peter back. He said, "What are you driving at these
days, Bell?"

"Nothing in particular right now." I was finished with one
job and not yet ready to start another.

"We could use some help over our ways. Some of the family is sick and we could use an extra hand."

Mr. Dumont advised me not to go, with a stern look and a shake of his head. "They have not treated you fairly. You have no duty to tend to them."

I can't say why I went but I felt the strangest need to go. I said I would help out as long as I was needed, they could pay me as they were able. I wanted people to forget their anger to me and to mend up.

I had a light heart as I worked that morning. I made soup for the ailing ones and set water to boil for the soiled linens. The day was dry and it was best to get the sheets out before the weather took a change.

A young Gedney cousin, Portia, came into the house with a fright filled face. "Heavens and earth, Isabella. Cousin Fowler has killed Eliza!"

The news came in a letter which she held crumpled in her hand. Right then Mrs. Gedney and her son Solomon came in. I could tell by the look on their faces that they had not yet heard the news. They had come to visit Mrs. Gedney's oldest sister who was sick with consumption. Here was the man who sold my son to Alabama and here was the woman who would not help me get my son back, who told me that my kind could not have the feelings that mothers have. Her daughter was dead, and for a few short moments, she did not know what was about to befall her, did not know that the air would fly out of her lungs and her ears would ring as if she was hit in the head. "What in the world is she doing here?" she asked, nodding her head in my direction.

"She's come to tend to your sister," said Portia. The girl looked helplessly at me, wanting me to do something.

Solomon and Mrs. Gedney went upstairs to the invalid's bedroom. Portia followed, straightening the letter to better read the awful news to the mother and aunt of the dead woman, Eliza. I suppose I must count Solomon too, he was her brother.

A servant is never to enter a mistress's room unbidden,

any fool knows that, and I had never done so before in my thirty two years. Yet I heard a voice, clear as glass, telling me to follow them, to enter and listen. I balked and held my ground. Then the voice rumbled in my ear, "Go and listen!"

I climbed the stairs and could already hear the steady tones of Portia reading. I opened the door and pressed my back to the farthest wall from the bed. The girl continued reading.

"...being a friend of the family, were it otherwise possible, I would not be bearing such terrible news. Mr. Fowler has been imprisoned for the murder of his wife, your gentle Eliza. Because of the fiendishness of his deed, which I must explain, or you will not understand the further action that was taken, I and others felt that it was best to remove the children from Alabama and the possible reach of their father who will no doubt be released from prison when his fortune eventually aids him. Eliza suffered increasing brutalities from her husband, yet none that I thought would take her life. I do not know what rage overcame him to carry him past reason. I will tell you plainly so that you shall know and not wonder, for that may be worse. He saw Eliza coming out of the kitchen; he had just arrived home from overseeing the punishment of several slaves. He jumped on Eliza, knocking her with his fists. He pressed his knees into her chest, broke her collar bone, and tore out her windpipe. When word of his deed reached town, he attempted his escape, but too slowly for the enraged men who apprehended him. He was put in an iron bank for safe keeping..."

Mrs. Gedney made an awful sound, yowling cat-like and all those in the room began to sob, even Solomon. I left the room as quietly as I came. Their grief was so great that I do not think they ever saw me enter or leave. I finished my work downstairs, doing all that I could for them and then left and did not return.

As I walked back to visit with my girls, I said to God, "I did not mean so much trouble, I did not mean this to befall them." I never sent a curse to anyone after this. Mrs. Gedney went deranged; she spent the rest of her days calling for Eliza and could not hear any of those around her.

A few months after, I accepted an offer from a Mrs. Gear to move to New York City. Mrs. Gear was a mild woman from the Methodist church and she recommended me to an employer. I did not think at the time that I was leaving the Hudson Valley forever.

I could not take all my children with me so I took the one who was grievously damaged and needed me most; I took Peter. I took Sophia, who was four, to live with her father and sisters at Dumonts so that she could be with her family. Dumont swore to me that no further harm would come to my children. "If they are harmed in any way, I will know it and I will come back here as fast as the wind can carry me," I said.

"Bell, there is not a person in the whole county who doubts that."

Soan came to the dock to see me off. I knew it cost her dearly to come so far from her job in Albany. She looked suddenly old. For the occasion, she let her white hair down and the wind picked it up and carried it like a thick flag. She told me that as long as she breathed, she would take occasions to look in on my daughters, who remained bound servants to Dumont, except for Sophia who was a free person. I watched Soan as long as I could, waving with one hand, holding onto my son with the other.

CHAPTER THIRTY

NEW YORK CITY

After some uncertainties with Mrs. Gear about where I should live and work, Peter and I settled in with a comfortable arrangement. We lived with the Latourette family for the most part and yet I worked for Mrs. Whiting over on Canal Street. Peter came and lived with me on Sundays and stayed at his work apprenticing to the carriage stables on Broadway. Learning to be a coachman looked to be a fine future for my son. I was determined to repair the damage that was done to him.

But there was the catch in my throat, that waited for me even in moments of sunlit, autumn days of pleasure; here was the price I paid to keep Peter, my most damaged child with shredded back. I had to pick between the most damaged and the youngest.

A newly freed black woman could not hope to keep her whole brood together as she set out to build a life beyond slavery. Both Diana and Elizabeth were indentured until their twenty fifth year. But Sophia, hands still round on top, eyes fringed with the thickest lashes, was as free as I was in the eyes of the law, her slavery paid off by the Van Wagenen. But no matter. Peter could not last in New Paltz where we had caused such a stir in courts. He had to come away with me.

* * *

I had trembled in front of Sophia's eyes to tell her she must stay. I knelt in front of my child, this child born of a fury that held no love between Tom and me. My face crumbled, starting at my chin, then my lips gave way and to save the day, I put on my stern face, the look that Diana said made the devil go faint. Oh, could not this child look away?

I took her face in my hands. "I am going to find work in the city. Peter will come with me. You will stay here."

"If you leave, I will follow your footsteps and the tracks of the wagon. I will follow the big boat too." Her chin stuck out and all her might came forward in the soft point below her mouth. I picked her up and heard again the voice of Mau Mau in a breeze that whirled around us. I took a breath.

"Sophia, if you want to talk to me, go ahead and tell God all your troubles and God will send me the message. The world is a big place with many rooms. You and I will be in the same house but in different rooms."

"I want to be in the same room as you."

I did not think that I could go on. And then her whims of childhood saved me.

"Diana tugs too hard on my hair. Elizabeth took away my corn husk girl." The doll made by Mr. Van Wagenen caused such a stir with my daughters.

"Well then, you and I can make another doll now that we've seen him do it. Let's get a bit of corn husk. I have a ribbon on my shawl that can be spared."

And we did. And I left my daughters.

* * *

My first job in the city with Mrs. Whiting was as housekeeper with cooking. The first time people ate my food, they started to get to know me. They tasted me when they licked molasses from their spoons, and ran their tongues over smooth cornmeal puddings. When they ate my pies, they tasted Mau Mau as well. I thought of her every time I rolled out a piedough: four big handfuls of flour, a pinch of salt, several spoonfuls of lard, some cool water to mix it together. If the day was moist, I dusted more flour into the dough, if the day was crisp, I added a few more drops of water.

I was a free bondswoman. Could they taste my freedom? Did my cooked ham taste different when I started wearing a hat and shoes? Could they taste my new name, chosen by me and no other? Isabella Van Wagenen. I took the name of Isaac and Maria to honor them for their kindness. They said I didn't have to do that but to me it meant a name of freedom. It was my choice to name myself and I reveled in it. They had saved me from more than they knew; I could not hold on to my hatred of white people after the Van Wagenens wrapped me in honest kindness.

I took to preaching a few words of my own on street corners. Could they taste the salt of my sweat when God's words filled me to bursting, taste the swelling of my heart when I saw that my voice filled a passing person with grace and everlasting light? I was thrilled by the power of spirit and I longed to share it.

I baked pies with the berries grown on the northern farming lands of Manhattan. Being new to the city, the filth of it was enough to make me cover my face at times, but when the farmers came to town, they sold the sweetest berries and the flavor of them was enough to wash away the filth. Children and women were the berry pickers; tiny strawberries that grow low to the ground, elderberries, blackberries, raspberries. As the summer marched on, new sorts of berries replaced the old ones that had gone hard and dry from the sun. Blackberries were the sturdiest and stayed the longest. I bought a small basketful from a young girl who sold them from house to house.

She was barefoot and I admonished her. "Take care to cover your feet in the city. There is much filth here." I bought her blackberries and slid a few of Mrs. Whiting's coins into her small white hand, dyed blue at the tips of her fingers, the backs lined with scratches from the tough vines.

"I won't sell enough berries this summer to buy shoes," she told me.

"Come back again tomorrow," I said.

In so short a time, I had come a long way. I was far from the Dumont farm, far from asking Sally to get me shoes and awaiting her decision. Far from standing barefooted before grand jurors in Kingston. Farther still from my days as a child with feet split open from the cold.

I talked to the mistress of the house and asked if they had any shoes that were too worn. I explained the situation of the young girl selling berries. Mrs. Whiting gave me a pair of shoes that were in need of a shoemaker's touch. "If she is clever, she can mend them herself," she said.

The girl came back the next day. I bought more berries, as well as two eggs. I handed her the shoes. "Wear these. It is better to cover your feet in the city."

The blackberry pie tasted of small white hands picking among the sticker stalks, feet covered in leather, protected from wheels and horses hooves, dung and worse. The pie tasted of the first pair of shoes that I was able to offer another.

The city was altogether an exciting place, filled with the hard working class of white people, such as Mr. Latourette who was a fur merchant, along with more colored people than I had ever seen before in one place. There were colored sailors, and carriage drivers, shop owners, and colored children going to school and reading the Bible like there was no tomorrow. I don't mean to say that this was heaven, because it was not. Even though New York was several years past the time of freeing their slaves, it was still possible to be kidnapped and taken to southern states where slavery was grinding Negroes into the dirt. I learned to temper my jubilation with wariness. I looked ahead and behind for kidnappers. They would have to kill me before I'd return to slavery.

The noise of the city was enough to rattle me senseless in the beginning. "Step smart," said a gentleman to me as his carriage jangled by on Canal Street. Indeed, one could not let the mind wander in the city for fear of being run over by carriages intent on flying people from one place to the next. It was not possible for men to keep up with the droppings from the horses. The mess created by the beasts was a nuisance.

My room at the Latourette house came complete with a bed, hooks for my clothes, and a wash stand. The last thing I did at night was to go outside, pump water, and bring it into my room to fill my basin. This was mine, this clear water to rinse my mouth in the morning and splash dreams from my eyes. The pitcher was chipped and did not match the basin, yet they looked to be the grandest china to me.

I did not have a fireplace in my room, as the kitchen did, the parlor, master bedroom and two other rooms. In the coldest months, I took thick embers and placed them in the long handled, metal bed warmer, running it quickly between the sheets so as to warm them without scorching. If I belabor these details of life in the telling, it is because I found them to be wonders and I felt rich beyond imagining. I saved much of the money that I earned. It was only when I had been in the city for a full year, and the coins of my wages were considerable, that I stopped to think about the years of my labors that were rewarded with nothing but difficulty and the marked lack of coins. All of my labors on the farm were gained by Dumont. Now I could choose my fate. Some days left me exhausted with choosing.

Many people in the city hailed from farms or countries across the ocean. They tried to make the city look like the farms that they left behind. Mrs. Whiting had the finest garden behind and to the side of her house. Her husband, Perez, liked to sit in the small garden and read. The walk to the privy was lined on either side first by peonies, then later in the summer by hollyhocks. I noticed that the air turned warm earlier in the year and stayed later in the fall so that we had a longer time with flowers. Larkspur grew on two sides of the well, coltsfoot and lavender grew in the crowded garden also. Two young apple trees filled the remainder of the back yard. Mrs. Whiting said they had already picked enough apples last year to make pies for the fall and apple butter that lasted clear to midwinter.

There were things that I did not do when I moved to the city. I no longer made soap from rendered lard and lye. Instead, we bought soap from a man who sold from his wagon. He sold good hard soap, which was difficult to make and I admired his work. I no longer did field work. At Dumonts', I had half come to think of myself as a brute field worker, a tireless animal on the farm. I knew nothing else. In the city, I was afforded comforts that gave room for grander thoughts in my mind. My work was hard enough, but I was also filled up by church and prayer meetings and the words of the Bible and the excitement of so many people searching day and night for the work of the Lord.

Mrs. Latourette was a religious woman of the first order and she opened doors for me that sent my mind spinning. I joined the Methodist Church on John Street, which was filled by Negroes and whites both. A terrible dispute broke out when the colored ones learned that we could be members of the church but we were never going to be allowed to preach. Why, some of us were already preaching. The colored Methodists left in a huff and formed our own house of worship on Church Street. We became the Zion Church, and it was there that I felt my life grow larger and a deep comfort spread over me. On most Sundays, Peter came with me, dragging his feet all the way. Depending on the day and how many people came to church and how much God spoke to each one of us, we could be there till supper. I often had to pinch Peter's arm to keep him from squirming.

More than a few people had prayer meetings in their homes, so on any evening, I might be seated in a parlor warmed by fervent bodies, listening to someone with a strong voice reading from the Bible. Then we all said what the

217

reading meant to us. The meetings were colored and white alike, though most people were white.

I was envious of those who could read the Bible. Church people offered to teach me to read but I never could get farther than the a b c part of it. The leap from little letters to the words of God was too far for me. Nor could I stop the letters from jumping about on the page, so I gave up on reading. I had strong powers of remembering. If I heard a song once, it stayed with me forever. When I heard the Bible, the words moved into me and never left.

There was no end to the people who Mrs. Latourette knew and no end to her kind invitations to me. When Mrs. Latourette told me that women from her church went directly to people who were most in need of preaching, I said that I wanted to go too. "Well then, Isabella, there are no souls more in need than the harlots of Five Points. Come with me to a prayer meeting tonight."

All sorts of people lived in the city. Some were driven by want and hardship, others were merchants by day and saviors by night. The women who lived in Five Points, the harlots, sold their flesh to men. Everyone agreed that these were the souls ripest for saving. As we walked from Bowery Hill to Five Points, Mrs. Latourette said that this could be my special calling, working with the harlots. I told her I was a poor black woman, but that had nothing to do with being a harlot. More women from her church met us there, in a stuffy room in the back of a storefront. It looked to me that about half of the people were from her church and the other half were a reluctant looking group of young women dressed with more ribbons and baubles than I had ever seen. Only two were colored, the rest were white. They looked hot with shame, then stubborn. One of them fired back an icy glare at me when I stared too long. Had I forgotten so quickly what it was to use your body to survive? My body had been a tool of constant labor, stronger than some men. Their bodies were used in another sort of trade.

One of the Methodist women began to preach and before

long, the spirit came into a gray haired woman across the room. She rolled her eyes up, fell against one of the harlots, and spoke a string of words that not a one of us understood. With the crush of people in the room, I thought this was a good time for me to go out and get some fresh air. I also didn't take to such antics. These folks were so wild with noise that God could have walked in and sat down and no one would know the miracle. I started to leave when someone stepped on my skirt and pulled me down to my knees.

"God has thrown her to her knees!"

"The spirit is in her!" shouted Mrs. Latourette.

I attempted to pull myself up, but several feet hindered me further by pinning down the other side of my skirt, pulling me further to the floor. "You're pulling me down!" I said to a sea of skirts and a few trousers.

"She feels the temptation of the devil! Lay on hands, Lay on hands!"

I was covered with hands all over me, people pressing me down. The close quarters and the heat from so many bodies made my head buzz. "Let the spirit take over, make room for the Lord," said someone from beyond the immediate huddle.

"I can't breathe. Please let me breathe," I said. I started to feel a sense of dread, a fear of being crushed by the weight of so many people pressing down on me. I gave a desperate heave. "Get off me!"

Several women staggered backward, giving me room to rise. I headed for the sweet release of the door. I looked back and saw the same harlot who looked at me with such coldness earlier. She cocked a questioning eyebrow at me and one side of her mouth pulled up in a crooked smile. I knew that I had disrupted the prayer meeting. I had to make apologies to Mrs. Latourette when she returned home, but I refused to go back to Five Points and I never again went to the sort of prayer meeting where people carried on so foolishly. I imagined that I could see to the heart of the true word of God, and surely, I would not lose my way.

CHAPTER THIRTY-ONE

On this day, the autumn air was finally free from stinging bugs. The noon day sun brought only drowsy flies, unable to dodge the snap of my dishcloth. I was filled with unexpected gratitude, the way a person can be when one part of the brain goes quiet and fills up with light. Could my parents see me? Could they see that not one of my children had been sold into slavery?

I had heard often enough growing up on the Dumont farm that I could not have the same longings in my heart as white people. I could not love my children, or not anymore than a sheep does when she bleats for her lamb.

I call this back door thinking. If an idea is so addled that it can't fit through the front door, then tip it sideways and slide it through the kitchen door. Selling black children from their parents made good farming sense if you believed that it was impossible for us to crumple from despair, to feel our lungs collapse and watery fear run through our veins instead of blood.

When I became a free bondswoman and traveled along the streets of Manhattan without a master, I imagined that I would one day find my brother. I pictured turning a corner, strolling through Five Points and a hand would touch my shoulder and would be Peter, a beautiful grown man, saying, "Isabella, it's me, Peter. I have missed you so much."

Would he be a sailor? Would he be a black jack, sailing to

Nantucket and Martha's Vineyard, down the coast of our country where slavery still held an iron grasp? One of the first things I heard when I came to New York was that a black man had become a captain of his own ship, that he circled the country like a swift whale carrying goods and more than a little human cargo from the south destined for the free lands of the north. On Sunday mornings before church, I sometimes stood at the docks and watched for a black jack who could be my brother. I asked as well. Had they seen a colored sailor named Peter, a bit younger than me, and just as tall? But I did not find him and this made me hang ever tighter to my son.

My son, Peter, would never again know the threat of a wagon pulling up to take him away. Never would someone be my master, claim my child and say, "Isabella, it is time for me to sell Peter. I can fetch a good sum. He'll be leaving tomorrow." That terror was gone for me and I could do for him what my mother and father only dreamt of giving their twelve children.

Yet here was the miracle: in Manhattan, Peter was an apprentice with a carriage stable and no foul word was spoken of him. Every Sunday night he came to visit with me and I checked to see that his clothes were mended and cleaned. And I was earning my way, sending new cloth back to my daughters when I could. The world was opening up and I would have my part of it through my own labors. And I would have my children with me one day in my own home.

* * *

Mrs. Whiting asked such a simple question while I worked in the kitchen. "Where is your home?" I sliced up cold salted ham and cold potatoes to leave for their supper. My hand stopped and hovered, knife blade sinking midway into the ham.

"My home?" I asked her. Her tendency to ask me direct questions still startled me.

"Yes, you and your family." Mrs. Whiting was a small woman and unless we were sitting down, a position that neither of us frequented, she would look up at me with her head tilted one way or another. We were getting on well enough. She had never had slaves, and with servants, she was clear and forthright.

"I did not have a home in the way that you might mean. I lived with my children and husband in the cellar of John Dumont's home." I let the weight of my arm push the knife the rest of the way through the ham and the blade struck a sharp chord when it hit the plate.

"I see. And your daughters remain there?"

"Yes, indentured until they are twenty five." I did not know the woman well enough to explain about Sophia. And I did not trust her well enough to tell her that one day all of us would live under one roof. I did not tell her because this day was far away and stood on wobbly legs like the newest of lambs. If she were to scoff, or raise an eyebrow, my dream might blow off like a storm.

But for right then, my home became buying strong calico for Diana and sewing her a skirt, wrapping it tight in paper and asking Mrs. Whiting to help me send it by steamer up the Hudson. Home was walking by the stable on a surprise visit to let Peter know that I was not so far away. Home was saving my small pile of coins until I was able to buy a chair of my own, purchased with my own free labor, of my own choosing. Home was where the chair would one day sit.

I ventured a risk with Mrs. Whiting. "There will be a day for me to have a home."

CHAPTER THIRTY-TWO

I had lived in the city for one year and half of another when Mrs. Latourette introduced me to Elijah Pierson. I had already entered the world of camp meetings and from there, my own preaching took off like a shooting star. I say preaching, but what I truly mean is speaking the word of God.

Mrs. Latourette, in her passion of the spirit, lead me to my first camp meeting at Bowery Hill and I knew within moments that I was turned top to bottom, and inside to out. All the parts of me that had been called beast, wench, wilden, black devil, all softened and slid off me like a snake skin no longer fitting. I stepped out of old scales and emerged blinking and new.

I don't know which came first because many people have asked and I can't find the answer. Did I hear the words of testimony from others and hear the resounding echo in my own ribs, or did my voice call out first, bounce off the souls of others and come back to rattle my own bones? Could the coming of my voice at camp meetings have happened as soon as I joined with all the rest of us drawn on hot summer nights? I will tell you this; when I opened my throat and I told my story, I did not know beginning or end or high or low.

I overheard Mrs. Latourette tell her husband that my voice rang out so loud at the camp meetings that her skin rose

223

up into goose flesh. The old voice of Mau Mau rang in my head, "Keep your voice quiet. It is better not to be heard but to do the listening." I prepared to be chastised.

"She has a way with the word. People stop and listen to her when she sings and when she speaks, they take heed."

"I am sure you exaggerate," he said. I heard a chair scraped into place.

"I am sure I do not," she said as a plate landed on the table with a clatter.

The next day, she asked me if I wanted to meet one of the most famous preachers in the city. She said he was a reformer and I suppose she was right.

My first meeting with Elijah came soon after. He was near fifty and made older by the sadness of widowhood. His hair was parted on the side, and from there, it took its own way, being the well curled sort. It was more gray than brown. His eyes were ashy blue, filled with passions of the spirit, drilling deep into me when we met. We stayed to hear him preach a sermon in his house. Not more than a dozen people filled his parlor.

What struck me most about his home was the lack of finery. There was no upholstered furniture, no pictures on the wall, no mirrors, curtains, or carpets. Despite the lack of these things, I could see that this was a wealthy home. The banisters were carved of rich woods and the doors were thick and heavy. Perhaps only a person who had lived in a dirt cellar could see that this was the home of a man who chose to go poor.

His words turned over in my brain the whole next week. He said churches were meant to be free and he railed against those he called the salt-water elite. They built churches only for those who could pay the dear rental of the pews. None others could attend. "Did Jesus ask people to pay in gold to pray with him? Never! Did He dress in silks and jewels? No! He attended to the poorest, the meanest of souls."

I knew that I wore God thin talking to him in any place I happened to be so I did not need a church to pray, and any fool could tell you that it was wrong to make people pay in gold to sit in a church. But I felt the heat of shame rise to my face about fine dress. I had gone to some great trouble to make my dress as respectable as I could. I wasn't able to do so immediately, but after a year or so, I put together enough money to rid myself of all my old clothes. I wore shoes every day, winter or summer, and my style of dress changed to fit the times. I had one dress made for me, and from that, I was able to see how to sew another one in a similar style. The dresses I wore back at Dumonts' were little more than sacks, flying loose all over. Now my dresses were filled with nips and tucks, pleats on the bodice, pulling close to my body. I wore corsets for the first time, and did not take well to them, but better dresses could not be worn without them. Of course for heavy work, I wore a looser dress and a servant's corset that allowed me to raise my arms. At prayer meetings and church, I wore a good skirt along with a blouse, over which I wore a fitted jacket with bright blue braid up the front. I felt gilded and trussed up like a harlot in his eyes although he never said a word about it.

From the very first, I was drawn to Elijah. He was bold with his words. He scorched the air with his demands for fasting and long, hard prayer. He looked into me and knew me, knew the part of me that loved God.

"God calls to you, doesn't He, Isabella? You are one of those chosen to herald the new day. It is not easy and not for the timid. But then, you don't strike me as timid," said Elijah smiling in his gentle way.

We spent increasingly more time talking after the prayer meetings. Then Elijah came and heard me preach. He heard me speak the words of the Bible as if they were emblazoned on my skin, heard me tell of ways that people trick themselves into thinking that stomping on another's neck is fine if enough gold is gained from it, heard me tell that slavery is the greatest trick that people have played on themselves, and that God wants us to learn more kindness. I was on fire with God.

225

"Isabella, you are the truth of all that I believe. Let us do our work together, side by side," said Elijah. My heart soared.

* * *

When Elijah's servant left suddenly I became his housekeeper and could do the work of the Lord without so many disruptions. Mrs. Whiting offered me more money if I would stay, but I needed to help the Prophet.

"Are you sure, Isabella? I worry that he leaves too much of the earthly life behind him. It's as if he doesn't understand the everyday sort of life."

"He is a prophet and the everyday business is not so important to him," I said.

I also had to tell Mrs. Latourette that I was no longer going to live with them. She took the greatest offense, as if I was forgetting all the goodness that they showed to me.

I became Elijah's housekeeper in the fall of 1831. By then, I had more sense of time. I had started keeping track from my freedom say in 1826, because I was born in true spirit then and my mind opened up. I wanted to learn everything. Elijah said I was like the fastest horse in town; I wasn't happy unless I was going full speed with the bit in my mouth. I would rather not be compared to a horse; those days were over for me. We could talk to each other like that, easy and honest. He said he meant it as a compliment. I said I knew he did but that it wouldn't hurt him to see it from my side.

My work with Elijah pulled away from the Zion Church. It happened without me noticing, but before I could turn around, weeks had gone by without me going to my church, or taking Peter with me. I saw less and less of my son during this time, though he told me that all was well at the carriage apprenticeship and that he had a warm enough place to sleep and plenty to eat. He did come and stay with me on Sundays. Peter was at an age that was treacherous for colored boys. He was a prime target for kidnappers from the south, the heinous black birds, and he was just as much a target for his own foolery. A flicker of warning went off in my head when I watched him walk away one day. It was the same walk that made me call him Little Rooster when he was younger; but it did not wear well on a boy of ten. Now he was one half cockiness and the other half fear. I said a prayer, as I did everyday, that his tortures in Alabama be avenged by Peter growing to a proud manhood.

* * *

I had just returned from a trip to visit my daughters and to pay a visit to the grave of old Tom. He hadn't stayed with Dumont and the girls after I left for New York, for what reason I don't know because Dumont said he would have kept him on. He died in his sleep at the Poor House in the midst of the winter when the Hudson was frozen over. Wouldn't he go and do just what Mr. Dumont said freed blacks would do; up and go to a poor house and die there. Soan died the same winter, after working all night to bring a breech baby into the world. She was as close to a mother as I ever had after Mau Mau died. She must have been ready to die or death would not have found her. I wanted her to live forever, or at least many years longer. That's how it is with the ones like Soan, we forget that death will ever find them. I was orphaned all over again.

If I don't sound sad over the death of my husband, well that is mostly true. I was sad that he got so beaten down and stopped believing that we all had a chance in this life. That's what I was sad about, not his death. Death was a release for Tom. I smoked my pipe a short time over his grave and a long time over Soan's grave. I stuck a circle of crow's feathers over her heart, all standing up straight. When I was done smoking, I tapped my ashes into the middle of the circle. Diana and Elizabeth took Tom's death the hardest and I understood that. Diana knew Tom as her father and the

227

death of a parent goes down hard, like being kicked in the belly every morning before your eyes even open. Peter said he had trouble picturing his father in his mind, but when I told him of his father's death, he clenched and unclenched his fists like he was pumping up his arms for battle. Little Sophia tried to act sad, but Tom had been a thin ghost for most of her short memory.

I returned to the city near the Pinkster Holiday, except I didn't celebrate Pinkster anymore. All the coloreds were letting it go by the way. I'd come to look at the old Pinkster time in a new light. It was when the Holy Spirit came into people. Elijah was preparing to be set on by the Lord; he said I should prepare as well.

I think life would have gone on for a long way with all of us trying to be as perfect in our daily lives as possible, eating simple foods, no butter, cakes, sweetmeats, no coffee or tea. I changed my dress to be plain and modest, no bright strips of ribbon or brocade. On a good week, we might have fourteen prayer meetings in the parlor, stopping only for brief respites to sleep. When we preached on the streets, my voice echoed off the buildings as if we were in a canyon and I could be heard three streets away. Yes, we would have gone on just like that, becoming more and more perfect, heralding the way for the coming of the Lord, going among the sick and the poor and taking away some of their suffering, were it not for the knock on the door in the spring of 1832.

CHAPTER THIRTY-THREE

A shaft of morning light, filled with street dust, illuminated a man in the doorway and I swear that the air around him shimmered. How is it that such men hold their shoulders with such sureness, that their coats hang as if bidden to do so? My breath caught and hovered like a gull over the south port, and all of me wanted to rest with him. My body turned, ever so slightly, to find a point of entry before my mind could catch up and pull back the reins. We stared at each other.

"Is this the house of Elijah Pierson?" he asked.

My body already opened and took in his voice and made a home for his deep, resonant tones. "This is his home, but he is away this morning," I said.

He turned one ear closer to me, no doubt sifting my Dutch accent around. I saw both storm and calm in his eyes. His face softened around the edges and he said, " You're from Albany way. Your Dutch tongue reminds me of home. Am I right about this?"

Already, from the first moment, he wanted to know me, and this was the rope that pulled me in. His beard flowed down to his chest, so unlike the men of Manhattan who were all shaved to a point of daily peril. I put my hand on the doorframe to steady myself and to give me time to adjust to the confusion of his looks that drew a quick comparison to drawings of holy men in the Bible. I pulled tall, my heart beating wildly, surely ready to burst from my dress.

His hair and long beard were dark and dashed with silver. His eyebrows had not been touched by gray and they ran thick and heavy over his dark eyes. He stepped closer to the threshold. I was accustomed to most people looking through me without seeing me until I often felt invisible. I was suddenly seen by this man and the shock of it sent heat to my head and neck.

"Please forgive me. I was so startled by the fond memories that your voice and accent gave to me. My name is Matthias and I have come to call on Elijah Pierson." He held me with his eyes and I did not lower mine. He face softened into a smile. "I am a prophet."

I gathered my voice, despite the unaccustomed sense of being seen and revealed. "I do not know of a Prophet Matthias, but you are welcome to come into the parlor and we shall talk."

I could not believe I spoke to him so, nor that I held counsel with him in Elijah's parlor. His eyes traveled over the room, taking in everything from the mantel to the garden beyond. Who can say why some people stick to us like a burr and others never stay more than a moment? I could not have known that Matthias was already burrowing deep into me and with less than that, Elijah would let him into his house. Elijah folded Matthias into our life without skipping a breath and I have no memory of how it happened, only that there was never a pause from the moment I opened the door until Elijah and I spun around Matthias like Lunar Moths.

The next night, Elijah held a prayer meeting as usual. He preached about the coming of the Lord and the Prophet Matthias. As he spoke, Matthias rose from his seat like a bear rising from a pile of leaves. Elijah handed over the meeting to Matthias. I could not have imagined that Elijah would never preach again, either from his own house or any other. Nor could I have imagined that my own voice would go unheard by the end of the summer.

He spoke with a smooth voice that poured over me. He

told of his search for the deepest meaning of life and heaven. I think he made us laugh once so that the air was filled with the community of us all being in on a clever take on words. Then he grew more serious.

"How can I begin to tell you the most wonderful and fantastical of tales? I have felt the touch of the Lord as sure as the touch of your own hand. I am the Spirit from the Lord, the spirit of truth. We are on the threshold of the end of the New Testament, the time of Christians is dying away and the time of the truth is upon us."

He paused and let his eyes burrow into every person in the room. I worried for him when the silence went on too long. Had he forgotten how to speak? Was he finished, was he a fool? He walked to a window and looked out, turned his back to the audience. Then he whirled around. "The truth should shock you! I was rocked from my feet. But this is the word; all real men will be saved, all mock men will be damned! Elijah is a true man because the Holy Ghost came into him. Know him now by his true name...he is John the Baptist!"

The room filled with lightning air, jumpy and dark. I saw the hair on the man's neck in front of me rise and stand out straight. Everyone looked to Elijah. They had all come because of Elijah and they waited to see if he approved of the bearded man. But Elijah never said a word and Matthias burned through the next few hours in a way that none of us had ever heard before. At the end of the meeting, Elijah came forward and knelt before him.

The crowds of people for prayer meetings grew to fifty or sixty people as word of Matthias spread. Some came to see him as you would a two-headed cow, if ever such a thing was born, and many went away shaking their heads. Others wept and asked for the touch of his hand at the end of the night. I kept to the back of the room. Each night, I felt he spoke directly to me, demanding that I let him guide me to the heavenly world that he described. Each night, I refused him by the thin threads that were left between him and me.

231

This was the problem. Matthias said women were not to preach because the devil sought out women, through no fault of our own, because of our caring nature. The true way was for men to guide women. I had never before seen a man as commanding as Matthias, yet he denied my right to hear the sweet words of God and to speak them to others. I was pulled to him even as I fought my way beyond his grasp, but I remembered when I believed John Dumont too, knew everything that flew through my mind, that no where on earth was a man more powerful and terrible, and at strange turns, given to strokes of kindness. I had cut those ties. So now, to prove that my will was my own, I continued to preach on street corners and camp meetings in open defiance of Matthias. The God I knew was a savior, filled with the deepest love, more love than I could imagine. I always told the story of God leading me from Egypt, from slavery. I ended my meetings in song, never knowing where the song would come from, never knowing the song until it was over.

One night, a boy, ripe with the after effects of cholera, walked up to me. "I feel good when you sing," he said. "Sing more, don't stop now."

I looked into the crowd and on the edge was Matthias, leaning against the side of the building. When I looked back at the boy to say a kind word, Matthias took his leave. When I saw Matthias the next day, he put his hand on my arm and said, "People are moved by your words and your song." I heard a cautionairy note in his voice.

* * *

Matthias's clothes took on a change with the help of Elijah's money. His old coat was given away to the chimney sweep and his own was now a frock of the best green cloth, lined with pink silk, gold braid, frogs and fancy buttons. His shirts were ruffled at the wrists and the throat. His vest was silk, finished off with a blood red sash cinched around his waist. He had two pairs of trousers; one green and the other black.

He wore tall boots and kept them highly polished.

Our food changed in the house from flat bread and dried meat to food so rich that Elijah could not fit into his own trousers in three weeks' time. Suddenly we were filled with butter and cream, cakes and sweetmeats. We were all swept up in the grandeur that Matthias wove.

But it was the talking and the nightly debating about the most important matters that I loved. I cannot tell you the joy of it, Elijah, Matthias, and I, huddled together til late at night, all wrapped in each others words and possibilities, grabbing the world and flaying it open before us.

* * *

Mrs. Whiting sought me out after attending a prayer meeting led by Matthias. She put her hand on mine. "Isabella, I fear he is of a troubled mind that is half tempting to believe. I worry for you and Elijah."

"People have always thrown stones at prophets," I said.

"You have never known me to throw stones. But look yourself. Elijah is giving him money to dress in finery while Elijah himself wears the most plain of frocks. Matthias rides in carriages all day on Broadway while Elijah tends to the poor souls of Five Points. Who truly speaks the word of God?"

With her every word, I needed to protect him more. "We are on the edge of a new world and we must be bold of spirit," I said.

She sighed. "Please be careful. You have come so far. Call on me if you need me." Mrs. Whiting was not the only person who feared that Matthias was a false prophet, but she remained kind to me and did not cast stones at him as strangers did when he walked among them.

He took every chance to sway me. "Fools have always defied the word of God, Isabella. Yet I know you are not among the fools. The light of your soul is bright. I can see it clearly, but it is covered with confusion, led astray in these last days by the Christians. You will come my way, I know it. Your trust in me will be repaid one hundred times."

I thought I stood so firm. I had already endured slavery and the separation of my children, and the death of too many loved ones. I could face any summer storm head on; I didn't know that the storm was coming at my blind side.

CHAPTER THIRTY-FOUR

Matthias accepted an invitation to dwell for a time at the home of Mr. Mills, a plump and wealthy merchant. When Mr. Mill's nephew heard of a prophet living in his uncle's house, he took swift and severe action. Matthias and Mr. Mills were arrested and taken to the prison for the insane, all based on the accusations of the nephew.

Elijah and I worked with a fury, knowing that Matthias faced a dismal life in a hay strewn cell among the lunatics. Elijah spoke the language of courts and magistrates and gained Matthias' freedom.

There was also the matter of Mr. Mills' nephew. We heard that the nephew had no plans of taking his uncle out of Bellevue and that he was going to manage his uncle's money. Perhaps the whole ordeal had less to do with Matthias calling himself a prophet and more to do with a useless nephew who wanted to fill his own pockets.

We drove Elijah's best carriage to the prison. Elijah handed the warden a writ of habeas corpus that he had gotten from a judge. For years after this, whenever anyone had legal problems, I'd tell them to get a writ of habeas corpus. I liked the way it sounded and the way people spun their heads around to hear me say it.

When Matthias came to the front door of the jail after being in prison for two weeks, he stared straight ahead. He was filthy and covered with fleas and lice. I smelled his

235

pitiful condition from across the room. Thankfully for all of us, the carriage had a seat behind ours, for I did not think I could sit close to his stench.

We returned to Elijah's house where I immediately heated water for a bath. I poured the water into the tin tub in the kitchen and left Matthias to do his bathing. When we heard no sound from the kitchen, I went to find him still and grim faced, sitting in the tub. His knees were pulled up with his arms around them. I did not speak but I pulled my hair tight and tied a scarf around it to keep the bugs from getting in my own thick hair and washed him from top to bottom, telling him to stand when I had done all that I could with him seated. Elijah came in and we both worked on the lice, picking them off him and tossing them into a small fire made for just that purpose. Elijah wrapped him in a blanket when we were done.

In the first few days he was meek, and I let him know that no harm would come to him. It pained me to see him flinch at the sound of horses clomping by or an abrupt knock at the door. I fed him strong soup stock and the fruit from the market stalls.

* * *

Peter did not like Matthias from the beginning, but I did not trust the eyes and heart of my son, who was tumbling through more employers than I was prepared to find. Peter grew silent when Matthias was about, flattening his back against a wall, facing the door as if harm would come to him.

"You treat him like he is the highest and you and Mr. Pierson are the lowest," he said. "I don't trust him and I am sorry to tell you that I shall not come to hear his words."

"You are not yet grown and your mother tells you if and when you come."

From August to late spring, Matthias and I lived in one of Elijah's houses and I will tell you only this of our time together. There is no one who knew him in the way I did. I understood his ways from waking to sleeping. He often stopped what he was doing to thank me. "The Lord sent you to me, Isabella. You are my light through the dark days of this world." I glowed in his gratitude. Thanks had come few times in my life.

He woke me in the middle of the night knocking at my door, and throwing it open, stood fierce in his cotton gown. "My kingdom among men will not last long, Isabella. I will stop preaching in two years."

I sat upright in bed. "What will happen? Will you leave us?"

He put his hand on the doorframe. "Of that I am not sure, whether it will be my leaving or that the world will burst to flames. I will be betrayed by those who claim to love me."

"My last year will be 1835. Everything must be in order by then. We cannot wait." He stepped into my room. "If you are with me, then we cannot wait longer for your baptism." He had urged me for months to be baptized. Out of old habits, I stood up. I did not like to have a man standing over my bed, even if it was Matthias.

"Are you ready to join me as a believer, to be assured of your place when all others will be consumed by the crumbling earth?"

I did not want to be left behind, either in flames or crumbling earth. But an old voice rumbled low in my chest. It was the voice I had spoken to since I was a child, who spoke to me when I was lost, who guided others to help me. A low rumble, like the muffle of a far away storm, pounded in my body.

"I told you, I hear a voice inside me and I can't give up on that."

"The voice you hear is mine. I am patient with you but do not wait past my patience."

He left my room and I knew he was past sleeping. By the time I woke to start our breakfast, Matthias had been awake for hours, sitting by the parlor fire.

The house on Clarkson Street held many prayer meetings,

but as the winter wore on, the crowds grew thinner. Matthias said that the faithful were few but strong and he must find the ones who were the strongest.

Among the most faithful were Ann and Ben Folger, who were as rich as any people I'd ever seen. Ann, always on the arm of her husband, led Ben to the front row each night. Ann nodded in agreement to the sermons. After they purchased a farm called Heartt Place, near Sing Sing, a small village thirty miles to the north on the Hudson, we saw them less and less. Elijah and Matthias let their eyes rest on Ann Folger on those rare visits in a way that I thought they should not. Ann never took her hand from her husband's arm, yet her eyes traveled from man to man. As she did, her glance left a trail of men with their fur raised like dogs.

In the midst of summer, Matthias told me he must make a trip and I was not to worry, nor was I to come with him. He was gone for not more than three days when Ann Folger herself came to the door.

"Matthias now lives at Heartt Place. I have come to fetch his clothes."

Ann was a handsomely dressed woman, still young with deep brown hair and with the blue eyes that gave me a start when I saw them on white people. Blue belonged on plates, in clothing, or in flowers.

"Does he plan on coming back?" I asked her.

She smiled. "No. He shall be with us now. He said he has found his new home."

Was this why Matthias' interest in baptizing me had fallen away when the ponds melted? Was this no longer his home? Was I no longer his housekeeper and the one to share his secrets? I wrapped his clothes and tied the package together with hemp cord. I handed the large package to her. "Did he send a message to me?" I asked her.

"No. He has not mentioned your name other than to send for his clothes."

I went that night to Elijah's home to speak with him, to pray with him, to seek solace from him. When I knocked on

Elijah's door. Elizabeth, his daughter, answered. "My father has moved to Sing Sing and I am preparing to go there tomorrow when a wagon can bring more of our furniture."

I was left behind. For days, I did not see the light of the sun. I pulled the drapes and collapsed on my bed. I did not cook. I dared not pray. My own lowliness wrapped thick blankets around me. Were it not for my children, I would have wished never to awaken from a deep slumber. I did not want God to see me with my weakened faith.

I cleared the cobwebs out of the house, thinking that only a few more days were left on the rent. I needed to find a new employer. I took a short handled broom to the doorframe to clear away the soot. A familiar voice startled me.

"Isabella, my kingdom lives and I have need of you."

It was Matthias. Tears pooled in my eyes and I quickly batted them away. "What need could you have of me? Is Ann Folger not taking care enough?" If I could have swallowed my words, I would have.

"It is Elijah. He is having fits. His body stiffens and trembles like a rabid dog and then he is better for a few days. No doubt it is the devil chasing him. You must come and take care of Elijah."

I did not think I would be gone long, perhaps a week. My good friend Elijah was sick with fits. There was little that was done for people with fits, except keep them from crashing into the mantle or chairs and hope that they pass. I would have done anything for Elijah, my gentle friend with his wish for poor people to be treated just as well as rich people.

I stopped at the mirror and straightened my collar. I ran my hands across my face, my lips, around the edges of my ears. Somewhere in the house was rose water. I went to find it to freshen my face, hands, and neck. Matthias waited in the parlor to go with me by carriage to the Folger's house. The early evening promised a fine sunset over the Hudson. The hours in the carriage with Matthias would be mine and his. We had much to talk about.

239

In no time, I saw that Elijah did need me and more importantly, Matthias needed me in his kingdom. As the front door at Heartt Place closed behind me, I entered into a house of seekers, of which I was one of many.

CHAPTER THIRTY-FIVE

The way to tell about my time with Matthias is to skip most of it. That's what some stories do, they skip over water like a smooth stone tossed with a deliberate hand and even though the stone touched down once, twice, three or four times if the person has a good arm, we know all along that the water is there without diving under. I can say that my heart soared too high and that the tumble from the sky was fearful. But for a time, I believed that I was home in a way that I had never been. Home in the heart and in the spirit. Here was gathering of people who dared to let the reach of our searching take the limit.

As soon as we all moved to the Folger's house at Sing Sing, Matthias changed the name from Heartt Place to Mount Zion and the property was put in Elijah's name. The house sat on a rise high enough to see the Hudson to the west. He allowed Ben and Ann to keep reading from the Bible for a short time. They knelt and read to each other from the Bible while Matthias sat stony faced at his place at the head of the table and the air grew thicker than I could stand. Before long, Ben and Ann left the Bible in a locked chest and Matthias let loose with the word of God. We were born anew into the family with Matthias the Father and we were his children.

Matthias was a different sort, and I knew him better than anyone. I don't often try to explain Matthias because once the newspaper men wrote about him, he sounded like a

241

lunatic, a fop who only wore fancy clothes and there was no substance to him, just air beneath his skin.

But here is what he offered me. It was if I was a bird who had never flown before, only hopped along the ground, taking safe glides from branch to ground. And no other birds around me did any different. We could flutter from ground to tree branch and that was our whole world. But Matthias commanded me to soar.

All the other birds said it was impossible, life was all about hopping, pecking, and twittering. But I tried it. I let loose and soared. I kept the feeling, even after he was gone and Mount Zion was folded up flat like a letter in a box.

* * *

Elijah, who had fits now and again, was given the job of walking through the kitchen garden, or so it seemed to me. It was true, he was not suited for field work and Matthias had assigned women to house duties, which left fewer options. Elijah's daughter was given the job of chamber maid, Ann Folger was given the job of dressing her small children, I took over all cooking and the heavy housework, with the help of Catherine Galloway, a white servant who had worked for Mr. Mills.

We all put our money into one pot that Matthias guarded for us. I took the money that I had saved for several years since coming to Manhattan, as well as the few bits of furniture that I called my own and brought them to Mount Zion and handed it all over to Matthias. If I had owned more, I would have given him that as well.

In the first few weeks of living at Mount Zion, I had finally consented to a baptizing in the way that Matthias said the Lord intended it done, in full nakedness. I said only if we did it at night so that I could keep my full nakedness to myself as much as possible.

I put it off until June was halfway gone. We drove to the farmland on the north side of Sing Sing and walked out to a pond that Matthias said called to him as the perfect place. We waited for the sun to run off. A riot of frogs erupted when darkness settled.

"Shame is a sin, and you are without the sin that plagues the hearts of so many," he said as I pulled off my dress, as well as my underskirts, petticoats, corset, and every last stitch. He took off his clothes as well.

"I am ready."

We both walked in the pond and the mud squished between our toes. The night turned cloudy and we were but a dim ghost figure to each other. When we were chest deep in the water, he put one hand on the back of my head and one on my forehead and pushed me back hard so that I went under the water, then he pulled me up just as quickly.

"The word of God is in me and I say you are baptized in the name of the one true God."

After all my stalling for months, it was as easy as that. There was no shame. We were two souls standing in dark water holding hands in the name of God.

* * *

Life at Mount Zion took off at a gallop. Ann started chipping away at me to siphon off all I knew about Matthias. She sought me out, and wheedled words from me that she soon used to put Matthias into a trance. I don't know what would have happened if Ann had kept to her own husband.

At the supper table, we all sat together, and Matthias took those moments to share words that God kept sending on down to him. "The false men in the city run like babies from doctor to doctor seeking cures for their pork filled bellies. The devil grows larger in every one of them who does not seek out the true God."

Before I could reply on the matter, Ann spoke up.

"On this very day, I have poured out all of my tonics. I am making way for the word of God." She looked straight at Matthias, not at her husband Ben. "I believe I have been misguided by doctors and now I see that I am seated in the presence of the word of God."

A fire started in Matthias that had smoldered for months, and for those of us who knew him well, we saw it plainly. I looked at Ben, who held his knife and pointed it at his wife. "You should tell me before you throw away your medicine!"

Ann held Matthias' gaze a moment longer than I thought all of us could stand, then dropped her eyelids in the way that some women do. "Of course Ben, but I was moved by the words of the Father."

And so it went. Each night Ann jumped in at just the right moment to show Matthias how much she knew about his words and each night his fire grew brighter. Ann took to sleeping in my room. Matthias said he was starting to see who was a match spirit for who and that all those married by a false Christian minister were not truly married in the eyes of God. So the women sleep with the women and the men sleep with the men until he got it figured out.

We bathed the same way too, women with the women and men with the men. Except we all took our bath in the kitchen at one time. I expect that if the townspeople knew we were taking baths so regular, they would have thought us peculiar. If they knew all the men and women got naked in our big kitchen and lined up to use the two tin tubs, why that would have caused a disturbance.

The way Matthias saw it was that shame was a sin and he was there to help us with our sins. If we were naked and didn't feel shame, we had tossed off the sin. So every Saturday night the women got one tub ready with hot water on one side of the kitchen and the men got the other tub ready on the other side of the kitchen and both sides tried not to stare at the other; if we did look, we looked straight at someone's eyes or their forehead.

On the Saturday after Ann announced she had tossed her tonics in the dirt, the air at bath time was tight with expectations. All the men had washed but Matthias and it was his turn in the tub. The women were done and Ann, who had been the last to bathe, dressed by the lantern. She suddenly stopped and looked right at Matthias. "Father, shall I wash you?"

The rest of the men had already left the kitchen; the women wordlessly filed out as Ann picked up a washing linen and headed for Matthias. I closed the door behind us. None of us moved from the other side of the door. Catherine and I stood with Elijah's daughter Elizabeth. Ben and Elijah were both on the stairs to the mens' bedrooms but they turned back when they saw us huddled near the door. For the longest time we could hear gentle splashing, then silence. Elizabeth turned to her father and said, "Don't you think the Father is clean enough by now?"

Her words, spoken loud and honest, broke the spell. Matthias emerged clean and wet haired, and appeared flustered. He went immediately to the men's sleeping room. Ann came out, flushed in the cheeks, looking at none of us but at the last place where Matthias passed, as if she could still see him in the air.

Late at night, I sat outside and smoked my pipe, watching the stars travel through the fall. It was my one time to be alone, to think over the day, and to steal a few thoughts of my own. I noticed that ashes needed to be thickly sprinkled in the privy to keep the smell down. I made a mark in my head to remind one of the children in the morning. I headed back inside to close down the house for the night, so that we didn't wake up with chickens walking on the table.

In the parlor, I found Ann and Matthias sitting close in front of the fire, rushing out words in the endless stream that can happen when you think you have found the perfect ears and mouth. As I entered, they both jumped up, looking as guilty as any pair of thieves I had ever seen. Ann followed me to our room and the bed that we shared. She twitched and quivered all night.

Matthias announced that God had spoken to him again and to his great joy, he learned of his own match spirit and that she was here among us. Ben, who had been unhappy without his young wife sleeping beside him, clenched his jaw making tiny muscles leap around his mouth.

Matthias turned to Ann. "Here is my match spirit and she is now the Mother."

What followed were days of debate and fury over the matching of Ann to Matthias. Do not think that we all followed Matthias like sheep as the newspaper men later said. Ben roared. Ann pleaded and cried. Elijah, widowed for too long, asked where he could find a match spirit. As a colored woman well into my thirties, I said that I saw no prospects of a match spirit and wanted none, so I entered the debate without hope of such, nor fear of a wrong match. I made them stop squabbling and I filled the house with my voice (or so Elijah told me later.)

Ann moved to Matthias' bedroom and nothing was the same after that. Matthias and Ann went everywhere together, sometimes with her three children, most often without. The little work that she used to do was given up completely. They took to sleeping in later than farm people ever sleep. Catherine Galloway was not a strong worker but she tried to help me with the heavy labors. What with Ben Folger and Elijah in a state of excitement, they also did less work than before.

But we had days of contemplation when we stopped fretting about match spirits. We had days where we sang and laughed. Of course those are the days that get much less attention when we think back, but I force myself to recall those as well. In the best moments, I felt that I belonged to a family of people who cared for me, who would not cause me harm, and who longed for the spirit of God as much as I did.

In the three months that it took for Ann Folger to wrap herself completely around the senses of Matthias, I found myself backing away from the center of life at Mount Zion and taking the view of a hawk. I kept my eyes open and my talons ready to grab, as I soared over the top of the farmhouse. If I could have, I would have reached my talons onto Matthias' shoulders, pierced his skin for a tight grip, and carried him away until the drunkenness of lust drained out of him and then I would have gone back for Elijah and left Mt.Zion behind.

CHAPTER THIRTY-SIX

Ann and Matthias stayed in bed until midday, calling to me for morning coffee or porridge. Catherine grew clouded over with moods so dark that her work was only half meant. Only when I pressed her for reasons did she tell me that for months, she had looked on Ben Folger as her husband.

"Isabella, I have slept with him for many nights, here and in Manhattan. God came to me in a dream and said he was my true husband."

I threw down a mixing spoon and it bounced on the floor. "Don't you think God has better things to do than to peek into our bed chambers and see who is sleeping with who? The voice you hear in your head is your own!"

Catherine was not alone in her dreaming; Ann had dreams that foretold of a holy child being born from her womb. By the time Elijah told me later in the day that the Lord came to him and said for him to find a spirit match, I kicked over the kitchen chair, grabbed my cloak, and marched out of the house into the snow. I did not come back until late into the night when the edges of my skirts were heavy with ice.

My peevishness was not long lived. I could not take this stand against Matthias any more than I could have denied that God had guided me from slavery. The next morning, Matthias rose early and met me in the kitchen. I was startled by his presence.

"You left us with no supper." He had a blanket wrapped around his shoulders and his breath jumped out in puffs of cloud. The kitchen smelled of cold, damp ashes.

"I think no one went hungry," I said. A fear crept up my spine from the old days. I tried to shake it off.

"You know better than all the rest of them. You know that I wrestle with the burden of God's word, you know that I despair and suffer from all the false teachings that tempt you. You know my word must be law." He came closer to me and dropped the blanket.

"You leave me no choice." His voice rose and before I knew what was coming, his hand snapped my head back. He quickly returned another blow and I dropped to my knees. He picked up the hearth brush and cracked it across my shoulders. I crooked my arm to protect my head.

The words came out of their own accord; I could not bear to be beaten by him and to disappoint him was a more terrible pain than I could have imagined. "Father, forgive me. It is not you I left, but the others." His arm stopped as if pulled tight by a cord.

"Do not make me send you away, Isabella. I need you, do not force my hand against you. The pain of it burns my skin..."

His voice broke and he fell to his knees alongside me. He hung his arms around my shoulders and collapsed in a heap of tears. "I need you, Isabella. Do not leave me."

"I won't, I won't leave you. I can be more patient with the others. God can teach me patience."

His tears stopped. "Let the teaching come from me." He held my face in his hands. "God comes through me and your place is by my side."

Then he did a strange thing. The skin near my eye had split open and blood rose and flowed. He placed a finger on my face and dipped it in the blood, then put his bloodied finger into his mouth. "You are part of me, you are inside me."

Without another word, he pushed himself up, picked up the blanket and walked out of the kitchen. I rose on shaking legs and promised myself that I would try harder for Matthias.

* * *

My greatest trials in the days ahead were Ann and Ben Folger. I longed for the day that both of them would load up their carriage in the middle of the night and ride so far away that their best dog would not be able to track them down. But that was not to be.

All matter of dark waters swirled around us, and none of us could clear our eyes enough to see the danger of drowning. Elijah had fits more than once a week, during which he had started to curse, much to the distress of all. Catherine Galloway grew more muddled by the day with her dashed hopes for Ben Folger. When all the men said they were going to Manhattan for three days, I could barely contain my words of thanks. If they had not, the walls might have fallen down.

With the absence of Matthias, Ann said she could not sleep alone and came to my bed. I wondered if Ann and Matthias did nothing but talk constantly to each other, for Ann could not pause in her talk.

Ann turned her head to me in bed. "He has entered the most holy of holy," she said. "He has entered the sanctum sanctorum. I was made holy and I carry the holy child. I have been cured by the Father in the most wonderful of ways."

I did not know what sanctum sanctorum meant and told Ann so. "It is Latin, but being an unlettered person, you wouldn't understand. But you must guess, my most holy of places." She paused here, narrowing her eyes as if dreaming. "The womb that carries the holy child." So Ann was with child. I did not have long to think on it. She pulled herself closer to me in bed. The night was cold and I did not mind the extra body heat at first.

Peter came only once to Sing Sing. Mrs. Whiting sent him to let me know that he was not harmed in the fires and riots that swept through Five Points. In a wave of pure meanness, men had burned down the schools and churches for blacks and the homes of many. I had not heard of the fires until Peter told me of them. He stood in the kitchen doorway, looking oddly at a point above my left eye. "You are hurt, Mama. What happened to you?"

My hand flew to my face and in a jumble, I pulled far from the truth. "I fell, tripped on my skirts outside." I turned away from my son, never having lied to him before. Here was the child who knew more about being beat than all the rest. This boy must not confuse my beating with the cruelty of a slave master from Alabama.

He was at my side, his hand on my elbow. At twelve years of age, he was not yet up to my shoulder, but I felt the bolt of his young strength for the first time in his grip. "Who did this to you? It was Matthias, wasn't it?" His eyes were wide open, ready to pounce, ready to decide.

I turned full forward to my son. "He is a man of God and I made a mistake and forced his hand. If there is blame, then it is with me." I saw his face change from love and concern to disgust. His chin pulled back, his eyes lingered too long on me.

"This is what takes you out of Manhattan? This is what keeps you from visiting my sisters? To be beaten by a man who calls himself a prophet?"

If there was any child left in Peter, the sight of my swollen eye emptied out the last drops.

Peter and I had gone beyond mother and child and I forced us back. "Remember your place with me boy. You are too young to understand all that you see. Take that look off your face."

He sat rigid and silent for the next hour while I fed him bread and soup. He answered yes or no to my questions. I fought back the sense of being naked and ashamed and yammered on about the freedom of the house and the great work that we were doing. After his bowl was emptied, Peter pushed back his chair said that if he hurried, he could catch the next steamer for which Mrs. Whiting had paid. I would not see him again until mid summer when all the nails blew from the house and the walls fell flat.

CHAPTER THIRTY-SEVEN

If I sound unseen, unheard, like a ghost making my way through Mount Zion, this is partly true. There was naught that I could do or say to change the passions of the household. I stayed because I believed Matthias was a man of God and because I cared for Elijah as an old friend and I feared that his health was worsening. Matthias and I still had our moments together when he was not ripped in two by the stirrings of his heart. In mid July, he sat outdoors with me when I smoked one night, both of us marveling at the clearness of the sky, the sparkle of the stars.

"Are you still a believer Isabella, that the Lord speaks through me, that he guides me to make this life a heaven?"

"You will not get less than the truth from me. I expect you know that. So hear this and know that I am still a believer; passions on earth can cloud even your eyes, even a man of God." I prepared for a sermon on my lack of faith.

"Should a prophet be denied his wife? She is mine, sworn to me by herself."

"Think back before we came to Mount Zion. You preached to all of Manhattan, sending out words of God to all kinds of people. Now you are huddled away with Ann. Elijah grows more troubled by his fits, and the townspeople are bound to come at you once again." We had attracted the attention of the men from Crosby's Tavern who heard stories only half as wild as the truth. Whiskey soaked men had gone

253

home and told their wives what they had heard and what they had made up. Now we could go nowhere without the open stares and taunts of even small children.

He touched my arm and gooseflesh rose up to meet his fingertips, then the palm of his hand. The damp air off the Hudson galloped up the hill and made the summer night cling to us. Matthias asked, "Why do you only smoke your pipe outside?"

I drew deeply on my pipe. "When I was sold for the second time as a child, I was sent a gift from my father. The only thing he had to give me was his pipe. I lived in the barn and my master said that they'd already lost one barn to a fire and that not far away, a nigger had been hung for burning down a house, so I had better smoke outside. I took to it and the way of smoking outside stayed with me."

Matthias shifted, pulled his arms across his chest to warm himself. "I'm not a smoking man. I was once."

"I used to smoke Kinnickkinnick leaf then, or Bear Berry, that's what some called it. Sweeter than tobacco. A slave child couldn't depend on getting tobacco. I could get as much Bear Berry as I wanted, dried it in the barn."

We had rarely talked alone since coming to Zion. So dear to me were the most plain of things: telling of a pipe, gooseflesh touches, a shawl to wrap around my shoulders, sitting in the dark on a summer night. Did I dare try to warn him of the doom that I felt circling us? The words rested on my lips, waiting to hop off.

He must have heard the words that spun in my head. "I know, you think my love is a folly and I cannot bear to hear you say the words, so I ask you, do not say them." This was the old Matthias, the one who knew what I was going to say before I said it. He closed his eyes and a shudder went through him. "The world will come to a fiery end by 1835. Many will turn against me, and even you, even you and I will take different paths."

I jumped up. "I will never turn against you! Do not speak of this."

"I have seen it. You will leave me too. There is work to be done before we go up in flames. I cannot rest."

"Now I say your sight is wrong and you do not know me as well as you think. I did not survive slavery, see two husbands die of broken spirits, to be put off so easily."

He opened his eyes. "Sit longer with me, Isabella. Do not leave me yet. I am soothed by you."

CHAPTER THIRTY-EIGHT

I first noticed a dramatic change in Elijah one evening when the Father was absent for several days. Elijah came to the supper table and instead of sitting at his own place next to me, he sat at the head of the table. His hair was a tangle, as he had refused to bathe with the rest of us on the evening past

"I am a man of God. A minister. I have been so for years. If I cannot preach, I will wither. I am sitting in the rightful place for me and if Matthias knows of this, then let him strike this house with lightning."

We all flinched, tightening up for the crack of thunder surely to come, blowing us from our chairs. When none came, Elijah began to preach, as in the old days, until a fit came over him. The fits tightened up his muscles, cranking hard on them, pulling his arms into spasms and twitches. His head jerked around to one side and his eyes rolled up, showing us the whites. We had come to accept the fits without such a scare as when they first started.

But this night his fit took a disturbing turn. One of Elijah's hands danced in his pants, opening his buttons, clutching himself, and he spoke in strange words, his eyes rolled back. We sat frozen, except for Elizabeth, who ran from the room covering her ears. The blood drained from Ann's face, her fork clattered to the floor.

"Control yourself man!" shouted Ben.

Elijah had worked open all the buttons on his pants and

his cock was straight up for all of us to see. I stood and slapped him hard in the face and threw a glass of water on his hand that worked fearsomely in his pants. Still, he did not return to his senses.

"Ben, help get him to another room."

We hoisted him, each of us grabbing an arm and dragging him to the parlor. We put him on the rug in the center of the room. He turned on his side, his hand locked on to his man parts and with a shudder that shook even his feet, he was at last quiet. Ben and I stood outside the door and looked at each other.

"I do not recognize my friend," he said.

"He does not recognize himself," I said.

Elijah slept solidly until the next day. I had covered him with a summer quilt before I went to bed. He rubbed his arms as if they had stiffened into wood.

"Why was I left sleeping on the floor?"

I did not spare him the cruel truth of his actions; I recounted for him the bad turn of his fit and the shame of his sin.

"No. I was preaching, no more than that." His eyes showed no trickery. He did not know.

"You were seen and heard by all of us. If you think I am lying, ask Ben, Ann, or if you dare, your own daughter."

At the mention of his daughter, his legs crumpled, sending him to a chair. "What is happening to me? I am a man of God."

He made me promise to slap him hard again, take him away if the devil tormented his soul. But the torment did not stop. With the return of Matthias, the fits only grew worse, leaving Elijah with sunken eyes.

* * *

The garden was surrounded by good dark blackberries. More often than not, if Elijah went picking, more ended up in his mouth, on his beard and fingers, than in the bucket. His trips out to the berry patches were a sign that his mind was clearing, that the old Elijah was coming back to me. If you believe the courts and the newspapers, they say it was July 28 when Elijah brought a bucket into the kitchen, filled with blackberries and handed them to me.

"All is not lost, I've some use left. This is my contribution to supper." He put the bucket on the table and he paused as if caught in the air the way birds look sometimes, wanting to go forward yet staying in the same place. We all ate the berries at supper, except Matthias, who was peevish about not being served first. I ate my fill, I always do, not that you'd ever know it to look at me. So did Ann and Ben. Elijah ate a handsome dish of berries with fresh cream, more than the rest of us. I was on edge, hoping that his fits would not come over him at the table, for those were the worst. His fit did not come at supper.

The next day Elijah appeared stronger than he had in months. He went out into the fine morning sun, reaching for more berries as he worked. I did not see him when he collapsed, but Elizabeth was in the garden when he hit the ground. By the time I was summoned, he lay on his back, his beard covered in purple vomit.

None of the rest of us took sick, only Elijah. He went to bed, gradually getting weaker in the next few days, losing everything that can shoot out of a body, so that no one but me would tend him and even I could barely stand the stench. If a person gets sick enough, or if the smell is bad enough, you can be sure that a colored woman will be tending. Ann did ask to have a doctor sent in, I'll give her that. Both Matthias and Elijah said no; prayer and prayer alone would be the cure.

In the end, I slept on the floor near Elijah, wiping him down, dripping water onto his lips, cleaning his sheets that he soiled like a baby, holding him when the last of the fits threw his body into knots that tried to break his bones. Matthias came in once to the hot bedchamber and slapped Elijah hard with the palm of his hand to bring him back from the grips of the devil.

Elijah died while I cut the hay. We were in the field the whole of the morning and Matthias would not let me go back to tend to Elijah. "Let the devil work his way out. We will pray for him at supper." He turned back to his work.

Ben called from the house. "He's dead! Elijah is dead!"

CHAPTER THIRTY-NINE

Elijah's death scattered us; each to their own safety. When last I saw Mount Zion, Elijah's brother was closing up the place preparing it for auction.

I returned to the city and contacted my old employer Perez Whiting. He and his wife welcomed me back without question and said that in all the city, they did not know of a better housekeeper. I had not heard simple words of encouragement in so long.

Mrs. Whiting read to me every day from the newspaper in the afternoon before Mr. Whiting came home. The heavy work was done by then and we both needed to put our feet up. The newspapers were filled with gossip, I can't call it much better than that, about Matthias and our time on Mount Zion. The reporters flocked around Ann and Ben Folger and took what they said as truth.

"Read me some more lies," I said to Mrs. Whiting.

"Oh, Isabella, can you bear to hear more? Spare your ears, be glad for once that you cannot read." I kept after her until she read every word that was printed in the Sun.

"Matthew Roberts, commonly known as Matthias the Prophet, stands accused of theft. Mr.and Mrs. Folger accuses the man of stealing $525 from them and defrauding them of an unknown amount of their fortune. He is suspected also in the murder of Elijah Pierson, who died under suspicious circumstances in August of this year. A negro woman,

Isabella, who was a servant to the group, lives under a mantle of suspicion in the murder." Mrs. Whiting put down the newspaper.

"Not one newspaper man has asked me what happened, not one, and I know the truth!" I said.

"They will take only white evidence," she said. The newspapers could drag my name through the worst of garbage, all on the word of a white person, but they would not come to me to find what my eyes saw.

Matthias was arrested and put in Bellevue, and the first thing the newspaper men did was to publish what Matthias said when he was asked questions by the police. I thought it a peculiar thing how wild words could sound in the newspaper, when I knew that Matthias was no more wild in his thoughts than a good many people. Who was more insane, Matthias who said he was a prophet or the mobs of people who burned down black churches and homes in Five Points earlier in the summer? Men from the mobs told white families to light a candle and hold it close by their face while standing in the window and they would know not to burn down their house. Now those are the words of someone who is mad as a rabid dog.

Mrs. Whiting kept me informed about the local talk about Matthias.

"Your Matthias does not help himself by what he says. Must he say that he is the prophet of God or that the city of New York will burn to the ground if he is convicted? He only harms himself further."

"He is the prophet of God." This was a point that found no rest between us. I could not be moved from my faith and she could not be moved from her doubt. But she never wavered in her support in me.

I stood accused, by rumors and newspaper stories that came straight from the devil himself, of stealing money from the Folgers and poisoning Elijah. I wished that I could talk with Elijah. I missed him, the way he was before we all went and lived at Mount Zion for the year. I was wild with anger

261

that anyone would think that I would poison my friend. But it was not me who New York wanted to hang, it was Matthias. I was not worth the bother.

Work kept my brain from burning up with the bitterness of hate. The Whiting family would never have laundry as clean, their lanterns were never smudged with black soot, and there were no ashes on their hearth. Mrs. Whiting said that if I washed the floor one more time, we would be standing in the cellar. After several weeks of worsening rumors and floors washed to splinters, Mrs. Whiting called me into the parlor.

" I have a dreadful fear for you. Ben Folger bought space in the paper to tell the story his way. This is getting worse by the minute," she said. The words brought me to my knees. He told the most terrible falsehoods, how Matthias tricked him into believing that he was a prophet, how he threatened them, forced them to live in unholy ways and finally how Matthias had swindled them out of their family fortune. And he said I was party to all of the evil events.

"Let me talk with my husband about finding a lawyer for both you and Matthias."

* * *

That evening, Peter came to have supper with me.

"Mother, did you really serve poison blackberries to Mr. Pierson? I hit another boy who said you did." His eyes were wide and his lips trembled. He suddenly looked small again, like I could hold him on my lap.

"Where would you get such an idea?"

"I heard the men talking at the carriage house. They said Mr. Folger said you tried to poison a houseful of white people. They told me to be careful what I ate." I could see that it pained him to tell me this. He was hurt from the shame but still trusted me enough to tell me. I grabbed both of his hands in mine.

"Listen to me. I have never lied to you. I moved a

mountain to get you back from Alabama. I am telling you that Elijah was my friend, but he was sick for a long time. Peter, I have no need of poisoning anyone, least of all a friend. As for the Folgers, they aren't worth the trouble. That is the truth."

Peter and I ate squash soup with plenty of onions and turnips. I asked Mrs. Whiting if Peter could stay the night and she welcomed him with a blanket. He slept on the floor next to my bed and I watched him sleep. It was terrible to know that the talk of the town was a lie about me, but far worse was the look on Peter's face, the wrinkle of doubt and fear that lingered near his eyes. I could not bear to have my children hear such vile rumors.

* * *

Perez gave me an introduction to a lawyer named Western. The October sun warmed my face on the walk downtown. I was already wearing a path in the cobblestones from Mrs. Whiting's house on Canal Street to Mr. Western's office. The first three times I sat in his office, I talked and he wrote down what I said.

"It is important for you to tell me the truth, exactly what happened," he told me on the first day.

"You will get nothing less from me," I said.

Sometimes his hand cramped up. We decided that he would hold up his left hand when I should stop so that he could rest. He put his pen down and waved his right arm around to get the blood moving and then we were off again. He asked particular questions about Elijah's fits, when they started, what they looked like, and how I took care of him toward the end.

"I tried to keep death away, but he got sicker no matter what I did."

He looked over his glasses. "We will get another autopsy report. Elijah was a sick man for more than a year. Your care gave him comfort in his last days."

Well that undid me. I put a hand up to my face to hide my tears. Then I had to use both hands. Mr. Western was the first person to notice how much I cared for Elijah except for Mrs. Whiting.

"Oh here now. You are upset and it is my fault."

His face was soft, sort of loose skinned like some dogs are, without much for eyebrows. The hair on his head was giving way to baldness and what was left was a coffee and cream color. One eye was green-blue and the other was blue-green. He gave me his handkerchief. When I came to the end of the story, he took off his glasses and leaned back in his chair. "No wonder Ben Folger is accusing Matthias and you. If the truth of this story gets out, he will look the fool and he and his wife will be banished from society in New York."

"Can he tell newspapers lies about me? Is there nothing that I can do?"

"Ben Folger is a bigger fool than I imagined. Yes, you have a right to protect your name Isabella. We are going to sue him for slander." He took out his pen and dipped it into the ink well. "Let me tell you what the Folgers are trying to do. Ben Folger wants his foot back in the door of the good society of New York. To do this, he must show your character to be at fault. In short, he will call you a liar, a cheat, even a devil. He knows that you are loyal to Mr. Matthews and you will speak kindly of him. He also knows that you have the truth of what happened and that you witnessed the shocking behavior of his wife. If the world thinks you are a liar, your words will matter little in defense. As a negro, there are inherent problems with your testimony. We will find white evidence to back you up. To start with, we will need certificates of character from your past and present employers. Can you obtain letters to this effect?"

"All of my employers, save one, will tell you that my work was honest and long. Only Mr. Latourette, who was disturbed when I left his employ to go work with Elijah, will not speak well of me. He swore he would never write a letter for me."

"Then we shall not ask him. It might be a sin of omission, but such sins are not law."

* * *

I traveled north to New Paltz and Kingston, welcome for even a brief time to see my daughters. When I heard that Sally was visiting relatives in Rochester, I let out old stale air from my chest that I hadn't known was there. I had not wanted to see her look of pleasure about my circumstances of public scorn.

I grabbed hold of my daughters after the two younger ones got over their shyness. Diana had been sick with fevers over the summer and her skin carried a dry and sorry tone.

"Diana, you go sit down and stop minding these two little girls. They are coming with me to find you some strong mint to cook up along with whatever else I can find." Elizabeth and Sophia galloped behind me, showing me this or that. When I found a green patch of mint that the frost hadn't blackened, we gathered all that we could. Sophia stood as close to me as she could get and I gathered in her smell. "Should I call you mother? Sometimes we call Big Sister our Mother."

I wrapped my arms around her and I did not cry. "Yes, you should call me mother. But Diana is the one who wakes every morning with you and sees that you have clothes and food and that you are well." I paused, wondering what I could offer them when I could not touch them at night as a mother should, or guide them or scold them. I sat on the ground and pulled them both to me. "I want to tell you about your grandparents, Bomefree and Mau Mau..." I sat with them telling them stories that Mau Mau told me. I was only getting warmed up when Diana found us and said that Mr. Dumont had just come home.

Mr. Dumont listened as I told him of the treachery of the Folgers and the sad death of Eliljah. "He died of fits? Well the man was ailing for over a year with fits. Ben Folger

265

agreed to his wife bedding down with another man? Ben Folger wants to look better than he deserves and your friend Matthias is far past peculiar. But Bell, how did you end up in the middle of this storm?"

Before I knew it, Mr. Dumont had dragged out two old chairs from the barn and we sat facing the river as the wind carried a chill from the north. I wrapped my shawl around my shoulders. Sophia stood at the door to the barn, pretending she wasn't listening to every word. At times he interrupted me to ask a question. "You gave him all your money? Did you take part in any of the match spirit foolery? Tell me again what he wore on his head?" As always, I told him the truth. When I was done, he told Sophia to bring us some new cider and I took notice that her bare feet were scuffed and thick soled as mine had been when I was a child.

In the end, I got certificates of character from Mr. Dumont, Isaac Van Wagenen, two of the lawyers in Kingston, and Mr. Whiting. When I returned to New York City, even Mr. Webster was startled by the letters.

"You only failed to get a letter from God himself."

"God is too busy keeping an eye on the likes of Ben Folger so he doesn't do any more harm."

Mr. Western accused Ben Folger of slandering me. He said that Ben did not have the right to ruin my good name. He offered as evidence the letters I had collected. I was not permitted to testfiy, but Mr. Western read my testimony and gave situations where people said the same thing as I did, all to prove that my words were true. The court made Ben pay me $125 for the damages that he had done to me. I thought Mr. Western's face was going to split apart with his smile.

"This is a good day Isabella, a good day for all of us. Now, let me get to work. The trial against Mr. Matthews is only one month away."

Two days before the trial was to start, Mrs. Whiting received a note from Mr. Western which said, "The trial is postponed until spring. The judge has taken ill and cannot leave his bed. Ann Folger is ill with chicken pox after the birth of her daughter." I stared hard at the note, marveling that so big a message could fit on the small, crisp page.

"Maybe this will give everyone a chance to forget Matthias and this charlatan will be forgotten," said Mrs. Whiting.

I stormed at the sudden rebuke from the usually gentle woman.

"He is no more of a charlatan than ministers who force people to pay rent to sit in a pew, no more so than the new preachers who spring up everyday, and he is trying only to bring the word of God to people. I think my faith is made of a stronger weave than yours, I am sorry to say."

"You are new to the power of charlatans and imposters. Most of your life was spent under the yoke of slavery. It is no fault of yours that you were taken in by Mr. Matthews, but you must begin to open your eyes." Her face was flushed red and the air between us was thick.

"You know little of my years of slavery if you think that I never met a charlatan before! Tell me if slavery is not the worst charlatan of all time, tricking white people into thinking they can own another person, that dark skin makes a lesser soul. And tricking black people into believing that there is no hope in this lifetime, that we must wait until we are dead to be free! Matthias brought words of freedom, that this lifetime is the heaven and he has come to make it so." I walked out to clear my head, hoping for cold winds to soothe me. When I returned we spoke no more of Matthias for days.

CHAPTER FORTY

In the winter evenings while I waited for Matthias' trial, I knitted two pairs of mittens for myself with liners, then I did the same for Peter. I hoped that Diana was teaching the two younger girls to knit. I took to walking outside to smoke my pipe, even on the cruelest nights of February. I lit the clay pipe, then I wrapped a scarf around my head to keep my ears from freezing, put my mittens on and stepped out into the night to have a few words with God. It had been a long time since I spoke to him directly. I told Him about losing my way, that I feared I was losing faith with the prophet.

Ben Folger did not use the winter for good works as most folks do. In February, Mr. Western sent a note to me through Mrs. Whiting. "Please be so kind as to warn Isabella that Ben and Ann Folger are helping Mr. Stone write a book about her and Matthias with the aim of prejudicing the citizens of New York against them. The book is not yet complete and we can only hope that it will remain unfinished until after the trial."

"Has everyone lost their senses?" said Mrs. Whiting with a voice more shrill than I had ever heard from her. "This Mr. Stone who I have heard to be a sour man, is writing a book about you and your Matthias? He has done so without any fact from you at all!"

I attempted to reassure her. "Who will give money for such a thing? Let's pay no mind to a book of lies." I could not have been more wrong. By nightfall of the next day, young Peter came breathlessly to the kitchen door, free of his duties at the carriage house for the evening.

"Mother, there is a book being written about you! Everyone is talking about it!

They say all the trouble in the world today is from the likes of you. But it's not true." And my big, tall boy took to crying.

"There can be no truth to a book when the foundation for it comes from Ben and Ann Folger," I said as I took his wool cap from his head and handed him a rag for his tears. To keep his mind away from the book, I gave him several lanterns to clean and I filled him up with soup before he left for the night.

* * *

In the days before the trial, I thought often of Elijah. I remembered the pull of his voice, the sureness of his hand on my shoulder, and how we had been matched, step by step, in our preaching. Yet not one person in the courtroom would know of this friendship, only that Elijah was dead.

The mud in April was fierce and thick when the ice finally melted. We gave ourselves plenty of time to get to White Plains for the trial and took up lodgings. A kind family from the Methodist Church was called on to give me a room when the local innkeeper turned me away. The innkeeper simply said, "I'll not have a nigger sleep here and surely not one who is a murderer."

The next day the courtroom was filled with the scratch of pencils as reporters scurried to write down everything about Matthias from his hat to his boots and his beard, which was once again full and long. I noticed that his beard had turned completely white since I first met him three years earlier. The desire to stand between him and his enemies was so strong that I rose part way out of my seat, and then with my heart pounding, I sat down.

The first day of court was taken up with the judge

269

deciding if Matthias was insane or not. He was sent off with doctors who came back and said he was peculiar, but not mad. The second day of court, Mr. Western brought in three doctors who had looked at Elijah's stomach after he had died.

"What is your conclusion regarding the cause of death of Mr. Pierson?" Mr. Western asked each doctor in turn.

One by one they answered, "I came to the only scientific conclusion that remained to me; Mr. Pierson died of natural causes."

I allowed myself a smile, not a big one, but a true smile. Matthias was innocent of poisoning Elijah. And if Elijah died from his own ailments, then I could not be accused of a crime. Mr. Western only had Ben and Ann left

Ben was called first. He leaped from the straight backed pew when his name was called and he was sweating by the time he was sworn in. "No, sir," he said over and over. "There was nothing at all suspicious in the ways of Matthias, except his peculiar views on religion which I momentarily looked into."

The last witness was called. The courtroom grew so quiet that I could hear the rustle of Ann's clothes from half way across the room. She wore a fine light wool skirt of the deepest blue with a matching jacket fitted snug across her chest with the big sleeves that all the fashionable women wore. Her skirt was helped along by a stiff horse hair ring on the bottom and her ribs were held tight by a corset that Catherine must have tied with all her strength. When she sat in the witness chair, she gave Ben a look of devotion, then tipped her head down slightly and lowered her eyes. The late afternoon sun shone in the west windows, getting in Ann's eyes so that she had to hold one gloved hand up to shield them.

The prosecutor, Mr. Nelson went first. Ann told the story from the start of her time with Matthias, and for the most part, I can't say that she lied, she just left certain parts out; how she sought after him and ran her hands across his chest in full view of her husband and me. He asked if she had children, how long she had been married, what church she went to before moving to Sing Sing, and if she was a Christian woman.

"Oh, I have always been a Christian woman and always will be. But I understand now how people can be led astray." By the time she was done, the sun had moved across the room and the newspaper men looked at Ann with soft eyes. I could have snapped her in half.

Mr. Western went next. "Were you not called the mother of the kingdom?" he asked her. And by the time he was done leading her through her story one more time, by a different path, she was also beaded up with sweat. With each question, Mr. Western let her know without saying as much, that he knew everything about the kingdom.

On the third and last day, the jury returned and gave their decision to the court.

"Robert Matthews is found not guilty of poisoning Eliljah Pierson." Shouts of anger dotted the air and I feared that a riot would erupt. Mr. Nelson jumped up.

"We have an additional charge against Mr. Matthews of assaulting his daughter."

There wasn't one man on the jury who cared about a daughter being whipped by her father, but if this was the only way to punish Matthias, then this was the road. So this was how he was finally convicted. He had beaten his daughter once at Zion, it was true, but he was convicted because the world wanted his hide.

The judge ruled on the end of the third day. "There shall be nothing in your favor, sir. This court will be severe with you. You led a group of people of normal bearing into a life that is too indelicate to speak of in proper society. I give you the harshest penalty that I can for the crime that can be proved. My advice to you, if there is any hope for you at all, is after you have served your imprisonment, to go to work like an honest man, leave off with your doctrines, and shave your beard."

Matthias was given one month for contempt of court, and

three more for the beating of his daughter. He had already spent seven months in prison. He would be released, at long last, by the end of summer and I would be there waiting for him. My doubts about him were nothing compared to my loyalty.

CHAPTER FORTY-ONE

On the day of Matthias' release, I was ready for him, waiting with a horse and wagon. Mr. Whiting permitted him one night in the house as a kindness to me. That night Matthias took me into his confidence. "This is no place for us, Isabella. The west winds are calling me. I need to find heaven away from the dark minds of those who call themselves Christians. There is no freedom in New York."

He didn't ask me but I said, "I'll come with you. Surely there is a place in the west for my children and me?" My memory fades here, I am not sure of his answer

When I left Mrs. Whiting's house the next morning she said, "I will go to my grave without understanding the hold that this man has on you. End it now, do not go further with him." She held both my hands in hers and implored me with such a look. Peter had come the night before and brought me a new pipe and a bit of tobacco. He and I spoke not a word of Matthias.

I did not tell her my dreams were filled with Bomefree and Mau Mau cursing me and banishing me from their home and that I woke in sweat and tears. I did not tell her that I feared being brave enough to stand by Matthias as we built the Garden of Eden. Instead, I covered my fear with stubborn plodding and I closed my ears to her as best I could. We left by coach the next day, traveling north, then west.

I was strangely at peace sitting next to Matthias in the

coach. He had dusted off his green trousers and shined his black boots. His pink vest showed frayed threads around the buttonholes. My devotion to Matthias when he was in prison made me feel like I had nursed a sick child for the best part of a year and finally, he was well again. I allowed myself to close my eyes as we bumped along the well worn road, kicking up a brown ribbon of dust behind us.

A woman with a tightly woven cotton dress sat across from us with her daughter, a girl with a strained expression on her face, perhaps from illness. When I opened my eyes, I saw that Matthias watched them. "You've no way of knowing madam, but I am Matthias the Prophet and this is one of my believers, Isabella."

The woman swallowed hard and let her eyes dart to her daughter. "It is our pleasure, sir." I could see that she hoped the conversation would end right there. She pulled out a small sampler for her daughter to work on, undoing a few careless stitches.

"False men kept me in prison, but they could not hold me in their deviled caverns. Only a prophet could walk away as I did. Do you travel to meet your husband?"

She looked up and his eyes caught hers, long enough for her to turn as red as Matthias' cummerbund. She nodded yes.

"In my world, no woman would travel alone. When I bind a man and woman together, their spirits are forever knotted. While we travel together, allow me to offer such care and protection that a husband might offer."

"Your offer is generous, but my daughter and I are safe enough with the Lord's blessing."

He leaned forward, bringing his face, close enough that she pulled her head back.

"Do not go down the road that has led so many of your sisters astray. Do not attempt to grasp the word of the Lord from Christian ministers, they are false men of evil institutions. Worse yet, do not consider knowing God by your self. The way is through a true man." Matthias pulled back again, and looked long at the woman, until she turned her head to look out the window. Hearing his words inside the coach gave them a different ring, like a bell with a broken clapper. I squirmed and fought the urge to explain what he meant, and that he was not so queer as he sounded. I did not know if it was I who had changed in the year or if it was Matthias.

If the ride was not marked by calamities of the road, Matthias might have preached to the woman endlessly, releasing all of his unchained thoughts. But the wagon ride had not gone far when we were forced to stop because one of the horses threw a shoe and had to be replaced. The stage had not taken us far after that when one of the wheels cracked a spoke hitting a stretch of road badly rutted from rain. It was late in the day, but our delays were many, so we had covered only half the distance intended. We were too far from the last town to walk and nightfall was already coming on us. The driver could not have been much older than Peter and I thought that he had been sent when there was still too much child in him. He looked weary from all the mishaps and worried that he would be blamed. We were given the choice, sleep in the carriage, or walk to a barn that was a mile or so back the way we had just come. Matthias chose for us.

"I've slept confined for too long. The walk to the barn is a trifling. Young man, will you be staying with the coach?"

"Yes sir. The horses and I will be here. Tomorrow, I'll take one of the horses and ride ahead to find a man to make repairs."

Matthias and I stretched our legs after climbing out of the carriage. I ached to take off my corset. I'm sure that if you come to corsets late in life like I did, you never get used to them.

When we got to the barn, the four of us settled into the main floor. The mother and daughter arranged themselves near a pile of clean hay and then stretched a blanket over it. I stepped outside to smoke my pipe. The fog rolled in making sounds carry loud and far.

"Madam, do you need my coat over you for the

evening?" Matthias offer the woman, a Mrs. Clayburn.

"No thank you."

"You'll sleep untroubled here. I speak the word of the Lord and you are one of the lambs who are protected in my presence." They had forgotten me for the moment, and that I had ears because I was out of sight.

"Is the colored woman you travel with your slave, or your servant? Is she protected in your presence as well?"

I put down my pipe, and thumped the bowl of it into my hand as I anticipated his answer. I waited for her surprise when she heard of my stature with the Prophet, waited to hear his gratitude to me for finding him the only lawyer in Manhattan who was able to keep him from being hung, waited to hear him explain my loyalty and my closeness to God. I was prepared to be humble.

"I've been bringing her along. I saved her from a life of sorrow and ignorance. We must be compassionate to all creatures," he said.

The fog wrapped tightly around my head and made my ears buzz. My mouth took on the taste of nails.

"Is it compassion to let one such as that carry on with the grand airs of refinement? Truly, she has given me a fright."

"Does she frighten you? I assure you, she is under my complete control and will do whatever I tell her to do."

"Still, I do not think that I shall be able to sleep with her near me. There has been too much trouble with the coloreds and I do not trust them."

I pulled open the door and let the fog rush in with me. Matthias leaned against a beam that was as wide as my outstretched fingers. With a shudder, I remembered just such a post when I was whipped for not speaking English.

"Isabella, it is best for you to sleep outside this evening. I saw a tidy shack by the road that should keep you warm for the night." He turned away from me and nodded to Mrs. Clayburn. A crush of knowing hit me hard in the chest, solid and thick and my ribs felt ready to crack.

"If you send me out, do not expect to see me when you

rise."

His head spun back to me. "Do you dare to threaten me! Who are you but a woman I saved from Christian fools who would still keep you in bondage?"

I took two steps toward him. He put his hand on a hayfork that leaned against the wall. Mrs. Clayburn yelled, "She'll kill us, she'll kill us all!"

I paid no heed to her. She was no more bothersome that a fly on my supper. My life was held in the air between Matthias and me, hovering in the fog and the dust from the hay. Both of us were ready to strike.

"Do not go against my word or you go against God. Get out of this barn! Do as I say!" His voice went straight into my bones and moved them around, shaking them into pudding.

"Then I will go no further with you. You walk without me." I wanted to say more but part of me was afraid that God was going to strike me down and the other part was so filled with rage that I could feel his throat crush under my hands. I backed out of the barn.

My blood changed course on the night I stood outside the barn, when Matthias scorned me. There have been many times that I have let the righteousness of rage come through my voice. My own children said they worried not that I would whip them but that I would kill them with my tongue. But any sound that I could make was too frail to form the word "betrayal." So I let my blood thunder, let my breath come back into me and pushed myself from the splintered barn wood door. I could not say further words of parting to Matthias. I thought only to get away.

I walked back to the coach, gliding on the bitter power of grief, and recovered my satchel. The coachman never stirred, and I turned east and began the walk which took me three days, back to Canal Street, back to Mrs. Whiting.

277

CHAPTER FORTY-TWO

I stayed in bed for two days, or so I was told. As soon as I came fully to my senses, I got up, not knowing that time had slipped by. Mrs. Whiting must have heard my feet hit the floor boards, for the latch clicked on the chamber door before I could fully stand. I wobbled and Mrs. Whiting took a firm grip on my arm and said, "You'll fall like a rock if you try to stand." I looked down at my feet, which had suddenly sounded an alert, and took note of blisters that had been sliced through to let out the hot juices. I felt no red hot lines coming up my legs so I knew that Mrs. Whiting had kept them clean.

I remembered shreds of walking back to Canal Street, seeing the front of their house and seeing Mr. Whiting coming up the street. And then no more.

"Isabella, I've tended many sick people, but none so wild as you. I feared you lived every hardship over ten times again in the last two days. I had to move the water pitcher far from the bed to keep your arms from crashing into it."

It was clear that Mrs. Whiting had tended to me after my long journey back to Manhattan. Her eyes were circled with shadows and lines of worry brought her eyebrows close together.

"I need to wash myself," I said.

Her husband brought a pitcher of hot water to the room and after he left, Mrs. Whiting helped me bathe. She brought

278

me to a straight backed chair. She was such a small woman that I could easily rest my hand on her shoulder while she gave me sturdy support. I let my sleeping gown drop to my waist and she dipped the linen cloth into the water, caught up some soap from the jar and began to run the cloth over the front of my shoulders, and then moved around to the back. She stopped and I turned my head to see what was wrong.

"Oh Lord," she said. She was face to face with the patchwork of scars on my back.

"That was long ago when I was a child. The pain of it was more than I thought I could bear. If I had known then that I would live to endure a far greater pain, I could not have lived. It is a blessing that we don't know what lies ahead."

She put her hand on my shoulder. "Matthias is finally behind you. But I see that he was not the worst of your tormentors."

With each passing day, I felt layers of my old life with Matthias fall off like thick scabs, always falling off too soon, pulling fresh new skin that did not have a chance to take root. By late fall, I was left with the freshest skin and even a breeze or a glance rasped me deeply.

I struggled in the darkest of places, one day feeling foolish for ever believing him, the next thinking myself abandoned by him. To be abandoned by the Prophet, the Father, who would create a heaven on earth as no other, sent me to a barren land. If we live only due to hope, then I do not know how I survived. I would not go to the John Street Church as Mrs. Whiting suggested. If they were Christians, and Christians had tormented Matthias, then I had no room for Christians and their churches.

"But you have said yourself that the Methodists gave you the greatest welcome," said Mrs. Whiting when she found me sitting up from another sleepless night. "They will receive you again. You must find a port and come back from the storm that threatens you."

I did not go north to visit my daughters during this time, nor did I go to see my son Peter. When he came to visit with me on Sunday evenings, he did not try to speak with me, giving up after weeks of my mumbled responses. He came and sat, brewed me tea, and left when the fire grew low. He stopped all his mischief during this time, and did not steal an apple or a candle.

When frost could be seen late into the morning, Perez Whiting handed me a package about the size of my palm, folded paper tied with string. "Tobacco," he said. "I don't smoke myself, it upsets my stomach, but I hear it is soothing to some." I slid it into the pocket on my apron. When I was done setting up the wood for the evening, I gathered the parcel of tobacco from Perez, took my pipe, wrapped a coach blanket around me and stood outside, and lit my pipe with a thin stick from the kitchen fire. For a moment I smelled the skin of Bomefree, his old feral scent thick in his coat, and saw his gnarled fingers bringing his pipe to his cracked lips. I pulled the smoke through the pipe and into my mouth, holding and cooling the swirl of gray, then letting it drop down deep into my body. Finally, I poured the smoke from my lips into three perfect rings that chased off into the night.

Perez brought home the book by the rascal William Stone and it was filled with lies about me and Matthias, all to benefit Ann and Ben Folger. Mrs. Whiting read the book to me over the next few weeks. The reading took so long because I shouted and jumped up at the first lie that I heard and each one after, causing much delay in the reading. I particularly disliked that he made it sound like I talked like a slave from Mississippi instead of a woman who spoke Dutch for the best part of her childhood.

I recall the most stinging parts of the book. Like scars, they stuck to me against my will. From the very first pages, Mr. Stone said, "Isabella, a black woman, entered into the delusions of Elijah Pierson and was, before the end came, among the most wicked of the wicked." He could call me wicked, for what black person was not called wicked and had not grown a shield around their hearts for such words. But to speak of Elijah as a madman, and to more than hint that I would act against my friend, that was the making of a scar. I didn't know it then, but his evil book was a tonic to me, better than all the kindness from the Whitings and Peter. I let loose with a healing rage.

Mrs. Whiting said she feared the story of Matthias would never go away, that New York City would still be talking about him as we entered our graves. When Gilbert Vale came to call on me because he wanted to write about the trial and set the record right, I sent him packing and would not let him in. I had no trust in writers; every newspaper man I'd run into made me out to be a devil who tried to poison people. It was only through the influence of Perez, who told me that Gilbert Vale was strong against slavery, had followed the trial and was disgusted that Stone and the Folgers tried to shift the blame to me, that I was willing to listen to him. In the end, I believed him and told him everything from the beginning, as I knew it.

I made him read every page to me and I corrected him whenever he made a mistake. He figured everyone in New York City would read it and that he would set the record fair and right for me. But he was wrong. There was a new scandal that took up the attention of the good people of Manhattan; a harlot from Five Points was murdered at the hands of a gentleman, and all old news was forgotten. The other reason that people stopped talking about us was the fire.

CHAPTER FORTY-THREE

December came on us like the crack of a whip and I knew we were in for a winter that would freeze tails off the dogs. The streets had finally become too cold for the colored women who sold hot corn out of a bucket for a penny.

We did not see the fire first, but smelled it, right about the same time that we heard the clanging of bells from City Hall and from a half dozen churches. The Whitings' house was shuttered up as tight as we could make it against the cold, and still wisps of smoke came in. We had been wrapped in our beds, hugging our soapstone bed warmers, but we tumbled out when the bells warned of fire. Like every house in Manhattan, we had several leather buckets in case of fire and Perez went straight for those. Mrs. Whiting and I dressed for warmth and left our stays off and went outside. What we saw did not prepare us for what was to come. "The fire is far to the south. We've no need to worry here. But I think the firemen will be pouring brandy in their boots to keep their feet warm on a night like this," said Mrs. Whiting.

The sky over the south seaport was glowing orange. Perez said he should go downtown to see to his business and he could lend a hand if bucket lines were needed. He left with a smile for his wife and said, "I'll try to bring you back some heat for the morning." We would not see him again until the next afternoon.

At around midnight, Mrs. Whiting and I grew uneasy

with the constant clatter of wagon wheels going down Canal Street and we began to think that the fire was fighting off the efforts of anyone who hoped to douse it. We opened the door and looked outside. The air was filled with smoke and the entire sky was lit up. "The whole city is burning!" said Mrs. Whiting. My first thought was that Matthias had done it, he was going to burn down the city, just like he said he would when he was held in jail and I had been too much of a fool to believe him. My very next thought was Peter.

"Peter sleeps in the carriage house on Pearl Street. I'm going to get my boy." I wanted Peter far away from the fire so that he wouldn't be killed but also because the whole city would soon be looking for a place to put the blame. A young rascal of a colored boy would be the easy target.

Mrs. Whiting tried to talk me into staying but she gave up when she saw me wrapping wool into my shoes and folding an extra wool blanket.

"Well, I see there is no stopping you. Go find your boy and bring him back here. I'll be waiting unless the fire takes the whole city and then God help us all."

I headed straight for Pearl Street, south of Five Points, where Peter slept in the loft over the horses. When I crossed Broadway, omnibuses filled with men flew past me. In the dark, I couldn't tell if it was firemen or the men who kept their shops down near the Merchant's Exchange. Church bells rang in belfries and it looked like every person in the city was awake. I cut through Five Points and headed for Pearl Street. The inside of my nose was frozen and sharp; my hands, although tucked into mittens with two layers and then held close to my body inside my cape, ached from the cold. When I got to the carriage house, only John, a small boy who couldn't be much help other than mucking out the stalls, stood inside whimpering.

"There's no one here but me," he said. "They took the horses and the carriages down to the fire, a man hired them to haul his bags of coffee from his store before the fire got to it."

I knelt down beside him. "I'm going to look for Peter. If the fire comes close to here, get out. Go up to Five Points. If you still feel the heat of the fire on your back, go to Broadway and go away from the city, up to the country. Do you know which way to go?" He nodded and shook so hard that I wasn't sure he could walk if he had to. "I'll come back and check on you at daybreak."

I was close to the East River when I heard people running toward me. "The fire is coming up Water Street! All the cisterns are frozen, they can't get water out of the river! Turn back!" I turned and made my way west, covering my nose with the blanket, my eyes burning with the thick smoke. I came near John Street and an explosion roared with a suddenness that took my breath away. Then another. A man on horseback clattered by. "They're blowing up buildings to stop the fire at Wall Street. God save us! Turn back, turn back!" I went forward, thinking only of Peter.

I went as close as I could, looking for the outline of my son against the flames. Every building I saw was lit up with fire waving like a flag. The firemen stood watching the flames, hanging their heads; they were helpless without water. I walked all night, keeping to the north edge of the fire, listening to the shouts of men and the screams of horses that begged to run from the fire. By daybreak, if you could call the smoke filled sky that, the fire still raged, and found buildings that it had missed during the night. Even the frozen river caught fire when a ship spilled its load of kerosene and flames ran across the river like a wild animal. By mid-morning, I turned around, fearing the worst for Peter. I remembered to stop by the carriage house and see the child left to watch over things there.

At first I thought that he was gone, but when I called his name, I saw a pile of hay move and he pushed away the warmth of the straw and stared at me as if I was a ghost.

"I didn't think you were coming back. I thought they'd all left me." He couldn't have been but six years old. I was dead on my feet and my throat was raw from the smoke.

"They don't think the fire will come farther north now unless the winds turn. I'll rest with you for awhile and then we'll go to Mrs. Whiting's house for hot porridge." I sat down next to him and pulled him near, covering us both with my cloak. I must have fallen asleep immediately. An urgent hand woke me later.

"Mother are you alright? What are you doing here?" My son had survived. It seemed like I always kept getting him back. The blanket fell from my shoulders as I grabbed Peter in my arms.

After Peter fed and watered the horses, Mr. Gulick, the carriage master, let him and the lad go with me to Mrs. Whiting's house. She fed them the hot porridge that boiled over the welcome fire. Peter told us of helping the men chop the ice off the pier for the fire hoses. No sooner would they get water into the hoses than the hoses froze. Peter jumped along the water hose to keep the water from freezing but it did no good. Then he helped Mr. Gulick and the other men drag bolts of silk and lace, cotton and hats from the stores because they knew the buildings could not be saved. When Tontine's Coffee House caught fire, Peter said all they could smell was billows of coffee filled smoke.

Perez Whiting came in mid way through Peter's story and he looked ready to drop. Perez did not suffer a loss of business; his shop was five blocks north of the fire. But he had stayed to help others.

"They've built the warehouses too tall, five stories, and the fire hoses can't reach those on the warmest of days, never mind when the water runs out like a dribble on the coldest night of the year. The fires started down in the warehouses." His wife sent him to bed and he slept one whole day and night.

Over six hundred buildings in all were burned and in the months that followed, New York talked about nothing else. I could imagine Matthias and God working up a fury of vengeance and cleaning out the tip of Manhattan, burning it like the brightest candle for all to see. It was not beyond his doing.

As spring finally warmed us, I went back to the heart of where the fire had been and stood among the blackened ruins. I picked my skirts up to keep the wet charcoal from staining the edges. Everywhere, men tore down the shards of buildings and hauled away piles of rubble to make way for new shops. I wanted someone to tear away the old shards of my burned out heart and make way for the new. I wanted the gnawing to stop that had not released me since Matthias and I blew apart.

What if Matthias really was God, wouldn't I have to give it a chance? When do you stop believing in the possibility of God? I have talked with God on most every occasion and I have looked for God in every leaf of every tree. Why not see him in the bearded Matthias? You see, I have no regrets about the choice I made, about giving him all the money I had saved from cleaning houses and doing laundry for two years. I went the limit with my search, I looked in every crevice. That part of me is satisfied. I don't have to search for a human god to be over me ever again. I am empty of such a desire. My only regrets are the dark years after Matthias, only after this did I dare ask God if I would be rejected for foolishness.

It is a terrible thing to sit in the mire of God's rejection. I know now that this is self made, the fear is created from within, but in the years of shame after Matthias was arrested, after I was his last supporter sitting proud with him on our trip west, I lived in my own shame as Matthias' illusion finally fell from my eyes. I closed up in those years, became the most quiet of my life. Until God and I had a long talk. "Isabella," he finally said, "few people have looked as hard for God as you have. Why, you even looked in Matthias. How many can say that?"

CHAPTER FORTY-FOUR

In the three years since leaving the side of Matthias, New York rebuilt after the fire, and I went back to Church, letting the word Christian take back a meaning filled with love and forgiveness and hope. I was not a fool, and I knew clear as day that all sorts of people call themselves Christians, like the ones who said Negroes could attend their churches, but we had to sit off in the balcony, nigger heaven they called it. There were those kinds of Christians. And there were the kinds who tried to shame people and drag them down.

I went to two churches. Almost everyone belonged to just one church, but I kept at two, looking for differences, looking for something that sounded like the words I heard when I talked to God.

Life for Peter grew more troublesome. New York squeezed him every which way and he started to look as beat down as if he'd been hit with a stick. I kept trying to prop him up.

New York had freed its slaves more than ten years back, but as each year went by, there were more and more jobs that didn't allow black men. They were turned away from apprenticing at all sorts of jobs as boys, and the men were not allowed to drive the coaches, and if we started our own stores selling calico and wool, we had best look out for late night fires. If we built a school to teach our children to read, the school was burned down. We were free as long as we didn't try to work or learn.

Peter lost his job at the carriage house when Mr. Gulick hired an Irish boy. Then he worked for a ragman for a time, then I don't know what but he fell further and further down. He was caught stealing fruit and the police brought him to me at Mrs. Whiting's house. The police said Peter was headed for trouble and I was lucky that he wasn't thrown in jail. I can't abide a thief. I taught my children the same as Mau Mau taught me: don't lie and don't steal, that's the starting place. I said, "If you catch this boy stealing again, you should throw him in jail and I won't come after him!" I was so mad at Peter that I picked up the cabbage I was chopping and threw it right at his head; then I did the same with the potatoes and the squash. He yelped and dipped around the kitchen. Finally Mrs. Whiting said, "Don't throw our entire dinner at the boy!"

There was one decent place left for black men and that was on the whaling ships and the merchant ships. Black sailors held their heads higher, walked with a sureness that Peter could only mimic.

Reverend Williams helped Peter get started in the Nautical School for Colored Men. That was the one school that they didn't burn down. I should have known this was more my idea than my son's, that it would have been better if he had come to me; instead I dragged him by his collar.

Months went by and I was proud of Peter, proud that one of my children was going to school, learning to read maps, and books, and stars. One day I saw the head teacher of the school taking a Sunday stroll through Five Points and I made a point to say a few words to him, feeling at last grateful for a turn in Peter's life. "You don't know how much this school has done for my Peter," I told him. "I want to thank you. I know Peter will make you proud of him."

He looked puzzled. "Forgive me, but I am not familiar with such a boy."

My heart grabbed at my ribs. "Peter Van Wagenen, he

started late last winter. Reverend Williams brought him in."

He squinted his eyes and looked off to the corner of his mind. "Yes, I remember now. I am sorry to say that Peter attended only once and has not returned."

Each time I had asked Peter to tell me what he was learning about the sailing ships, he had lied about reading the stars and the maps. My boy had looked in my eyes and lied to me. I wanted to thrash him, but he was too tall and strong as eighteen year old boys get. I did not have to wait long to find Peter; the police brought him to me. This time they did arrest him for stealing, or for looking like he was stealing which was the same thing.

I looked at my ruin of a boy, squeezed hard by New York, his lips tight to keep from crying.

I promised to find him another job, someone to take him on, in order to keep him free from working off his time as a night man, the lowest job in the city. They mucked out the privies, loaded it on carts, and took the loads to the river.

The end of summer had turned the city into a cauldron of steam and stink and nights brought no relief. I lay sweating in my bed, sleepless with turmoil over Peter. We were faced with a terrible choice on summer nights. We could keep our windows open to let out the hot air of the day, all our stale breath and sweat and take the chance of catching a cool breeze rustling our curtains in the hours before dawn or, we could get caught in the middle of our dreams by the night men. I came to learn their songs and if I heard them far off in another block, I would get up and close all the windows in the house so that the unbearable stench wouldn't stick in our throats. What sweet boy ever dreamt that when he was a man, he would shovel the shit of New York onto wagons and drive it to the rivers, scorned by all the good people of the city?

That was how I came to send him off, my only son, on a ship that agreed to take him on, and would not come back to port again for three years. The ship was a Nantucket whaler called the Zone. I did not know how else to save him, for I feared the city was about to slice the last bits of his life away. Instead of keeping him near me, I sent him to the farthest reaches.

I watched his ship as she set sail but Peter was too mean and angry to wave his hand. By the time his first letter reached me, nearly one year later, all the meanness was boiled off him, and nothing was left but longing to hear of his family. Four more letters reached me and then no more.

CHAPTER FORTY-FIVE

It was a summer morning, unremarkable on Canal Street, except that my clothes had not yet begun to cling to me. Mrs. Whiting and I had spoken just the day before about the need to pull down the winter drapes, which due to the illness of Mr. Whiting, we had delayed along with most of the heavy spring cleaning. I stood on the smaller ladder to get to the curtain rod and smelled the smoke and grease that had soaked into them from the lanterns all during the winter and damp spring.

I felt a rumbling beneath my ribs and gripped the ladder; my knees grew unsteady and I thought only that I must get down. As soon as my feet touched the floor, my knees gave up their job and let me fall, landing on my backside, my feet spread in front of me. The light in the room suddenly grew dark, a swirling grey, and my stomach sickened as if I would faint. I heard seagulls and the crashing of waves where there were none, and the burn of saltwater in my throat where nothing had passed but my own spit.

I pulled myself together and made for the front door to get air, only to feel the ground buckle beneath me again. This time I was certain everyone must feel the calamity, but as I peered at the street, I saw the rest of the world bustle by in usual fashion. Only I was struck. I pulled my knees up and wrapped my arms around them, resting my head as I tried to understand. The certainty of the message gradually branded itself into me. I stood up, knowing that Peter was dead, only such a passing as his could knock me to the ground. My son was gone. I had tried every which way to save him from slavery, from black birds, from the worst jobs in the city, from jail, until I finally sent him off to the sea. I had not seen him in four years. I knew Peter was not coming back, he would not walk down the pier with coins in his pocket, a new scar over his eye, fresh from the life of a sailor.

I think he died a violent death. There was no ease for him in this life; he would not die with loved ones at his side or a clean blanket over him. He died a hard death with salt water in his throat and that is what dropped me to the ground.

You ask any mother what was the hardest thing in her life and it won't be that she went hungry or was beaten or lost the love of her life even though at the time, those were all terrible pains to her heart. No, the thing that every mother will tell you (unless the world beat her soul right out of her body) was the most unbearable pain is the death of a child, and it doesn't matter if the child is three or thirty. I was denied a mother's job of cleaning and preparing Peter's body and taking him to rest. I would have buried him next to Bomefree or Mau Mau, not in the city. I would have sung a song about the trials in this life and how he was learning to be a man and how I wanted God to take him into his arms since we couldn't do that for Peter anymore.

Mrs. Whiting said that I didn't have written word from the sailing ship that he was dead so there still might be hope. I said I didn't need the written word; a mother knows when her son is dead or alive. I went down to the dock just as the sun was coming up, where Peter left four years before. Several of the Black Jacks checked the thick coils of rope on their ships. I stood at the edge of the dock and I sang about a mother losing a son at sea. I don't know all the words now, I couldn't find the words again if I tried. This was a song to be sung one time only. I opened up my heart and let the sorrow come out of my mouth. When I was done, the Black Jacks had taken off their hats and bowed their heads.

Anyone knows that the days of grief have no time. I didn't stop living or working, but there was a time when I couldn't tell one day from the next and it just kept on like that until they grew large enough so that I could taste my food again and smell the lavender growing along the kitchen walk.

* * *

New York grew harder for poor people, black and white, but being black made life not just hard, but dangerous. The kidnapping black birds were driven by greed to sweep up slaves who escaped from the south and bring them back. And if they couldn't find a fugitive slave, they were just as likely to kidnap a free negro and cart him off to the south and collect a rich sum of money. In church, the ministers called for mothers not to let their children out of their sight, not to send them alone to the well for water for fear of black birds getting them. We all knew who they were; some fine black men made it their job to know the whereabouts of each kidnapper. We had our own newspapers and you would have thought the world was going to fly apart when the names of all the black birds in the city got published.

I went back to camp meetings again, slowly, watching my step, looking for people who said they were more than what they were, like Matthias. I was looking for words of God. I heard of Matthias once or twice. Someone said that he tried to take up with people called Mormons who thought men should have as many wives as they wanted and that women had no say so about anything. Someone else said he was dead.

I could have gone on with my churches, my camp meetings with the Whitings, and I might have if I had not been called. Those people who have never been called or had the sense to listen if they were, won't know what I'm talking about. God came to me on the Pentecost, the first day of June in 1843. Back when I was a slave, we celebrated Pinkster on the Pentecost because that was all we had, a day to drink and dance and tie bright ribbons in our hair. Ever since coming to Manhattan, I knew the day to be a time when the spirit of God came into us and spoke with us. People said we were living five minutes from midnight, that the world was coming to an end and we had best be prepared. Well, I had heard those words before and knew that for us to pick the day for the world to end was foolishness.

I was full of arguments and vinegar when my day of spirit came around. It was the sort of day that a smart black bird prayed to stay out of my sight and false prophets were better off not claiming their glory in earshot of me. I was ready for a fight. Wouldn't you know that was just the day that God would pick to call on me.

The air was comfortable and filled with breezes from the Hudson River, a different air than the sea breeze, noisier I'd have to say, more filled with the voices of people and deer and birds and white birches that live up north along the Hudson. I was bringing out the wool clothes to air before putting them away for the summer. And that's when I filled up with light, a soft light, not one that made me squint. I looked right in this light and I could see everything, the whole city, my daughters up north, every single person in my life plus some I didn't know. And then God said I was ready to go east and I didn't need to stay in New York any longer, I was done living there. He said this through my body so that even the hair on my head knew it. He said the world wasn't going to end, what would be the point in ending the world? He loved us and he loved the world.

"Take your new name and go east. Take your name as you now know it and will know it forever. Take the name Sojourner Truth." Even after his voice stopped, I was filled with the sweetest of sounds, the joy of gratitude.

My one regret was telling Mrs. Whiting that I was leaving. "What's wrong? Is one of the girls sick? When do you plan on leaving? For how long?" A good part of her hair was white and I had noticed that she was shorter than she used to be when I first started with her, a dozen years earlier.

"I'm leaving as soon as I pack a satchel to carry. That's all I'll need. I'll send word to my daughters." I was getting the words out too chopped up because it was harder to say goodbye to her than I thought.

"Isabella, this is very inconvenient for me. If you leave now, I will have to hire help for the heavy cleaning," she said in a peevish voice. She pulled her head back and held her lips tight.

I thanked God that she was so peevish in that moment, which was not like her. She was as good a woman as I had met in New York, not as wise and laughing as my old friend Soan, but good and solid, brave enough to let fugitive slaves hide in the attic on their road north, which only now do I dare to say. If she had not sounded peevish, I might not have been able to leave as I did. I pulled her close to me and kissed her on her forehead, which I had never done before. "My name is Sojourner now, Sojourner Truth."

I left the city as I said I would. I carried two shillings and some clothing in my cloth satchel. I did not look back.

CHAPTER FORTY-SIX

From that day onward, I let God be my guide. I was not shy about asking Him which turn in the road to take. I took the ferry to Brooklyn, and from there walked each day and preached where I was able. The world was on fire with preaching back then, so it was not hard to find people who wanted to talk about God. But like now, it was harder to find people who lived as well as they talked.

From Long Island, I took a ferry to Bridgeport. I wandered along the docks and watched the handsome young black men working the ships. For every three white sailors, there was one black one, standing out like the great hope that they were. We were well into summer, coming down the other side of it. I rose from the crate where I rested, ready to start my journey to New Haven, when a colored man approached me from one of the ships. He wore a red kerchief around his neck and stepped smartly, as if he owned the world. He was full of swagger, but I saw that he rubbed his thumb and finger together in an agitated fashion. He was not what he seemed. I must have gazed longer at him that I knew.

"May I have a word with you?"

"I'm filled with words. You've come to the right person," I said. Seagulls floated on the morning breeze and called to each other.

"We're unloading our ship, a merchant ship, fresh from Maryland and North Carolina before that. We have fresh fruit from the south of the darkest sort. I was told to look for a woman on the docks who would know where such fruit could be shipped." His eyes latched onto my soul. I was not the woman he sought, but I understood his meaning. Any dark skinned person of the time would have understood, as well as those white people who helped us.

"The woman you seek is not me. I am a traveler and it is only my weariness that brought me to this spot for a moment's rest. But if your fruit can last one more leg of the journey, there is a sure place in New York City." I gave him the name of Reverend Williams and directions to the houses that saw the faces of so many run away slaves. His face drooped, disappointed that I did not know of a safe house in Bridgeport.

"Can they hang on a day longer?" I asked him, all talk of fruit done.

"They have worried the flesh off their bones. They are in the worst hold of the ship, desperate for fresh air." His eyes darted up the street.

I took hold of both his rough hands. "Tell them they are close and that friends await them in New York. Find Reverend Williams and he will go to the ship at night, that's his way. He won't fail them. Tell them one more day, they have waited a lifetime, let this day be one of reward for them."

"Thank you," he said, getting ready to go back to his ship.

"One more thing. Did you ever see a Black Jack by the name of Peter Van Wagenen on the Zone?" Despite knowing in my heart that Peter rested at the bottom of a cold ocean, I sought any word of him. I described him to the sailor.

"No. We sail mostly from here to New Orleans and back. The Zone is a whaler and they sail around the Horn to the Pacific. We don't cross paths with them often."

I thanked him and went on my way. He would not be the last sailor who I would ask. It is a mother's yearning to know of her child, even if it is to know their last hours. I watched the colored sailor walking briskly back to his ship, risking life, limb, and freedom for his precious cargo.

I left New York thinking it was a Sodom, like Mount Zion or a slaveholder's farm. But New York was not a Sodom, it was a place of hope for people who came from worse hells, and it was a haven to the poor wretches on the ship in Bridgeport

I spent the rest of the summer going from churches to camp meetings, preaching and listening. I often ended what I had to say with singing, reaching people who couldn't be touched by talking. Singing reached right down into the blood and bones of a person whether they liked it or not. I had my favorite hymns, and I had my own that came with words that fit the moment.

If you're a preacher of the traveling sort and you've given yourself over to God, the path is always lit for you. There are surprises along the way, turns that seem like the hard way instead of the easier way, but my faith grew stronger with each passing day and I knew I was being pulled somewhere as sure as I knew that I needed breath to live.

If I had not attended the most foolish of camp meetings outside New Haven, I would not have found my new home, the place where I would feel truly at home for the first time since I was a child under my parents wings. I knew that if they could speak from the grave, my parents would have said that a muddy slave master's cellar was not a home and they did not regard it so, but a passing through place. I would tell them no, home was by their side.

Matthias taught me lessons through the back door that he never intended for me to learn. Having faith does not mean sitting still while the preacher tells you what you should believe when in your heart, you disagree. When I took the name Sojourner Truth, part of the arrangement with God was that I spoke the truth wherever I saw it. Matthias didn't like to be questioned, he said he was the prophet and he should have the final word. What I learned from Matthias is that his sort of talk is the surest way to ruin and that I didn't need to spend one more minute in ruin. I could now see clear through preachers who leaned in Matthias' direction.

I forget the name of the town where the Millerites were meeting outside of New Haven, but I know the katydids were in high form, so I know the time of year. When I went in, I heard too much talk about living five minutes to midnight, too much talk about what to do when the world ends; this preacher was going to take off down a road where I didn't want to go.

The preacher was a thin nervous sort with his bones nearly poking through his face. He wore the plainest of dress, a dark jacket and white shirt that needed more laundering than he allowed it. The trouble with people who think the world is ending in five minutes is that they stop living their life and don't do the rest of us one bit of good and they certainly let go of cleanliness, as if God would welcome a gang of Christians who didn't have sense enough to wash their clothes.

His sermon was simple enough; the way to God, who was galloping down the road any minute, was to throw away all earthly goods. This man was a master at whipping up a crowd and this crowd came expecting to cut loose. They knew their minister; they waited for the sweat to pop out on his forehead. And the faithful sheep did as he asked, they pulled off their buttons, tore off their bonnets, ripped ribbons from their children's clothes, throwing them at the feet of the preacher. He stoked their fires until the men took off their suspenders, yowling and moaning all the while. When two old men spit out their false teeth and added them to the pile, I could stand it no longer. I stood up and pointed my arm at the preacher.

"The Lord might come in, move through this camp, and go away and no one would notice him for all the noise. He'd be the one keeping his teeth in his head and his suspenders on. He'd be the one picking up that bonnet to find someone who needed it. He'd be the one walking away looking for people to live this life and fix what's ailing it."

I got their attention, I knew how to do that. It turned out
that there were folks who wanted to talk about fixing up this
life and I talked all night with them. The preacher went to
another place with the few people who saw the road to God
strewn with all the best part of their clothing and some of
their teeth. The ones who had kept their bonnets on offered
me a place to sleep and food to eat if I stayed and talked
more, which I did. When I finally left, they pointed me in the
direction of people further north, giving me a letter of
introduction to a friend, saying that I was a preacher and bed
and food would be a great comfort to me.

I edged my way north into Massachusetts and spent the
night of the first frost in Springfield. The people there had
good strong soup with beef and potatoes and I ate two bowls
of it. They had a particular interest in hearing about my time
in slavery. As it turned out, slavery did not have the iron
grasp on Massachusetts that it had on New York. Slavery
ended there long years before New York could bear to loosen
chains on colored people.

After listening to my stories of slavery and the strength I
found by listening to God, they pointed me north again.

"If you are looking for people who are throwing open the
windows to the fresh air of all religions and all colors of
people, then there is a place or two you must see. One is near
Boston, called Fruitlands. The other is not but twenty miles
from here. They have a longer name that my tongue keeps
tripping over. Northampton Association of Education and
Industry." My host was a gray-haired man of the Quaker
persuasion, but he told me that he sorely missed hymns and
had enjoyed my singing like a drink of cool water.

"A name is an important thing. What in the world made
them pick a name that clunks like chopped wood? I like
Fruitlands better." But in the end, I did not pick Fruitlands,
because the cool air had woken the arthritis in my right hand
and I did not relish a longer trip. I headed north to
Northampton and seeing that it was only twenty miles, I
walked. If there was no trickery and men proclaiming

themselves as prophets, I thought I might stay a few weeks. I did not know that I would grow roots as deep as the mulberry trees.

CHAPTER FORTY-SEVEN

L et me tell you a few things about the folks in
Northampton. And it must be only a few because I'm
going to stop soon. Others have told the stories in
newspapers and such. You might know about my speeches
from here to high heaven, about the way I met with the
Presidents, about fixing the wagon of those fellas in
Washington who wouldn't let one old tired colored woman
ride on their street cars, about telling men to give women
their rights. Oh, and paying back the slaves for all their labor,
I'm still petitioning the government for that and I won't stop.
I'm not done with my life so I can't tell you all of it. I expect
to vote someday without getting arrested. I expect the
government to pay back the old slaves with land out west.
But I don't know if those grander times would have
happened if I hadn't hiked up the hill from the dusty
downtown of Northampton back in 1843. That's so long ago;
I must be one hundred years old, but Sophia tells me I'm not
but eighty-three.

When I met Samuel Hill I must have looked like one
scowling woman. Samuel was a founder of the Community.
That's what they called it, which was a relief to me because
the other name was too long and we all thought so. I didn't
trust Samuel and all the people who had congregated in the
Community, which had to be about fifty adults and near that
many children when I first knocked on their door. I was on

the look out for the likes of Matthias but no matter how hard I looked, I never saw him. Samuel said I was welcome to stay as long as I liked. Everyone was expected to work for the group and have equal voice. He said they welcomed me.

When I first got there, they all lived in a brick factory that brimmed with people of the most refined sort but they were doing the labor of the lowliest kind. I took a few weeks to consider what they were about before I stopped my scowling. They lived as simply as I ever had; more so, given my last years among city people. Most of the adults worked in the silk mill, tending the cocoons, working the silk thread. Children too when they were done with school. Other people did the cooking, or the tending of the small children. But that was not what kept me among them for years; it was the largeness of spirit and liberty of thought, speech, and deed. My soul garden was planted on the day I left New York City. My friends in Northampton helped me grow my garden that was strong and would feed many.

Every person there was an abolitionist; they said slavery was a sin and any religion that twisted the words of God to bolster up slavery was a blight on earth. The voices of women were as good as the voices of men and no one voice had more value because he was a man or a richer man than another. Samuel and the others had come to Northampton from all over creation, bringing one common thread: the rights of all are equal and it didn't matter about sex, or skin color, or religion. I thought I had fallen through the clouds and landed in heaven.

I did the laundering, but I was not expected to do it alone. I had two others helping me most of the time as well as the children who were sent to me after school. If I thought the clothes were too soiled to get clean, I walked them right back to their owner and directed them to soak the clothes in the Mill River before they brought them back again.

To give a feeling for the place, picture a heart on fire with the sureness of hope, add in the finest of people, every abolitionist from here to tomorrow, lecturing about the way to make the whole country united in freedom for all, and the truest caring from others who told me to speak and keep speaking because my words about my life could heal even the worst soul. Picture black living with white, high living with low, poor with rich, and when it came time to debate, every voice was equal. For the first few years we all lived in the top floor of the factory as easy as you could imagine. Maybe I'm forgetting the cold mornings or the times when the influenza dropped us all on our beds, or when we argued about the silk mill losing money, or how much lollygagging the young people should be allowed. But even at our worst, we were far better than I had ever lived before. My mind and heart had to be held by a tight cord, for they felt like they would soar away.

I sent word of my whereabouts to my daughters and Mrs. Whiting in late fall after I was sure that I would stay. By the next summer, I received a letter from Mrs. Whiting that Sophia was being treated scandalously by a widow man in New Paltz. She and Perez were on their way there to help my baby. When I talked to Samuel and the others, they said that we must get the girls here. For all of my life, tending to my daughters from a far distance, no one had ever offered to let them come to me, no one had ever offered to take them in, and yet those were the first words spoken from my friends in Northampton. Elizabeth and Sophia soon joined me.

My girls lived with the rest of us in the factory. They were appalled at how hard we were all working. Sophia was particularly slow, and I let her be at first, knowing that she had been lied to and used shamelessly. A few years back, John Dumont had relented on the long years of servitude that my daughters must pay; they had been given the choice to seek their own lives. Only Diana chose to stay with him. Sophia was quiet and kept to herself and wouldn't say what had happened back in New Paltz. Then after a month or so, I saw her face change. Her tight skinned face softened and filled out and her eyes took on the look of deep rivers or oceans. She was with child; there was no mistaking the change and I knew it in my bones.

The first frost turned the tops of the trees golden and in the hillside, the purest of reds were coming on. After all the work was done one evening, I took Sophia aside.

"Walk with me daughter. Let's go down to the Mill River."

She was a child born of a rape, and even though I never told her this, nor anyone except Soan who was long dead, I could not help but wonder at the strange way of fate. We had not said the words to each other yet about the pregnancy. Sophia's face was round and looked more childlike than my other girls. But I was like any other parent; my first inclination was to rage at her.

"What were you thinking? Or were you thinking at all? You have shamed all of us." My head was on fire and I stepped back from my daughter lest I strike her. The Mill River was low but the rich smells of soaked earth rose up to meet us.

"I'm the same age you were when Diana was born," she said. Her chin jutted out at me even as she quivered. I was expecting more contriteness. Her bold stare took away my last bit of control. I grabbed her by the shoulders and shook her until her scarf came loose. Her eyes grew wide and scared and she reached up for my hands.

"Stop it, Mama, stop it!"

I stopped shaking her and we stood face to face with my hands close to her neck and her hands gripped on mine. Then we both started to cry and we dropped to our knees and held each other. And then, I don't know why, but I told her all about Robert and how much I loved him and how Diana came from me and Robert and how slavery made his masters into rabid dogs who crushed his spirit until nothing was left. Sophia curled up on the ground like a baby with her head on my lap and I stoked her face.

"I can't understand why things have to change so slowly when I can see how they should be, how people should treat each other. But at least this baby won't ever be torn from you. You won't be feeding white babies at your breast. That's something anyhow."

"What will people here say about me having a baby with no father and not being married?"

"Nothing they would say could change the course of things. You are having a baby and that's bigger than all of us. Being good-hearted folks, they probably won't say anything and act like it's not happening. That's what we'll do too and then the baby will be here and we'll all do what it takes to keep another child safe in this world."

And that's what we did. When James was born in the spring, he was a welcome sight. We needed another boy in our family to take the place of all the ones who had died at sea, been sold to places unknown, been crushed by slavery, or had died in frozen misery like Bomefree. I vowed to keep a closer eye on this boy.

* * *

With the exception of my father, I met the two finest black men of my life at Northampton and I was glad for young James that he had such men to look up to. I knew of David Ruggles in New York City, every colored person did. David ran circles around the slave catchers, taking more runaway slaves to freedom than any of us could count. But he had started to go blind and his abolitionist friends like William Lloyd Garrison said he had to stop tending to the runaways. There was a bounty on David's head from people down south, dead or alive and he didn't stand a chance against them if he was blind. Mr. Garrison brought him to Northampton and he joined up the year before I got there. He ran a store and then later a water cure hotel. Mostly, he handed out hope to the runaway slaves who came through our way. He was sweet on Elizabeth for a time but to be honest, Elizabeth was a farm girl and she couldn't get over David being so far above her. Her feeling so far down kept her from acting natural with David and he finally gave up courting.

The other man was Frederick Douglass. David had helped him to freedom years back when Frederick was running from Maryland. Frederick took to reading and writing early on and he spoke like an angel. I told him, "Don't you dare get yourself killed. I've seen too many black men die. You and I have too much work to do here." That man was dangerously handsome and men and women, black and white always said so. He always thought I worked him too hard, challenged his thoughts, and argued with him. He said I was put on earth to make him sit up straight. He wasn't part of the Community, but he was a regular visitor. He wrote a book about his life as a slave and I suppose that's where I got the idea for my book.

I like to think I would have gotten around to my book sooner, if the Community hadn't ended and if the letter from Diana hadn't come. Diana didn't read nor write either, so we had to go through two extra layers to send letters to each other. I took the letter to Mrs. Benson and asked her to read it to me. Our silk mill business was going under and some of the families had moved away. Mrs. Benson looked like she was in mourning; she'd put all her hopes into the miracle of abolitionists living and working together. When I brought her my letter, her eyes were swollen from crying and she said, "Sojourn, I hope your news is good. All of our news had been sorrowful." She read to me.

"*Dearest Mother. I am well and I long to join you and my sisters in Northampton. But I am helping Mr. Dumont tend to his wife. She is gravely ill and coughs blood every day. In her fevered state last night, she called to you in such a way that made me drop the water glass. She is dying, Mother, and none but me heard her call to you. If you won't come, no one here will know that I asked you. A neighbor woman wrote this letter and she is sworn to silence. We could all use your help and you always brighten Mr. Dumont. Your daughter, Diana*"

"Is this not the man who kept you in slavery?" asked Mrs.

Benson. She handed the letter back to me.

"Near to twenty years ago I walked away from slavery and it was John Dumont who was the slave master. But he and I have since found a middle road of understanding. There was no such road with Sally Dumont. She was as ruined by slavery as my broken spirited husband Tom. And the man I would have picked as husband, Robert. But she had a choice, and my men had the choice beat out of them. She was cruel in ways I cannot speak about." I folded the letter and put it into my skirt pocket.

After a sleepless night, fighting with the bed covers, I stood waiting for the stage that roared through town. I knew how much trouble Diana had gone to in sending me a letter. I headed west to New York State.

The demons of childhood are the worst. They rise up in our dreams and choke off the pure, sweet light of day when we are long past being children. Sally took as much from me as she could. Now she was sick and dying but try as I might, I could only picture the raging woman who had me tied in the smokehouse.

The Dumont farm had lost some of its shine and the prosperity of the early days was gone. Mr. Dumont was white haired and although his spine stayed straight, I think it was only through his will; he was not a man to bend with age. I walked into the house and Diana dropped a pile of linens to wrap her arms around me. She kept an iron lock on her emotions so I knew that she had been taken to her limit by the prolonged illness in the house. Mr. Dumont stood in the doorway, and his shoulders gave a sudden sag when he saw me. "Bell, how could you have known? You are a welcome sight for this old man."

Death sat in every room, pulling the heat from the parlor fire, draining the freshness from the water, and stealing all the taste from the food. A flock of crows crowded on the elm trees, awaiting the funeral in their satin coats.

"You've done fine, daughter. Go rest now. Go outside and get fresh air," I said to Diana.

"Gert has been here for days. She just left. Her own husband is sick and Mr. Dumont made her leave." Diana was uncomfortable with resting or any sort of idleness. I knew she would follow me from room to room and continue to work herself to exhaustion. "Does mint still grow past the orchard? Take a walk and gather some for me. We could all use a freshening drink," I said, guiding her to the door.

I sent Mr. Dumont to the barn to gather eggs from the few chickens he had left so that I could make a custard for us. I took a breath to steady myself and went to their bedroom. Her rasping air filled the room. I covered my nose and mouth. She was asleep, mouth gaping open, cheeks sunken without her back teeth. Her white hair was thin and braided off to one side. I opened a window to let in a trickle of clean air. I pulled a chair close to the bed and sat, waiting for my old tormentor to wake.

What would my old friend Soan do, who paid back her cruel master by treating him roughly, when he could finally hurt her no longer? Sally was as brittle as old newspaper. She would crumble if I picked her up and dropped her. Perhaps the pillow, she'd be dead in moments if I placed the pillow over her gaping mouth. Death would come running and relief would pour into the house.

She opened her eyes. One was covered by dense clouds of cataracts. I didn't know if she could see me, less because of the cataracts but because she hovered between this world and the next. I had seen it enough in my forty-nine years; the dying don't know which world is the true one and they look at you like you were a ghost. "It's Bell. You're dying, Sally, and I've come to help. Here, I'm going to put some water on your lips." I dipped a clean linen towel into a cup of water and dripped it on her lips. With thick, slow movements, she forced her tongue to go from one side of her bottom lip to the other.

She turned her head to me. "You're the one I helped. I gave you something, didn't I?" A terrible sound came from her lungs, a rattle heralding death. Was this the death bed confession that I had sought from her, begging for my forgiveness?

I pulled my face close to hers. "What do you think you gave me old woman?"

"Spinning, I taught you how to spin. Made you useful." She closed her eyes, exhausted from the effort.

I was stunned beyond words as my mind whirled back to the slave days, of the briefest time when Sally did instruct me on the finer points of spinning. I had all but forgotten those few days on the farm. In no time, I had gone beyond Sally in my spinning. Her teaching was something that I endured; it was never easy for me to be close to her.

I put my face near hers. "When you go to meet God, what will you tell Him of slavery? Do you think He has a special place for slave holders?" I spoke loudly; I wanted to be sure she heard me. "Do you think God will be pleased that you taught me to spin so that you could steal my sweat and muscle, so that you could grow fat off my labor?" I was ready to tell her more, but her eyes opened wide and she gasped as if something lodged in her throat. The woman could not breathe. I heard death stand up in the next room and begin his slow shuffle to the bedchamber. "Don't die yet Sally, I'm not done here," I said. But her choking was pitiful and I pulled her up to a sitting position. She was too weak to hold her own body up, so I slid onto the bed and held her up. She relaxed into my arms like a baby and leaned her head against my breast. Her hands were as cold as china. All muscle was gone from her arms. Only the thinnest layer of chalky white skin covered her bones. I could not help myself; I wrapped my arms around her chest to warm her. I pitied this poor creature, her mind filled with lies, and as torn apart in spirit by slavery as the rest of us. She shuddered and went still. I heard the scuff of boots in the kitchen, eggs placed in a bowl, and the still familiar footstep of Mr. Dumont. He stopped in the doorway when he saw Sally and me in bed.

"She's gone now, John. Come sit with us."

I did not stay for the burial. Mr. Dumont asked me to sing

at the funeral but I would not. He drove me to the stage. Toward the end of the drive, he said, "I did Sally a great disservice by bringing her into the world of slavery. She knew nothing of it before we married."

"She made the worst of it," I said. There was no point in saying otherwise.

"I see now that slavery is a wicked thing, the greatest curse that we have ever brought on ourselves."

"Well, there are people that still think that way today."

"But now all the world despises slavery and cries out against it! Now there is no excuse for not knowing the sin of slavery. When I was a slaveholder, few spoke out against it and those who did seemed a queer bunch who mattered little. There is no going back now, I see that." He steadied the horse after a pheasant flew up in a startle of leaves. He stopped the carriage and turned to me. "I should have emancipated all of you. I could have saved Robert, freed you both when you were young. That's what should have happened." He slapped the reins and the horses danced to a start.

I recalled the lectures that he used to give us about not stealing and not telling lies. Mr. Dumont stole sixteen years of my life, stole the chance to marry who I wanted, and stole my own work from me. I took his words as a confession, as close to a confession as he would ever get. I could have asked for more, but I took this moment in all its sweetness. This old man, this old slaveholder, turned to brother. Oh, I thanked God for this moment. But I neglected to ask Him to go easy on Sally when she arrived.

* * *

The Community was two years dead when I started looking for someone to help me write my book. I'm still sad when I think about the Community ending. We couldn't make the money part of things work, we had too many disasters with the silk worms, too hot, too cold, too many other people starting up silk mills in other places. In truth, we got tangled up in our ideas, none of which were bad. Some of the young people left, said we were too hard on them and wouldn't let them play cards and loll around on each other. Some might say I was the hardest on young people because I knew all about drinking and cursing and dancing, I wanted them to skip that part and go straight to the important work of life. Our country had slaves in bondage and I was on fire to get them free. What good would it do to play cards? So, the Community flew apart, and people scattered. There were one hundred and one reasons why people moved on, but my heart broke when the Community stopped because never in my life had I been so equal in thought and deed, one person, one vote.

Northampton captured some of the members; their roots had gone deep even without the Community and many stayed. I lived on with the Benson family for a few years and I continued to preach and sing. I talked about telling my story in a book, throwing out the bait until I hooked a writer.

Olive Gilbert was an abolitionist who also lived with the Bensons. She had traveled down south and saw the sort of evil that went on with slaves who were kept like dogs. She said no God and no religion should have anything to do with one human enslaving another. Olive and I took to each other right from the start. I told my story and she wrote, each of us doing what we did best. I told her everything, spared her ears not one moment of despair. We worked mostly at night, when our work was done elsewhere, when no meetings were held, when no terrified fugitive slaves needed our help on their journeys to freedom. Olive said that the trouble with writing books is that life gets in the way of writing.

David Ruggles saw that we were getting tangled up with our words and he gave us a few days at his water cure hotel. By then, his business had slowed down because a new water cure hotel had opened up down the hill from us. He put his hands on us, that was his way of telling what was wrong with people. That was one of his gifts, was his hands, and he could tell if someone was sick on the inside before they even knew it. Even through the cotton of my dress, I could feel the heat of his hands clear through to my collarbones.

"What's wrong with you? Do you have a fever?" I asked him.

He said no, his hands always grew hot when he tried to help people. David was a little bit of everything, and you'd have thought he would have been stronger in his own body but life doesn't necessarily work that way.

He let us have plenty of cold water baths over in the women's part of the hotel. I told Olive that I'd had too many cold water baths as a child and I didn't see what good it did to sit in cold water. She said let's try it anyhow. As we each sat in our own tub of cold water with a sheet over the top of the tub for privacy sake, we finished off the hard parts of the book. Olive said we had to leave out the parts that would seem indelicate. I said there was nothing delicate about being a slave and being a woman, delicacy never rose its head, and I wanted the world to know about it.

"Some things cannot be said in a book. We'll have to talk around Sally Dumont and that terrible Neely man and most of Matthias too. Learned people are smart enough to read between the lines," said Olive.

I let my head slip under water, holding my breath as long as I could because I was done talking. When I came up, I heard Olive crying. "How did you stand it, Sojourn? I would have died, I know I would have died." She didn't try to hide her face as most do, she simply gave way.

I rested my chin on the edge of the tub. "One of the worst parts of slavery is that it makes you hate. I hated white people and I used to dream that all white people would die, with nothing left for seed. And the next worst thing is that it makes white people get so small and rotten on the inside. Now I pity the poor slave owner. What will he do when eternity comes? Does he think God will welcome a rotten soul?"

Olive had stopped crying. "I don't know how you do what you do with words. I can say the same thing that you just said about slaveholders and I sound like I'm teaching adding and subtraction. You say the words and I'll remember them always. I think you could turn a Black Bird into an abolitionist."

We finished the book and I followed Olive's advice about leaving the parts out that would make people faint. The Bensons were the first to help us celebrate when the final words were written.

I borrowed money to publish my book, which took off like a steady mule, walking a sure but slow pace and it continued for as long as I lived. I suppose it was helped along by William Lloyd Garrison's part that he wrote for the beginning of the book. He wrote one speck about me and four pages about the brutishness of slavery. The book, *Narrative of Sojourner Truth, a Free Bondswoman,* was enough of the truth for back then. As I see it now, it was a weak tea. We held back what we thought people couldn't understand and I held back to protect some people who in their ignorance treated me beyond sinful.

The book put me in place to do something that at one time was beyond imagining. I bought a house in Northampton. A house, who would have thought that I could buy a house? And right across from the cemetery. No fussing from my neighbors when they were all as stiff as planks. The Bensons had a little bit of furniture for me, a table and a bed. Samuel brought a straightback chair and Olive hauled over a rocking chair that I right away dragged out to the small front porch. The Lord could have sent a lightning bolt through me right then and there and I would have been satisfied because life could not have gotten any sweeter; me with my daughters, grown as they were, and a fiery grandson, all together in a house that I owned and that I could wrap around us. My head was filled with light and my feet would not touch the ground.

"Diana," I told my oldest, "hold onto my hands or I'll float away!" Diana had moved in with us too after John Dumont moved west. She couldn't seem to work up to a level of joy and it grieved me to see her so. Sophia and Elizabeth, the younger ones, were in the full flower of their time. They squealed and waltzed through the whole house and I clapped my hands to keep them going. This was my house, and even when I tried to sleep, I floated on the light of the full moon.

JACQUELINE SHEEHAN

CHAPTER FORTY-EIGHT

If the slaveholders had not turned up the flame for their
hatred of black flesh, I might have stayed in my house
forever, my precious house, bought with the sweat and blood
of my book and my life. Seems like we had only a few
moments of rest. Diana was the serious one. She was born
with a furrowed brow.

"I remembered how you said we'd all be together one day
and I believed you back then. Growing up made me forget.
But now you've done it." She had a weakness of the lungs
when she was a child and it stayed with her.

Olive came to tell me the awful news first. The
newspaper hung from her hands like a dead child.

"They did it. They passed the Fugitive Slave Law. I
thought we could get rid of it! All of us are criminals in the
eyes of our own country." I pulled her inside and made us
coffee. I knew the night would be long when everyone heard
the news. So there it was; our own country said that to help a
runaway slave was against the law. And the worst part was
that any citizen could be appointed by a marshal to help a
black bird kidnap a runaway slave. This was now the law of
the land. When I heard that part, I went out behind the privy
and threw up.

Samuel and George came next to tell me.

"We must disobey this law. We must resist it!" said
George, and then he sank to my porch floor and sat with his

316

head in his hands. They all looked like they had been mule kicked.

"Well now we know the worst of it. Our government says we are criminals. But Lord, I've never seen such a fine bunch of criminals as those before me." They lifted up their heads and looked at me. "If it is a crime to help a runaway slave, then let us be the grandest criminals and tell the whole world to join us!"

Samuel stood up. "You won't let us get weary, Sojourn, that's why we have collected on your porch like flies."

I didn't have time to stay long at home with my daughters. We were off to meetings in Providence, Worcester, even back down to New York City where the worst of the Black Birds still circled about. And I'd have to say that from that time on, I never stopped, still haven't. I should thank someone, the worst slave owners of all, for getting that law passed, for letting us all see the worst face of evil. Let the devil be seen, I always say.

David Ruggles was one year dead when the worst of the law came. His body was worn out at an early age and his people from Connecticut came to take his body away. I wished that he could have been buried across the street from my house, I would have liked that. I know what he would have done if he had lived, I had learned that much from him. He would have doubled his efforts and brought more slaves through here than he already had. He would have been clear in his heart that a law had been passed that was as wrong as walking backwards. We all knew it was wrong.

Lloyd Garrison talked me into traveling with him and a friend of his from England. I nearly choked when he told me that his friend was a member of Parliament. George Thompson, that's who he was. At first I said no, I could not go lecturing with two such men. I was a poor colored woman and people would only want to hear the refined words of the two men.

Lloyd kept after me. "You have the power of words. I've been spellbound by you on many occasions, under the arms

317

of your favorite pine tree in the Community. You told a crowd in Worcester that goodness was everlasting, it was only evil that had a beginning and so it could have an end. You gave everyone hope," he said.

"I was not sure of myself on that day. Frederick spoke so well, every word was polished until it shined like silver. I felt like an old dented up pewter bowl and you and Frederick were the fancy china," I said. I admired Lloyd because he understood that unless women had our say, nothing in the world would be right.

"All stories of slavery are not the same. You tell a woman's story that Frederick cannot know." In the end I agreed to go with them, and in the winter of 1851, we headed to Rochester. I told Diana and the girls that I might be in a river that was too deep for me with such fine company. Diana laughed and said it did her good to see me wonder if there was something I couldn't do.

"Oh daughter, I wonder all the time. But God keeps whispering in my ear to take the road ahead. It's not time for me to stop." If I had known how long the road was, I might have rested up more; it seems like I never did get to rest after that. I sold my book everywhere I went.

We stayed in Rochester with friends and I saw that the world was growing bigger and abolitionists were everywhere. Women's rights people were sprouting up too but their crop was thinner. Some of the abolitionists said that women should not speak. Some of the women's rights people said that colored women would take away from the chance of women getting their rights. They wanted rights for white women only, leaving colored women behind. Lloyd, George, and I looked at the question every which way and we came to one decision. You couldn't free just the colored man; if the colored woman was left behind, she would be crushed. It had to be all women and all men, black or white.

In spring, we went to Ohio and stayed with friends there. The big women's convention was in Akron. The call had gone out, I don't know how. Carriages rolled in from all directions, women came on foot, and I saw one young woman with the last green of a black eye and I knew that her coming was hard won.

The church could not hold us all and the air grew thick with our breath and excitement. Dark stains spread under the arms of all the women, and I was glad that my handkerchief was not of the fancy sort, it was good strong cotton, home for the sweat dripping off my face. Men were there too, men who thought like we did and men who hooted and hissed each time a woman got up to speak about voting, owning her own property, about slavery. I could smell fear all around me like we were standing on the edge of a cliff getting ready to step off.

Most of the women had never before in their lives spoken one word in public. Their voices quivered and grew thin so that the hissing men from the balcony drowned them out. I saw that some of the worst men were ministers. The women who tried to speak grew red in the face, their hands shook, and their legs were ready to buckle were it not for the steadiness of the pulpit. Then God nudged me and told me to get up.

When I rose to speak, I heard a woman say, "Don't let her speak, oh don't let her!" She was afraid that the little piece of earth that the women gained on this day would be taken away by my black face. That's how the abolitionists and women's rights people were back then. Some were still saying: don't let the women speak at abolitionists meetings, others said don't let the abolitionists ruin it for the small piece of pie that women are fighting for. I turned and looked at her poor mistaken face as I rose to speak.

I asked Mrs. Coe, who was running the meeting as best she could, if I could speak and she said yes. I looked out at the church filled mostly with white women, and a sprinkle of men. I let them take a good long so that their eyes filled up with me. A few men in the balcony laughed loud enough to be sure I heard them. I looked up at them and saw that they were young and old alike, bound together in their need to bully women.

"I only want to say a few words," I told them. Only those who had heard me before knew that my few words often turned into many. "I have as much muscle as any man," I said, pulling back the sleeve of my dress, getting their attention before they knew what happened. "And I can do as much work as any man. I have plowed and reaped and husked and chopped and mowed. Can any man do more than that? I have heard much about the sexes being equal. I can carry as much as any man and eat as much too if I can get it. I am as strong as any man now. Then there is the intellect." Men were forever measuring their big heads with a woman's smaller head, saying that any fool could see that our brains didn't hold as much intellect. "If a woman has a pint and a man has a quart, then why can't she have her pint full?" I gave them a wink and further confused those quart-sized heads up in the balcony. "Don't be afraid, cause we won't take more than our pint will hold." Oh, they laughed then. I was getting them ready.

"The poor men seem to be all in a confusion and don't know what to do. Why children, if you have women's rights, give them to her and you will feel better." Then it was the women who laughed and clapped.

"I can't read, but I can hear and I have heard the Bible and learned that Eve had a part in Adam sinning. Well, if woman upset the world, do give her a chance to set it right side up again." I glanced to the balcony and the man with the white shelved eyebrows had cocked his head to one side, trying to figure out if I was making fun of him. "Women here today talk of Jesus and how he never spurned woman from him." I felt my true voice open up, the voice that my mother had warned me about. She had said to never use my true, large voice around white people. I let it open and did not try to damp it down. I wanted them to hear me outside the church and down the road. "When Lazarus died, Mary and Martha came to him with faith and love and besought him to raise their brother. And Jesus wept and Lazarus came forth.

And how came Jesus into the world?" From the wide-eyed looks from the women, I knew my voice was strumming their ribs.

"From God and a woman! Through God who created Him and woman who bore him! Man, where is your part?" There were gasps, and I swear by God that I heard a growl. But God was with me; his hand touched my cheek. I softened again.

"Women are coming up, blessed by God, and a few of the men are coming up too. But man is in a tight place; the poor slave is on him, woman is coming on him, and he is surely between a hawk and a buzzard." I let them toss a blanket of laughter over all the ice of truth. It is good for people to laugh now and then; it opens up their brains. I thanked them and sat down. I was finished with my lecture.

A reporter came up to me afterward. He said, "Did you really mean to say that Jesus came from God and woman and that man had no part in it?"

I sighed deeply. "Child, you need to read your Bible."

CHAPTER FORTY-NINE

I see the world different from most folks. My vision takes in a bigger view. Some people see what's in front of them; the garden they're weeding, the butter thickening in the churn, the horse below their legs, and every bit of their thinking stays right there, six inches in front of them. I'm not that way and I'm not putting myself higher up because of it, but my thinking always leaned in the direction of seeing how one thing effects another, and I only got more that way as time went on.

Take the Fugitive Slave Act. After I got done fuming and raging, then I said, let's look farther out and see what this looks like. I had a vision of a woman sick with a terrible illness and she was getting worse. Then she got a boil on her chest, right over her heart. It was clear to me that if she could keep that boil open and draining, she'd get better. All the poison would flow out of her. That's how I came to see the Fugitive Slave Act as a big boil, a sickness that could kill us all if we didn't keep it open and draining. That boil was a place for all the evil and poison of this country to be seen in its true form. The men who put together that law were ignorant and shortsighted. If they really wanted slavery to last forever, they never should have passed that law. Once the law was passed, people had to choose, they had to debate, think, argue, and take action. There was no room at the back of church to stay silent and slip away.

I made it my job to keep that boil open and spewing. I traveled all over, from Massachusetts to Michigan and as far south as I dared, all to tell people about slavery and what must be done. I can't tell you how many times I crisscrossed this country. I lectured mainly to white people, the colored ones didn't need talking to. They understood what was happening. I kept going more and more to Michigan until in '57, I bought a house there in Harmonia, right outside Battle Creek. Sold my house in Massachusetts, although every time I was in the area, I stopped in and stayed with some of the old friends from the Community.

I got braver as time went on. After a few years I took to traveling alone for my lectures, or I brought along my grandson James. I wanted him to see what the world was about. There was another grandson too. Elizabeth had a boy after she finally married a good enough man from New Bedford. Little Samuel. When he got old enough, I took him along because he was more agreeable than James and less prone to mischief. I had neither of them with me when I went to Indiana in '58, which was just as well. I couldn't have done what I did if one of the grandsons were sitting out there.

I was going full forward by then. I wanted people to understand completely what was happening. So I told them about being sold from Bomefree and Mau Mau and about the beatings from Neely and I wouldn't stop at showing them the scars. Some people only believe what they see so I had plenty to show them. Just the scars on my arms were enough to scare the dead. I could get most people to see a point or two, and if nothing else changed, that was enough. Every time I saw a man or woman nod their head when I asked them if it was wrong to own another human being, I saw one less child taken from his mother in a slave state. I wasn't making clever jokes the whole time; I was severe with the ministers. Churches are the kettles for the stew and if the kettles are old and rusted out, the stew doesn't stand a chance. We lived in a country that said black people could not become citizens, that we had no rights in court, and that it was perfectly fine to carve up a black girl's face in Georgia so she can be more easily recognized by the scum who hunt her down with dogs. So when I heard ministers drone on about what happened thousands of years ago, while their eyes stayed shut to the boiling cauldron of suffering going on right in front of them, I tended to be severe.

When I went through Indiana, I stayed with abolitionists, brothers and sisters who offered me a bed and a meal and news of the day. They often wrote letters for me so my family wouldn't forget me.

When I stepped off the train, I saw posters with my face on them announcing a lecture by me. Sometimes they called me the Libyan Sibyl. I wished they wouldn't call me that. With a name like that, thanks to Harriet Beecher Stow who came up with that all on her own without asking me, people expected someone with long Grecian robes and bare feet. They were frightfully disappointed to see an old woman of sixty years with a thick layer of road dust. As I looked at the poster of myself I wondered what I was going to say that night. I figured I'd have to go and find out.

There was no point in me lecturing if everyone agreed with me. I knew my job and had long ago accepted that people say and do the worst things when presented with ideas that ask them to regard their world in a new way, to change. These are holy moments and miraculous births came from the most difficult pain of changing.

The depths of my bitterness about the days of terror and fear weren't what the people heard when I spoke in their churches, granges, parlors, and town greens. You show the true package of bitterness and old hatreds to white people and one of them will kill you. I roared and cajoled and dragged them along, and let them think that they were the clever ones for understanding me. But if they ever saw the pit of despair that lived in the dark cellar of my heart, they would have run screaming from the hall and struck me down with an axe.

I had just received news that black men had been burned to death in front of their families for teaching children to read, that Frederick Douglass was telling coloreds to take up arms because he saw no end to this evil other than bloodshed, and that the underground railroad was clogged with women with a child in each arm and a memory of her children left behind. Every white abolitionist faced prison when they were caught helping a fugitive slave. Every black abolitionist faced far worse. I was in no mood for small minds when I stepped into the church crowded with men and women, every single face as pale as a hazy summer day.

"I have known slavery's whip and lash. My children were slaves for one reason only; they were born of my body. What do you think God will say to the man who let innocent babes be turned into the battlefield of slavery? What will God say to the slave master when his life is over? Is there any man or woman here who stands in judgement of God for making some skin dark and some skin light?"

I sensed trouble was ready to strike. Ask any person who was beat unmercifully as a child and they'll tell you the same thing. I felt the warning in my belly like an orange globe firing up sending out black threads all over my arms and legs. And not one woman had spoken since I arrived in the hall. I was the first woman they'd ever heard lecture.

"If you don't like it here, I've got an idea for you. Get on a boat and go back to Africa," said a young man who believed he was the first idiot to come up with that idea. He was flanked by two other young bucks, all with their arms folded across their chests like bony shields.

The pit of despair in my heart grew larger. Could this foolish white man cut off the ear of runaway slave? Would he put a brand on my back? If he saw a Black Bird drag off my grandson Sammie, would he unfold his arms and come to our aid? Or would he ask the Black Bird about the weather this time of year as my little one howled in terror?

My throat opened up and my voice rose up from my feet. "I am a citizen of this country! For all its faults, this is my country! There is something rotten at work in the government. You know how the weevil eats the sweet center

325

of the plant? I think the weevil has gone to Washington and it might be at work in your mind right now."

Laughter. I caught some of them off guard but the golden globe in my belly still tingled with warning.

"I am glad to redeem the white people from the curse of slavery, for few of you are strong enough to stand up to the temptations of it. Slavery has made a mess and any time there is a mess, you can be sure a colored woman will be sent in to clean it up. God said to me, 'Sojourn, this mess will take some powerful cleaning. You can't do this alone. You'll need help.'"

The curly headed man with folded arms said, "Well, Auntie, my barns needs mucking out. You can clean it." The trio guffawed and looked around to see who was looking at them. I suddenly had no patience for him or his sort. I saw myself with a pitchfork tossing that pea-brained runt as far into the sky as I could. The world would be the better for it.

I extended my arm and pointed my finger at him. "Who are you?"

He stepped forward and puffed out his already overworked chest. "I am William Bates, the only son of my mother."

I rolled my eyes heaven ward. "Well thank the Lord there are no more."

The hall erupted in laughter and William turned red. But William had friends, and one stepped forward, an older man with a barrel belly straining his buttons. The scuff of his boots was quick and sharp, not what you expect from a large man. He walked right up to the front of the room with me. If he wanted to challenge me to a debate, there was nothing that I wanted more at that moment. He stood not but two feet from me and I could smell his breath. He smelled like a raw onion left out in the heat.

"This is no woman before you. The gentle sex doesn't speak in this manner. This atrocity is a man disguised as a woman to win the sympathies of our women and to soften the men. This man is a fraud and a danger!"

Good Lord. Where do some men get their ideas? I was ready to debate the man. His brain was so small there was nothing to work with and the little that did rattle around in his skull was lacquered hard with hatred. I should have pitied him but I did not.

"There is only one way to prove my point," he said and for the first time he turned to me and looked me dead in the eyes. "If you are a woman, show your breasts to the women of this church. They will find you to be a faker."

The whole place broke loose. Those who were as shocked as I was stood up and shouted their outrage. His comrades, and there were many, cheered. I held up my hand to silence them after I regained my voice.

"I will not shame these women by your sin." My hands began to work on the top buttons on my neck. "Your mind is so clouded that you haven't the sense to know a woman when you see one!" My fingers opened the buttonholes on my collarbone. I turned to him so that he could see what I was doing. I heard a woman cry. I undid the front of my dress and untied my camisole. I opened up the top of my clothing down to my skin and laid open one side. Dry air puckered my nipples.

"These breasts have suckled my own children and many a white babe. Is that what you never got? Were you not born of a woman? Do you want the milk of my breast as well?"

He yanked his head back and his skin turned mottled and red. His mouth opened and no sound came out. I know if he could have killed me on the spot, he would have. He stumbled from the raised platform where we both stood and marched out of the church. I turned my back to the audience and closed my dress. I had gone past the limit and I knew that all in the church were turned against me. I faced them when my last button was secure again.

"There was shame here tonight, but it was not mine. I am done for tonight and I will not leave you with a hymn. All of my songs are silenced with sadness. Goodnight to all of you." I was exhausted from the foolishness of proving that I was a woman. I gathered up the pile of my books that I had intended to sell, and looking straight ahead, walked down the center of the aisle.

I was at the third pew when a thin woman stood up. She leaned over the man sitting at the end of the pew and reached out for my arm. "God bless you," she said. Another woman and a man stood up and began to clap, then more of them did the same. Not all of them mind you. A fair bunch kept their hindquarters in the pews and glared at me, but the rest of them warmed my weary, bitter bones. They bought all the books I brought along too.

CHAPTER FIFTY

War. The boil erupted and the country choked on its own blood. My grandson, James, joined up with the Colored Regiment in Massachusetts. War changed everything and when President Lincoln finally let the black man fight for the Union, I wished I was younger. I would have bound my breasts and taken up a gun. That's how much war changes everything.

Back in Michigan, I collected food for the colored troops, brought it to them myself and stayed with the boys on many nights trying to brighten them with songs. They weren't paid as much as the white soldiers and their supplies were worse than pitiful. But I thought I'd die from love and pride when they marched out. I gave them their own song, a hymn to carry them home.

One young soldier who looked achingly like my Peter, said, "We could win this war with your voice. If you sang to all the soldiers, Confederate and Union, all at the same time, I think the fighting would fall away." He was so young, everything about him was fresh, even the scar on his jaw was still new where something had taken a finger-sized bit out of him.

As much as I wanted to be with the colored regiments, when I heard that freed slaves were pouring into Washington like a thick river, I knew I had to go there to see the gush of freedom. And I dreamed of talking to President Lincoln. I had to thank him for what he'd done, proclaiming the emancipation of slaves.

I don't know what was wrong with me, certainly I was old enough to know better being a hair's breath from seventy, but I thought Washington would be the center of jubilation, hearts soaring about the city. It wasn't like that at all. The thousands of slaves who made it through after the president signed the great proclamation, were bone and spirit weary, living in the Freedman's Village which was another word for swamp, sickness, and fear.

I took one frightful look at the mess and saw that this was where I had to be, in this knee-deep mud with screaming babies and young men acting drunk and foolish just because they could. People came north with naked children and not much more for clothes on the mothers and fathers. Field workers gawked at the possibilities. Let me say this, a camp filled with the remnants of slavery and war carries with it all the weight of the worst of both and none of the joys of freedom because nobody knew what freedom meant.

I found out who was in charge and I settled in, teaching cleanliness, knitting, and preached as long and hard as I could about being industrious. "God tells us to be doers, not watchers! Take a hand out only until you are strong enough to stand up and work!" No one ever said I was too easy on people. I sent word to my friends all over the north that these people needed respectable clothes and most of them needed to learn how to read. Winter made swift work out of those who couldn't find clothing and shelter. Houses were made only of strips of wood leaned every which way.

Blackbirds from Maryland tried to make their way in and sweep up the children to sell them deep into the south. For the most part, I don't believe in killing but I might have killed a Blackbird or two and accepted any judgement from God that He saw fit to hand out. It would have felt that good. The Freedman's Association gave me a little house to live in while I worked. One night I opened my door to attend to a noise, and I saw three men trying to stuff the smallest girls into canvas bags. I grabbed my walking stick and waved it over my head as I yowled and thundered. I ran straight at them. My swearing came back from the old days and I let loose with words that I'd nearly forgotten.

The men looked up and I could tell they counted on me stopping, and when it was clear that I was going to run through them and that my stick was large, they dropped the bags and the girls. But I didn't stop, and a few men from the camp woke up and they took chase. "Blackbirds in the camp! They're stealing the children, drive them out!" Each time we chased out the Blackbirds, we got part of ourselves back. Each time we kept a child, each time the marauding blackbirds fell into the mud, our bones stacked up straighter.

The first fall in the Freedman's village, I wanted to meet the President. Among the abolitionists, we argued about Lincoln day and night. Was he friend or foe? Would he hand over the colored people if he thought it would save the union? Was he strong enough to stand up to the sickness in our country? I dreamt one night that he and I sat under a white birch tree and we were as free and easy as if we were brother and sister. Then a snake came through the grass and struck at Lincoln. I grabbed the snake before it could strike but it grew bigger and stronger and I didn't know if I could keep it from him. He looked sad and said, "Sojourn, you can't hold the snake away from me forever. It will bite me eventually." The next day I made contact with Mrs. Lincoln's maid and she said that I could get a meeting with Mr. Lincoln. I had to wait until the end of October.

We sat outside his office for an hour. I didn't mind waiting. By midmorning, we were called in and my heart flipped like a fish. I smelled smoke from a man's pipe and I was suddenly warmed by the memory of Bomefree and what he would think of me walking into the President's office. Mau Mau's breath poured into me and kept my knees from buckling.

He was a sad man; I could see that immediately. He stood up when I approached him. He was taller than me by a good deal, but bone thin and his skin had a poor look to it. The war had wrenched nearly everything out of this man.

"I have heard of you, even before you began to work in Washington," he said after introductions were done.

"I hadn't heard of you until you were President," I said. He looked startled and then one eyebrow rose up, followed by a crooked smile.

He showed me a bible that was given to him by black people in Washington to thank him. He was proud of it, but he showed it to me because he didn't know what else he was supposed to say to me.

"God chose well when he appointed you," I said.

"If God has chosen me for anything, it is to watch as we all go up in flames in this war."

I don't know news he had just received, but it was not hopeful and the deaths of soldiers filled all the space in the room.

"God appointed you to end slavery, the worst evil in this land."

He rubbed his hand across his brow as if to tend to a wound. "I would not have freed the Negro if I could have found another way to save the union."

"That's why you were appointed by God. You were the one who couldn't find any other way. This was your holy moment, Mr. President and you chose well."

He blinked and really looked at me. "I heard that you have the gift of orating. You turn even a pessimist like me into something finer than I am."

He sank into a chair that seemed too small for him. "I fear this war will kill me. If certain people came in here, they'd shoot me in the head and cheer so loud they'd be heard in New Orleans."

"Yes, Mr. President. They'd shoot me too. But the difference is, then they would sell my children and grandchildren into slavery after I lay dead."

He pondered this for a few heartbeats. That was a good sign. I told him about the freed slaves in his city and that trouble was brewing there. I told him that people in the north were sending clothes and supplies for the people but government men were stealing them or worse, selling them to the colored people.

"They need jobs and land. Staying bunched up like this is going to ruin them," I said.

A man came in and said that the news from the war was bad and the President had to leave. The President turned to me. "We will talk again. I had not intended to make your visit such a grave one."

I never saw him again. He was killed in the spring. Not by a snake, but by a coward of a man. The whole city wept but the keening from the Freedman's village was enough to tear off my skin. Women threw themselves on the ground and wailed. Men doubled their patrols to keep out kidnappers. I went to the river; I always found it easier to talk to God near water and the Potomac was swift and full of God the spring of Lincoln's murder. My pipe soothed me too. I stuffed it with tobacco and let the smoke flow down my throat and back out again.

People asked me, how did I know when it was God talking to me and when was it just me thrashing over an idea? By the time I was an old woman, I had worn such a well traveled path talking with God that sometimes I wondered the same question. And then along comes a day like the day Lincoln died when I wandered with my tears and smoke along the river and God came over me, just as brilliant as the day he told me to leave slavery, or to take my name of Sojourner Truth. Suddenly and without question he showed me a picture of how things could be. All the colored men and women filed out of the Freedman's village and they were given land, good farmland where they built strong homes and schools for their children. It was so glorious that I gave a shout. Of course! If the slaves were paid back even a small portion of what they were owed in land, they wouldn't need anything else from the government.

My plan was so simple that I knew everyone would

understand it, even politicians. The country could not begin to pay back the slaves for all that was taken from us. There was not enough gold in California to do that. But the government was giving away land to railroads and for people to settle. Why not offer something on the terrible debt to black people and give them land out west? Families could stay together, children would not be taken from parents again, husband and wife would not be separated. Bring in teachers to get all the children reading, then each one of them could teach another. I left the riverside in a rush, nearly dropping my clay pipe, to tell my idea to my friends in the city.

I spent the next number of years collecting signatures on a petition that said give the freed slaves this tiny payment for all their years of working and living that were stolen from them. I traveled from Michigan across to the east coast and after the war, I went as far south as Virginia. I took my grandson Sammie with me. We collected thousands of signatures, everyone of them saying that yes, this was the right thing to do. Surely the Congress would stand up and take notice when I finally presented them with the weight of people's wishes. I could barely wait for the day to come.

CHAPTER FIFTY-ONE

BATTLE CREEK 1880

I look up at the night sky and I am joined to all the people I have ever known, loved, hated, forgiven, and not forgiven. My mother got me started in this way, using the sky as her church when she was allowed no other. Maybe she just liked a bit of fresh air at night. Maybe she held on to a fine thread from Africa that kept her attached to her homeland, and then she wove it into a shawl with her stories. That's what I see when I look up.

When I look at the sky with the full power of a crisp night, no fog dimming the view, I see my mother and father, long dead, my twelve brothers and sisters, and my boy Peter. I see my boy with my brother Peter, two stars side by side. I see me and Robert making a baby, and another star sparkles. I see the troublesome times too, the hard, lean, barren times until I fully awakened and walked away from slavery. Oh, that was an unlit space of time. The sky won't let me forget.

I begin at the North Star because it's the easiest to find and it has led so many; sailors on the ocean, slaves running north for their lives. I say to the sky, "That's me, I'm the North Star." Then I go out from there. I can read my whole life in the stars around the bright one. That's one way to remember I'm still here and alive. Don't think I'm making too much of myself because I call myself the North Star. I know my part of the sky is small. That's the fine part of this whole plan of life; I only have to take care of a small part of the sky. I'm only one woman, and I can only do a small bit. Then I start thinking too hard and I don't think my brain can manage it all. I start to think about all the bits that everyone does, all the forgiving and forgetting, all the sadness and the tears, all the dying, and I wonder if there is room in the clearest sky.

I have three more years before I die. Don't ask me how or why I know, but I only have that much sand left. I stay at home in Battle Creek these days. That's where I ended up. I found such fine people here in Battle Creek, people of the highest order. My whole family is with me, grandchildren too. I don't go so far to lecture. When the weather is fair, I pick blackberries and sell them to the ladies in town. I'd like to talk to one more President before I die. Right before I went off to see a President the last time, I picked berries and sold them as always. One Mrs. Lathrop, who bought a quart of my berries, asked me if I'd be around the next week and I said no, I was going off to see the President and she laughed like I was a crazy old colored woman.

She didn't know me well. She doesn't know that my first President was Abraham Lincoln. If he hadn't been killed, he and I would have done a thing or two together. He died before I could tell him how things needed to go to begin to make things right for the freed slaves. I collected thousands of signatures on my petition. I took it to Congress like the splendid gift that it was, a gift of righteousness. All those signatures saying, let's try to at least make things a little bit right. But the Congress treated my petition like old news and they swept over it as if we have been un-named, the way Mau Mau could un-name someone and stop seeing them.

The next Presidents, I told them I needed to vote. "Women need to have their say. It's only right," I told them. I've been saying the same thing, let women vote, and pay your debt to former slaves. They keep calling me Auntie. I won't stop.

I don't preach so much anymore in far off places. Old ulcers, long healed, have cropped up on my legs again and cause me to often lay abed. Growing old is not something that happens all at once. It's bit by bit and the body gives out this way and that. I am still the girl who was sold at an auction with sheep and I am still the woman who sits with the Presidents to tell them what needs to be done.

I kept the signatures, stacks and stacks of paper etched with ink, names of good people who tried to help. And on nights when I have regrets that my part of the sky was not enough, I run my hands over the yellowed paper and even these old bones are warmed. And the sky is filled with stars.

ACKNOWLEDGMENTS

I could not have written this book without the generous
support of people who cared so much about Sojourner's
story. They include friends and writers Sharron Leighton,
Toni Brandmill, and Patricia Lee Lewis. I am grateful to
those who offered manuscript critiques: Millicent Jackson,
Anna Marie Russo, and Martha Sheehan.

I have been supported by the following writer's groups:
The Rebecca Boyd group, Eden River Writers, Third Wave,
Writer's Block, and Patchwork Farms International Writing
Retreats. Historian Paul Gaffney provided historical editing
and a detailed understanding of the Fugitive Slave Law.
Corinne Nyquist of the Sojourner Truth Library in New Paltz,
New York, escorted me on the path of Isabella's walk to
freedom. Alayne Heishman, computer scientist, rescued
Sojourner's story from the ether of cyberspace.

In New York, the following organizations freely gave me
the most intriguing information about the 19th Century:
Esopus Museum, The Fireman's Museum in Manhattan, and
the Ossining Historical Society. In Massachusetts, I was
thrilled to read original letters and newspapers at the
Antiquarian Society in Worcester and at Historic
Northampton.

I am grateful to my agent Jenny Bent and my editor, Amy
Scheibe. My family gave me encouragement and my
daughter, Morgan, was an inspiration.

THE COMET'S TALE

A CONVERSATION WITH JACQUELINE SHEEHAN,
AUTHOR OF THE COMET'S TALE

Q.   What inspired you to write The Comet's Tale?

A.   Several things came together at once. I was
writing more fiction, mostly short stories, when we
moved from Chico, California to Massachusetts. I
quickly learned that Sojourner Truth had lived in the
same town in Massachusetts. Even though I had known
only small bits of her life prior to that time, she had
been a powerfully inspirational figure. I slowly started
to read about her life, first her own Narrative that she
dictated and eventually other accounts of her life.
When I first started digging below the surface, I was
shocked that she survived with her spirit not only
intact, but large enough to help heal a nation. I was
especially moved by her tenacious attempts to save her
son, Peter. I spent the next four years researching and
writing about Sojourner.

**Q.   Sojourner was a real person. How did you
combine history and fiction?**

A.   This is a work of fiction based on the life of one of our great American heroes. It was important for me to do as much research as possible to provide the authenticity that this project deserved. I needed to be comfortable with the 19th Century world; the clothes, the food, the sensibilities, and with her physical environment. Then I had to gain an understanding of slavery that, despite what I previously thought, I never really had before. Basing a novel on true events also meant not being too heavy handed with the historical information. For example, I did a week of research about women's clothing, and corsets in particular, only to be able to let Sojourner make a few comments about adjusting to corsets. Although it was a balance between fiction and historical fact, in the end, telling a strong story always took the lead.

Q.   **You wrote this novel in the first person, in the voice of the main character. How did you decide to do that?**

A.   I wanted this story to be told close to the bone, inside the skin of Sojourner (or Isabella as she was first called). From the beginning, this story demanded to be told in her voice, as if she was finally telling us everything about her life.

Q.   **Being a white writer, how did writing about a primarily black experience affect you and your writing?**

A.   This is a primarily American experience and one that we, both black and white people, have been denied in most history and fiction. We have skimmed over it, which is quite amazing. Some of the most courageous people emerged from one of the worst time periods of our history.

When I first began writing, I heard a constant, nagging voice in my head that said I shouldn't be writing this because I was white. I was faced with the choice of giving in to this voice, which was really the collective unconscious of our country's racist guilt, or to be what I am, which is a writer. And writers create stories and characters and unless we are writing autobiographies, these stories are not about us. We have to be able to know our characters exquisitely, both the sympathetic characters and the characters who appear to be beyond redemption.

Q.   Why does most of the novel focus on Isabella when she is a child or a young woman and less on Sojourner's life when she is older and famous?

A.   If people know anything about Sojourner, they know her as the fiery orator who could outwit and outtalk anyone. What I wanted to know was how she survived the abuses of slavery to become one of the most famous women of the 19th Century. For me, the process of becoming was even more interesting than the woman she became.

Q.   You are a psychologist. How did this affect your approach to the novel?

A.   I can't think of a better background for writing fiction than psychology. My knowledge of psychology helped with character development and motivation, and it was the true foundation for understanding why she was not crushed by slavery when so many others were. I worked for years in California and spent a lot of my time working with women who had been sexually and physically abused as children. I knew the kind of nightmares they had and the roadblocks they faced. I developed an enormous respect for the unlimited potential of the human spirit to survive and to thrive. I was also sobered by seeing the unlimited potential that we all have to inflict unimaginable pain on others.

Q.   **What was the hardest part of the book to write?**

A.   I was completely surprised by my reaction to her relationship with her son because so many other parts of her life were brutal. But I realized that her drive to save her son was the compelling force of a large part of her life. When she finally learned his fate, I was in tears and I had to stop writing. I surprised myself even more by going to a church, which would not normally be my destination, but I knew that's where Sojourner would have gone. Of course the church was locked, which jolted me right back to the present day.

Q.   **What are working on now?**

A.   I am working on something completely different. It is a novel about a woman who is a psychologist who completely loses her grip when she is unable to save her husband's life. She tries to run away from her life, changing who she is, but finds that she is confronted by the very things she hoped to escape. There is a dog in the story that is currently stealing the show. We'll see how that goes.

Q.   Who are your favorite authors?

A.   We have a wealth of fine contemporary authors. Barbara Kingsolver changes me every time I read one of her novels. I remember changing my understanding of family after reading Animal Dreams. I was at the check out counter at the grocery store right after I finished Animal Dreams and I was suddenly unable to see the clerk in the same anonymous way; whether we liked it or not, we were both part of the same large family.
        Dorothy Allison's novel, Bastard Out of Carolina has also changed me. Up until that time, I was unable to understand the women who chose their abusing husbands over their children. If I had any understanding, it was only an intellectual one. Dorothy Allison gripped me with the desperation that some women feel. She changed me on a deep, emotional level.

FOR FURTHER READING ABOUT SOJOURNER TRUTH AND RELATED TOPICS

This book, From God and a Woman, is a fictionalized imagining of Sojourner Truth's early years. The author drew from a multitude of reference materials including original newspaper entries, letters, bills of sale, and grave stone etchings. The author was also fortunate to have works available by the finest historians, who have dug far deeper and with more tenacity than the most of us would dare.

For more information about the life of Sojourner Truth, the following books are suggested:

Carleton Mabee, Sojourner Truth: Slave, Prophet, Legend (New York University Press, 1993).

Nell Irvin Painter, Sojourner Truth: A Life, A Symbol (New York, W.W. Norton & Company, 1996).

Margaret Washington, Narrative of Sojourner Truth (New York, Vintage Classics, 1993).

For more information about Matthias, or Robert Matthews, the following book is a most complete, and enlightening read:

Paul E. Johnson & Sean Wilentz, The Kingdom of Matthias (New York, Oxford University Press, 1998).

The important role of African Americans in 19th Century Seafaring has long been neglected. The following book brings this part of our history to a glorious light.

W. Jeffrey Bolster, Black Jacks: African American Seamen in the Age of Sail (Cambridge, Massachusetts, Harvard University Press, 1998).

And for a comprehensive and highly readable study on the history of New York City, the following book is recommended:

Edwin G. Burrows & Mike Wallace, Gotham: A History of New York City to 1898 (New York, Oxford University Press, 1999).

CPSIA information can be obtained at www.ICGtesting.com
Printed in the USA
LVOW131226240912

300042LV00001B/86/P